The Rapture Don't Be Deceived

FIRST PRINTING

Billy Crone

Cover Design:
Chris Taylor

To Reid & Debbie Rucker.

*It was really a no-brainer
to whom I should dedicate this book.
With license plates that state Luke 21:28,
I believe common sense prevailed.*

*Thank you Reid & Debbie
for your tireless dedication and service
to our Lord Jesus Christ
and the ministry of Get A Life.*

*Little did you know
that on the day you showed up in my driveway
and "snatched away" all that equipment
that you would become a "blessed hope"
to me, my family, my marriage
and the ministry of Get A Life.*

*Thank you for being the "hand-picked" of God
to provide a friendship and partnership
at a time when it was needed most,
in helping to share the wonderful Gospel
of our Lord Jesus Christ in these Last Days
here in Las Vegas and around the world!*

I love you both.

Contents

Preface

Believe it or not, I used to be one of those guys. You know, one of those Christians who said it wasn't necessary to teach and equip the flock on Bible Prophecy let alone the Book of Revelation. I had the same rationale too. "Oh, there are plenty of other things to preach and teach on in the Bible. No need to bring up something so 'divisive' in the Body of Christ." The sad irony is that the very first verses in the Book of Revelation clearly inform us that the teaching of Bible Prophecy is a "blessing" to the Body of Christ, not a "divisive burden." However, I still persisted, as many unfortunately do.

Yet, God had a "spiritual spanking" waiting for me in Seminary. I was lovingly and bluntly reminded that one third of the Bible deals directly or indirectly with Bible Prophecy. Whether it's the Old Testament or New Testament, the First Coming of Jesus, the Second Coming of Jesus, the Prophetic Promises made to the People of Israel, the Millennial Kingdom, the Final Judgment, the Eternal State, you name it, Prophecy covers a *huge* portion of the Bible. Therefore, the challenge put forth to me as a Seminary student was, "How in the world can you call yourself a faithful shepherd of the flock, feeding the Church the "whole" counsel of God, when you deliberately leave out "one third" of the Bible?" I must admit, it stung, and still stings to this day that I would ever, as a Christian, have an attitude that basically states that it's perfectly fine to deliberately skip over one third of the Bible. In essence I was taking a magic marker and "blacking out" massive portions of the Bible from the Body of Christ. It's stunning and shameful when I look back on it all. All of God's Word is "good" for us. Yet, it wasn't until this "spanking" and the "shock" of the events of 9/11 that I began to be that faithful shepherd, one that preached *all* of the Bible to the Body of Christ. The very next week, I began teaching on the Book of Revelation and other Bible Prophecy related issues and have never looked back.

I see now that part of my faulty rationale was frankly due to a lack of working knowledge concerning Bible Prophecy and so "fear" of the unknown won the day. If that's you reading this, then learn. Apply yourself to this Biblical truth and the fear of it will go away. Also, I witnessed a lot of "immature" behavior in Bible College concerning the different positions on the Rapture. I used this "bad behavior" as an excuse to refrain from sharing the "Blessed Hope." Yet, two wrongs don't make a right. A mark of maturity is to agreeably disagree on secondary issues, like the Rapture, yet not divide. God's people need to know *all* of the Bible, not just some of it. Otherwise they end up half-baked and it's this half-baked Christianity that's messing things up.

Therefore, the purpose of this book is not to merely hand you yet another book on Bible Prophecy, specifically the Rapture, but to encourage you to obtain that "working knowledge" of this Biblical subject so you can get busy "teaching it" to others so they can be "blessed" by it. It is also a clarion cry to those who are being "immature" with their views on the Rapture and who *are* causing division in the Body of Christ. May this book encourage you to demonstrate your "maturity" by agreeably disagreeing on secondary issues yet not dividing. We both agree we're living in the Last Days, so let's not miss out on the main task at hand; that of working together as Christians, sharing the Gospel with as many lost people as we can. One last piece of advice. When you are through reading this book then will you please *READ YOUR BIBLE*? I mean that in the nicest possible way. Enjoy, and I'm looking forward to seeing you someday!

Billy Crone
Las Vegas, Nevada
2016

Part I

The Introduction to the Rapture

Chapter One

The Importance of the Rapture

Imagine the following scenario. You wake up one morning only to realize that your family has totally disappeared. You scramble, look around, run into the living room and turn on your TV to see what in the world is going on. There you watch a special worldwide global news report declaring that millions of people all over the planet are missing, and not just your family, but literally millions of people. As this slowly begins to sink in, you look down and spy your loved ones' Bible sitting right there on the coffee table and so suddenly it dawns on you that your Christian family was right after all when they kept telling you over and over again about this Rapture event. To your horror, you realize, oh no, *you have been left behind* and you will now be catapulted into the 7-year Tribulation that is coming upon the whole world. Maybe that initial news broadcast will look something like this.

"Christina Bronson reporting on today's Breaking News. We are getting last minute reports from all over that world that thousands of people have just vanished. I repeat, thousands of people from all over the globe have just disappeared.

The total number of people that have disappeared has not yet been confirmed, but it is expected to be a lot higher than what had been initially reported. According to authorities the number is expected to be in the millions.

Many flights have been cancelled because of security fears. According to reports, there have been plane crashes all over the world because some pilots have simply disappeared midflight.

Chaos has also spread to the road with a great number of traffic accidents being reported. Hospitals have not been able to cope with the number of patients coming in. Many parents are in complete despair about their children who have also disappeared.

Many believe that this could have been an alien attack and there are those that believe that Jesus Raptured these millions of people. Witnesses report having seen a bright flash followed by huge thunderous sounds and a being like a man in the clouds.

Here are some images caught on CCTV cameras showing people literally disappearing. The images you see now are from CCTV cameras all over the world. These images have been analyzed by experts and they are genuine. CCTV footage from parks, shopping centers, parking lots, Churches and traffic monitoring systems are indeed real and frightening. We are receiving images like these non-stop from all over the world.

We have yet to hear from heads of state all over the world who are in shock and have not released any statements. Members of various Churches are saying this is the Rapture of the Church. When asked why they also hadn't disappeared, many cried with regret that they hadn't taken Jesus more seriously before.

We are closing this new bulletin here and will report more news as and when it happens."[1]

Now, you can laugh and scoff all you want, but a news broadcast just like that really is coming to our planet, and dare I say, much sooner than most people realize. So the question is, "Will you be around to see that kind of news broadcast yourself? Will you be left behind?" This is part of the reason why we've entitled this book, not just *The Rapture* but *The Rapture: Don't Be Deceived*. If there's one thing you don't want to be deceived about, it's the truth concerning the Rapture. The Bible says for those who are left behind, they will be thrust into the 7-year Tribulation and it is not a party. Rather, it's an outpouring of God's wrath on our wicked and rebellious planet, literally mankind's worst nightmare! In fact, speaking of news broadcasts, maybe this will be one of the weather reports during that horrible time frame the Bible talks about. Let's tune in.

"We've got some big changes here for the upcoming workweek. Starting tomorrow, we are going to have a volcanic eruption right near Charlottesville and it's going to make things rather toasty across the area.

We are going to see lava spill out into Central Virginia which makes temperatures in Richmond at 350 degrees, Fredericksburg at 345, Charlottesville the hot spot at 400, not as hot off towards the tide water. A little bit more comfortable with highs near 100 degrees. The reason is we're going to have tidal waves moving in.

Ahead of this, a global super storm is developing in the Atlantic Ocean. This thing is headed our way. We can see maybe about 1 to 200 inches of rainfall with wind gusts up to 1000 miles an hour.

Overnight it looks calm but going into the weekend there will be some slight changes. Starting Friday the Southeast will see heavy rain and wind speeds topping 700 miles per hour. That will start an F5 tornado headed westward across the southeast all the way to the west coast.

In the west, temperatures will decrease to about 300 degrees below freezing. It says an ice sheet has been forming in California. This would be a good time to stock up on food as this extreme weather will compromise the food supply indefinitely.

Those along the Canadian border, look out for zombies. They're moving southward out of Canada.

Saturday would have been a great day for beach goers in the east but with the Avian Flu outbreak and the recent Zombie attacks, you may want to stay indoors for a while.

Don't forget to wear your masks and only drive in the daylight hours if you're driving along the I-95 corridor."[2]

Now, that doesn't sound like a very good time! All kidding aside, the Bible really does talk about that kind of crazy searing heat, volcanoes exploding, massive weather problems and even a drug induced population acting like a bunch of zombies during the 7-year Tribulation! However, that's still just the tip of the iceberg! You tell me if you want to be around during that time frame! Let's delve deeper into what the Bible says about that horrible time.

CHARACTERISTICS OF THE 7-YEAR TRIBULATION

Seal Judgments

- 1st Seal - White Horse – Global False Peace
- 2nd Seal - Red Horse – Global War
- 3rd Seal - Black Horse – Global Famine
- 4th Seal - Pale Horse – Global Death – 1/4th of Mankind Killed by…
  - Sword
  - Famine
  - Plague
  - Wild Beasts
- 5th Seal - Altar of Souls – Global Persecution
- 6th Seal – Beginning of Great Tribulation which unleashes…
  - A Global Earthquake
  - Sun Turns Black
  - Moon Turns Red
  - Asteroids Fall to Earth
  - Sky Recedes
  - Mountains/Islands Removed from their Places
  - Global Fear of God's Wrath

Trumpet Judgments

- Opened by the Seventh Seal – Silence in Heaven
- 1st Trumpet - Hail/Fire - 1/3rd of Earth/Trees & All Green Grass Burned Up
- 2nd Trumpet - Huge Asteroid – 1/3rd of Sea Dies & 1/3rd Ships Destroyed
- 3rd Trumpet - Blazing Comet – 1/3rd of Rivers & Fresh Water Bitter – Many People Die
- 4th Trumpet - Solar Smiting - 1/3rd of Sun, Moon & Stars Struck – 1/3rd Day & Night without Light
- 5th Trumpet - Satan Releases Demon Horse of Locusts – People with Mark Tortured 5 Months
- 6th Trumpet - Four Angels Loosed from Euphrates – 1/3rd Mankind Killed

Bowl Judgments

- 1st Bowl – Ugly Painful Sores on Receivers of the Mark
- 2nd Bowl – All the Sea Turns to Blood – All Sea Creatures Die
- 3rd Bowl – All the Rivers & Fresh Water to Blood
- 4th Bowl – Sun Scorches People with Fire – People Curse God
- 5th Bowl – Kingdom of Antichrist Plunged into Darkness
- 6th Bowl – Euphrates River Dries Up
  - Prepares Way for Kings of East for the Battle of Armageddon
  - Three Evil Frog-Like Spirits Deceive the World for Armageddon
  - Out of Mouth of Satan
  - Out of Mouth of Antichrist
  - Out of Mouth of False Prophet
- 7th Bowl – Final Pronouncement – IT IS DONE
  - Greatest of all Earthquakes
  - A New Look for Jerusalem - Split in Three
  - All Cities Collapse
  - A Cup of Wrath for Babylon
  - All Islands and Mountains Gone
  - A Massive Hailstorm – 100 lbs. each
  - Angel Harvest of the Righteous
  - Angel Harvest of the Unrighteous – Blood as High as Horses Bridle (4 feet deep) for 1,600 Stadia (200 Miles)[3]

Now, I'm kind of thinking, that's a time frame you want to avoid, amen? That's precisely why the Bible has been warning about this event for the last 2,000 years! You don't have to be there! God loves us, mankind, and He's provided a way out of this horrible time frame through Jesus Christ. Unfortunately, many scoff and refuse to listen to Him and reject Jesus Christ as their Lord and Savior. Therefore, they are headed for that time frame and it's their fault, not God's. Please, this is not a joke! *Don't Be Deceived* about it! In fact, Jesus said in Matthew 24 the 7-Year Tribulation is going to be a "time of greater horror than anything the world has ever seen or will ever see again" and that "unless that time of calamity is shortened, the entire human race will be destroyed." That's why we're producing this book to keep you informed of the ultimate rotten day of being left behind. You don't want to be there! *Don't be deceived*! This is not a game!

But we've also entitled this book, *The Rapture: Don't Be Deceived* because there's a multitude of opinions out there it seems, concerning the *purpose* and the *timing* of the Rapture. Because of this, it's starting to cause a lot of unnecessary *confusion* and *division* among people, concerning this next major event on God's Prophetic time calendar. So let's take a look at this event called the Rapture, and observe what the Bible has to say about this prophetic event where Jesus comes back and rescues His Church, from this horrible End Times destruction. Let's *not be deceived* about that either!

Chapter Two

The Basis of the Rapture

The **first thing** we're going to look at to avoid being deceived about the Rapture is the **Word Rapture Itself.** What does it mean? Well the English word "Rapture" comes from the Latin noun "raptura" which is a translation of the New Testament Greek word "harpazo." "Harpazo" is used 14 times in the New Testament and the basic idea of the word is to, "remove suddenly or a sudden snatching or a sudden catching away, to seize, to carry off."[1] Therefore, it's become the perfect illustrative word to describe the event, the Rapture, where God suddenly takes up or snatches away His Church from earth to heaven. Jesus comes in the clouds, He catches or snatches us away, the Church, from the earth, then we return to heaven with Him.

Which leads us to the **second thing** we're going to look at to avoid being deceived about the Rapture and that is **Where Does the Rapture Event Appear in the Bible**? Right? I mean you have to have a Biblical basis for this. That's precisely why we see the Apostle Paul giving us a clear description of the Rapture in his letters to the Thessalonian and Corinthian Churches.

1 Thessalonians 4:13-18 "Brothers, we do not want you to be ignorant about those who fall asleep, or to grieve like the rest of men, who have no hope. We believe that Jesus died and rose again and so we believe that God will bring with Jesus those who have fallen asleep in Him. According to the Lord's own word, we tell you that we who are still alive, who are left till the coming of the Lord, will certainly not precede those who have fallen asleep. For the Lord Himself will come down from heaven, with a loud command, with the voice of the archangel and with the trumpet call of God, and the dead in Christ will rise first. After that, we who are still alive and are left will be caught up together with them in the clouds to meet the Lord in the air. And so we will be with the Lord forever. Therefore encourage each other with these words."

1 Corinthians 15:51-52 "Listen, I tell you a mystery: We will not all sleep, but we will all be changed – in a flash, in the twinkling of an eye, at the last trumpet. For the trumpet will sound, the dead will be raised imperishable, and we will be changed."

We even see Jesus referring to the Rapture in John 14.

John 14:1-3 "Do not let your hearts be troubled. Trust in God; trust also in Me. In My Father's house are many rooms; if it were not so, I would have told you. I am going there to prepare a place for you. And if I go and prepare a place for you, I will come back and take you to be with Me that you also may be where I am."

In fact, what's interesting when you put these passages together, 1 Thessalonians and John, you see Jesus and Paul completely agree and have total unity concerning this teaching on the Rapture.

THE RAPTURE

JESUS	PAUL

Comforting Words

"Do not let your hearts be troubled"	"Encourage each other with these words"

The Necessity of Personal Faith

"Trust in God; trust also in Me"	"We believe that Jesus died and rose again and so we believe that God will bring with Jesus those who have fallen asleep in Him"

We Can Take God at His Word

"If it were not so, I would have told you"

"According to the Lord's own Word"

The Promise of His Coming

"I will come back"

"For the Lord Himself will come down from heaven"

The Removal from Earth

"And take you to be with Me"

"We who are still alive and are left will be caught up together with them in the clouds to meet the Lord in the air"

Forever Present with the Lord

"That you also may be where I am"

"And so we will be with the Lord forever"[2]

So as you can see, the Bible and Jesus and Paul are obviously in complete agreement. The Bible does not contradict itself about this Biblical event called the Rapture. It's real and it's really coming!

Chapter Three

The Purpose of the Rapture

Which brings us to the **third thing** we're going to look to avoid being deceived about the Rapture and that is **What is the Purpose of the Rapture**? Why is it that Paul, Jesus and the Bible in general talk about this event? Why bring it up? What's the purpose in the first place?

Well, the **first reason** the Rapture is brought up in the Bible is to **Comfort the Living about the Dead**. You see, when Paul was writing his response to the Thessalonica Church about the Rapture, many years had gone by since Jesus was on the earth. He had not yet come back for His Church and so some Christians had already died, leaving the still living believers with questions concerning their loved ones in Christ who had already gone. These Christians, knowing that their departed loved ones were present with the Lord, 2 Corinthians 5:8 "Absent from the body is to be present with the Lord," wondered how they would share in the coming of Christ. How would they be resurrected from the dead? Their bodies were in the grave, but their spirits were with Christ. How do they share in the Rapture with those who are still alive? This is why Paul responded the way he did. Let's look at that again.

1 Thessalonians 4:13-18 "Brothers, we do not want you to be ignorant about those who fall asleep, or to grieve like the rest of men, who have no hope. We believe that Jesus died and rose again and so we believe that God will bring with Jesus those who have fallen asleep in Him. According to the Lord's own word, we tell you that we who are still alive, who are left till the coming of the Lord, will certainly not precede those who have fallen asleep. For the Lord Himself will come down from heaven, with a loud command, with the voice of the archangel and with the trumpet call of God, and the dead in Christ will rise first. After that, we who are still alive and are left will be caught up together with them in the clouds to meet the Lord in the air. And so we will be with the Lord forever. Therefore encourage each other with these words."

FIRST, Paul says, Jesus will come down from heaven and He will bring with Him the souls of those "who fall asleep," or in other words, those who have already died in Christ. SECOND, those who have died in Christ will rise first, that is, their bodies will be raised from the graves and they will receive their new resurrected bodies first. THIRD, those believers who are still alive (you and I the Christian unless we die first) and remain until the coming of the Lord, i.e. the Rapture, will be caught up or Raptured and receive our resurrected bodies as well.[1]

Which means, our Christian loved ones who have already died, along with us who are still alive when the Rapture occurs, will meet together, the Lord in the air, and be with Him forever. That's why Paul says "comfort" or "encourage" one another with these words and why Jesus says "don't let your hearts be troubled." Our loved ones in Christ will be just fine, *and* we who are still alive at that time will be just fine. We'll never be separated again. Don't worry about it.

The **second reason** the Rapture is brought up in the Bible is to **Comfort the Living about the Day of the Lord**. Now, even a cursory reading of the Bible and what it says about the Day of the Lord in the Old or New Testaments will show you that it does not concern the Church. Rather, it's speaking of the horrible time frame when God's wrath and judgment are being poured out upon this wicked world. It's not a literal twenty-four hour day, or a single event, but rather a period of time which starts after the Rapture of the Church and incorporates the entirety of the 7-year Tribulation period. Therefore, the Day of the Lord does not mention and has no application whatsoever to the Church. It concerns Israel and the Gentile nations of earth.

This is precisely why the Thessalonians were freaking out so much about a fake letter saying they were in the Day of the Lord and why the Apostle Paul had to respond a second time to them concerning the Rapture and remind them that Christians are not going to be a part of this horrible day.

2 Thessalonians 2:1-5 "Concerning the coming of our Lord Jesus Christ and our being gathered to him, we ask you, brothers, not to become easily unsettled or alarmed by some prophecy, report or letter supposed to have come from us, saying that the Day of the Lord has already come. Don't let anyone deceive you in any way, for that day will not come until the rebellion occurs and the man of lawlessness is revealed, the man doomed to destruction. He will oppose and will exalt himself over everything that is called God or is worshiped, so that he sets himself up in God's temple, proclaiming himself to be God. Don't you remember that when I was with you I used to tell you these things?"

So here we see the Apostle Paul **comforting** and **reassuring** the Thessalonian Church from a misconception going around at that time by some false teachers saying that these Christians missed the Rapture because the Day of the Lord had already come! But Paul says, "No! No! No! No!" Christians are **not** going to be around during that time frame and he's very emphatic about it! Why? Because the Bible says the Day of the Lord is all about God's judgment and bringing people low. It's a time when He pours out His wrath, and anger, and desolation, and vengeance, and destruction, and it's terrible. It's a time of gloominess and darkness and distress and trouble, and refers to the cataclysmic final judgment of God upon the wicked, not the Church![2]

That's why Paul says "Don't be deceived" *and* you should know better! "Don't you remember I already told you this?" In essence, "Why are you falling for this? You know you can't be there! I already went over this with you guys. Christians are nowhere around in the 7-year Tribulation! We left at the Rapture, prior to the 7-year Tribulation!" So he says, "Don't freak out and listen to these false teachers!"

Besides, if the Thessalonians thought that the Rapture came *after* the 7-year Tribulation started, and then received a letter from Paul saying that the Day of the Lord had already started which occurs during the 7-year Tribulation, then would they not have been excited beyond words? Of course! They would have been hopeful that the Rapture was at the door because the 7-year Tribulation had already begun! They wouldn't have been troubled or fearful. They would have been excited! Yet that's precisely the point. The Apostle Paul is writing to alleviate their *fears* and *troubled hearts* concerning this fake letter that said the Day of the Lord had already begun and thus they were in the Tribulation. This *lie* is what freaked them out because they *knew* the Rapture occurred *before* this horrible time frame.

This is also why Paul says *comfort* or *encourage* one another with these words. You're not going to be here. Calm down. The Rapture occurs before all that! Or as Paul says here:

Titus 2:13 "We wait for the blessed hope – the glorious appearing of our great God and Savior, Jesus Christ."

The Rapture is our Blessed Hope. We are rescued from God's wrath and eternal hell and this horrible time frame called the 7-year Tribulation. As one man stated:

"The Rapture is a soothing balm for troubled hearts. It's a blessing and consolation for the Lords' people. Stop and think about this for a moment. If Paul taught a mid-trib, pre-wrath or post-trib Rapture would the truth of the Rapture really be that comforting?

If God's people have to endure 3½ years, 5½ years or all 7 years of the tribulation before He comes, how much of a comfort would the Rapture be? If we must face the 7-year Tribulation before He comes, Jesus would have to change the words, 'Let not your hearts be troubled' in John 14:1 to, 'Let your heart be troubled.' Knowing we had to live through the 7-year Tribulation would be troubling to say the least.

Ask yourself these simple questions? How comforting would it be to know that Jesus was coming after 3 ½ or 7 years of hell on earth? What would it be like at the graveside of a loved one, to hear the Pastor read the beautiful words in 1 Thessalonians 4:13-17, and then say, 'And after we endure part or all of the Tribulation, Jesus will come and Rapture us to heaven and reunite us to our loved ones – comfort one another with these words?' Could you honestly get excited about the Rapture if you knew that you had to endure a time on earth when the judgments of Revelation 6-16 were being poured out? A time when the Antichrist will be enforcing his mark and you and your family would be denied the right to buy or sell.

Furthermore, we would expect the Thessalonians to be rejoicing that their loved ones had already died and gone to heaven because they wouldn't have to endure the terror of the 7-year Tribulation. However, in 1 Thessalonians 4 the believers are grieving because they fear that their loved ones will miss the Rapture. Only a pre-tribulation Rapture makes sense out of their grief.

Also, we would expect the Thessalonians to be upset about their own impending trial in the 7-year Tribulation rather than sorrowing over their deceased loved ones. We would expect them to be asking for details about the 7-year Tribulation and the Antichrist. However, the Thessalonians have no fear or questions about the coming day of wrath or the Antichrist. Why? They were looking for Jesus Christ, not the Antichrist.

Finally, we would expect Paul, in view of their grief over their deceased loved ones, to remind them that their present grief was inconsequential in light of the future time of trouble that's coming. However, there's not even a hint of any impending tribulation for them.

Therefore, what we find in 1 Thessalonians 4 fits the pre-trib position like a glove. However, it's totally incompatible with either mid-trib, pre-wrath, or post-tribulationism. The blessed hope of the Rapture is that Jesus will come and take us to be with Him forever *before* the time of worldwide devastation is unleashed. And what a comfort and blessing it is!"[3]

This is precisely why the early Church used a common greeting to boost their morale and that was the word, "Maranatha!" It eventually replaced the Jewish greeting "Shalom" that meant "peace." "Maranatha" meant, "Come, O Lord," or "The Lord is coming."[4] Dare I say we need to use that same morale booster in the Church today! Amen? We are rescued from that horrible time frame, the 7-year Tribulation. Comfort one another. Be encouraged.

The **third reason** the Rapture is brought up in the Bible is to **Remind The Living of Their Current Life on Earth**. You see, the reason why we're still here is because God has a plan for us. This is what Paul says in:

Ephesians 2:10 "For we are God's workmanship, created in Christ Jesus to do good works, which God prepared in advance for us to do."

We are not saved by our works but God has prepared for us in advance good works to do in the meantime. One of those good works is to share the Gospel, the Good News that people can be saved though Jesus Christ. This is what Jesus said right before He went to the right hand of the Father.

Matthew 28:18-20 "Then Jesus came to them and said, 'All authority in heaven and on earth has been given to Me. Therefore go and make disciples of all nations, baptizing them in the name of the Father and of the Son and of the Holy Spirit, and teaching them to obey everything I have commanded you.'"

This is what's called the Great Commission, not the Grand Suggestion. Jesus orders us as Christians to get out there into the world and get busy sharing the Gospel, the Good News of salvation through Jesus Christ, making disciples of all nations. This basically tells us that God wants other people saved besides us, and hopefully that's not news for you.

But He also wants us to back up that sharing of the Gospel with holy lives. Why? Because God is Holy and people need to understand God's holiness if they're going to be saved. This is why Peter says:

1 Peter 1:15 "But just as He who called you is holy, so be holy in all you do; for it is written: 'Be holy, because I am holy.'"

God wants His Church to back up what we say about Him, and His Holy character, with our holy lives when we share the Gospel, otherwise we're sending a duplicit message. If we don't take sin or consequences for sinning seriously as a Christian, then why should a lost person? Apparently it's no big deal for us, therefore it's no real concern for them. Yet, sin *should be* a huge concern for all people because this is what separates us from God and places us under His wrath! And it is precisely because of sin that God's wrath will be poured out on this planet during the 7 year Tribulation and that's also why there's a place where people are punished for all eternity called hell.

So people need to know, by our Christian lives here on earth, that *sin is serious* and has *serious consequences*. Then when we *do* share the Gospel, they will understand why it really is *Good News*. That is, you really can be saved from all your sins that are separating you from God through Jesus Christ. Furthermore, it's a gift! It can't get any better than that!

Now here's the point. The Pre-trib Rapture position is the only position that sends this truth home about our need to share the Gospel to the lost! If we know that the Rapture could happen at any minute, then it gets rid of any sense of laziness or procrastination in sharing the Gospel. Why? Because this might be our last day to share with those around us. It also means that Jesus could show up *at any moment* and how do I want Him to find me? Sinning? Goofing off? Knowing that the Lord could come back at any moment dispels all that. As Paul states:

Titus 2:11-13 "For the grace of God that brings salvation has appeared to all men. It teaches us to say 'No' to ungodliness and worldly passions, and to live self-controlled, upright and godly lives in this present age, while we wait for the blessed hope – the glorious appearing of our great God and Savior, Jesus Christ."

God knows that we the Church have an unfortunate tendency to procrastinate and get lazy and get caught up in the sins of this wicked world system, *but* the Pre-Trib Rapture cures all this. It creates what's called the Doctrine of Imminence. Or in other words, the truth that the Lord Jesus could return at any time and get us at the Rapture. It could happen at any time. There is no prophetic event that needs to take place prior to this event occurring. It could happen today. It could happen before you finish this book.

Therefore, be encouraged and take stock of your current life. Is it holy? Is it aiding the Gospel? Are you sharing the Gospel? How will Jesus find you if He comes back today, because one day will be that day, and it could be today, it is imminent!

Now, it is important to note that all the other positions on the Rapture *do not* produce this cleansing effect on the believer. For instance, if I thought Jesus *wasn't* coming back to Rapture the Church until the midway-point of the 7-year Tribulation or ¾ the way through the 7-year Tribulation with the Pre-wrath position or all the way to the end with the Post-Trib position then I *do know* when He's coming back. There is *no imminence*. In essence I *could goof off* and *procrastinate* in sharing the Gospel because I know exactly what prophetic events *have* to take place *before* He comes back with all those other positions. All the Seal Judgments, the Trumpet Judgements, the Bowl Judgments, the Antichrist, all that stuff, all the events mentioned in the Book of Revelation about the 7-year Tribulation. All I have to do is calculate it all based on those events. That's why these positions *destroy* Imminency and its cleansing effects.

The Pre-Trib position is the only one that says there is no heads up warning and therefore you better get ready and be ready at *all* times! It could happen *now* so get busy sharing the Gospel *now*. It could happen *today* so get busy living a *holy life today*! It's also something we should even be longing for as the Apostle Paul says here:

2 Timothy 4:8 "Now there is in store for me the crown of righteousness, which the Lord, the righteous Judge, will award to me on that day – and not only to me, but also to all who have longed for His appearing."

Are you longing for His appearing? If you are it has a way of cleaning up your life and it causes you to get busy sharing the Gospel. Don't delay He could come back today! Also, by longing for His appearing, your life will not be wasted because Imminency motivates you to be faithful to the good works God has prepared in advance for you to do. Then you get rewarded in the end.

One of the best ways to hear from Jesus the words, "Well done, thou good and faithful servant" is to simply acknowledge the Pre-Trib Rapture position, that the Rapture is Imminent, it could happen at any time. Jesus is coming back and it could happen at any moment and I need to get motivated for Him. Time is short. *Serve Him now*! That's what keeps you faithful and being that faithful servant.

The **fourth reason** the Rapture is brought up in the Bible is to **Remind the Living of Their Coming Reward**. Again, as we already observed, when Jesus, Paul and the Bible talk about the Rapture, it's a good thing. Jesus said, "Don't let your hearts be troubled," and Paul says, "Encourage one another or Comfort one another with these words." You're going to be fine. You're not going to be around during that horrible time frame of the 7-year Tribulation.

But leaving the earth at the Rapture and escaping God's wrath poured out on the planet during the 7-year Tribulation is just the beginning of all the good news and bright future that the believer receives at that time.

The **first benefit** for the Christian at the Rapture is **We Get New Bodies**. This is what the Apostle Paul talked about in the same passage in 1 Corinthians where he mentions the Rapture. When Jesus comes back to get us, Paul also says we get new resurrected bodies.

1 Corinthians 15:50-54 "I declare to you, brothers, that flesh and blood cannot inherit the kingdom of God, nor does the perishable inherit the imperishable. Listen, I tell you a mystery: We will not all sleep, but we will all be changed – in a flash, in the twinkling of an eye, at the last trumpet. For the trumpet will sound, the dead will be raised imperishable, and we will be changed. For the perishable must clothe itself with the imperishable, and the mortal with immortality. When the perishable has been clothed with the imperishable, and the mortal with immortality, then the saying that is written will come true: 'Death has been swallowed up in victory.'"

So here we see that we the Church will not continue to exist in the same bodies that we have now when the Rapture occurs. This is just one of the benefits. We get new *imperishable* bodies. Simply put, they will never die, they will never rot, they will never decay, they will never break down, they won't even age. Is that incredible, or what?

Think of it. That means, there will be no more back aches, no more broken bones, no more disease, and yes ladies, no more anti-aging creams, to the joy of many. Why? Because our bodies will cease to wear down. Which means, there's going to be no more wrinkles, no more crinkles, no more age spots, none of that stuff! Make-up companies will be bankrupt. In fact, no more will you wake up and go to the breakfast table and you hear snap, crackle, pop and you discover you're not eating cereal. No more will you go to bed realizing that you and your teeth don't sleep together anymore. No more will you wake up looking like your driver's license picture. And no more will you look for your glasses for half an hour before you realize they were on your head the whole time. You won't need to remember them because you're not going to need them! We won't need glasses![5] Our bodies in heaven are going to be *perfect*!

The **second benefit** for the Christian at the Rapture is **We Get a New Home**. Now we've already observed in John 14 where Jesus is talking about the Rapture that there are many rooms in the Father's house and He's going there to prepare a place for us. When He's done, He's going to come back and get us at the Rapture and take us to be there with Him. And when you look at the descriptions of the Father's House, i.e. Heaven, in the Bible, it's an incredible place to live!

Revelation 21:1-4 "Then I saw a new heaven and a new earth, for the first heaven and the first earth had passed away, and there was no longer any sea. I saw the Holy City, the new Jerusalem, coming down out of heaven from God, prepared as a bride beautifully dressed for her husband. And I heard a loud voice from the throne saying, 'Now the dwelling of God is with men, and He will live with them. They will be His people, and God Himself will be with them and be their God. He will wipe every tear from their eyes. There will be no more death or mourning or crying or pain, for the old order of things has passed away.'"

Wow! What an existence! Our new *heavenly home* is not only going to be a place prepared for us by God Himself, as Jesus stated before, but it's also going to be totally decked out and absolutely awesome! Think of it! No more death, no more mourning, no more crying and no more pain! What a life! But that's still not all. The Bible gives us *even more* information about how wonderful this place called heaven is. Let's take a look at that.

CHARACTERISTICS OF HEAVEN

- The Dwelling Place of God: (Psalm 2)
- The Dwelling Place of Angels: (Matt. 18)
- A Heavenly Country: (Heb. 11)
- A Holy Place: (Isaiah 57)
- An Eternal Paradise: (1 Cor. 12)

- A Place with Streets of Gold: (Rev. 21)
- A Place with Gates of Pearls: (Rev. 21)
- A Place with Foundations of Precious Gems: (Rev. 21)
- A Place of Eternal Rest: (Rev. 14)
- A Place of Eternal Joy: (Rev. 7)
- A Place Without Wickedness: (Rev. 22)
- A Place Without Darkness: (Rev. 21)
- A Place Without Sin: (Rev. 21)
- A Place Without Tears: (Rev. 21)
- A Place Without Mourning: (Rev. 21)
- A Place Without Pain: (Rev. 21)
- A Place Without Death: (Rev. 21)
- A Place of Absolute Purity: (Rev. 21)
- A Place Filled with the Glory of God: (Rev. 21)
- An Everlasting Place: (2 Cor. 5)[6]

Now, I'm kind of thinking, that heaven is one place you really don't want to miss, anybody else? Yet, this is what we get, and where we're going at the Rapture!

Oh, but there's more! The Bible says *heaven is so awesome* that we can't even imagine all the things that God has prepared for us there.

1 Corinthians 2:9 "However, as it is written: 'No eye has seen, no ear has heard, no mind has conceived what God has prepared for those who love Him.'"

The Bible clearly says that even though we can understand *some things* about heaven which are absolutely amazing, God has still prepared for us things so out of this world, so amazing, so wonderful, that we can't even *imagine* or *conceive* what they are yet.

So let's try to expand that imagination by taking a look at heaven from a *scientific* point of view. Maybe we can get a sneak peek of what this text is telling us, 'No eye has seen, no ear has heard, no mind has conceived what God has prepared for those who love Him,' as this man shares:

"The electromagnetic spectrum contains all the different wavelengths, like radio waves, microwaves, and including a small piece called light. Now your eyeball can see the colors, red, orange, yellow, green, blue, violet, that's all.

The spectrum goes forever in both directions beyond that. Suppose we get to heaven and God gives us new eyes that can see the entire spectrum. That means there will be brand new colors, trillions of them. Not new shades of our current colors…but brand new colors! That's why heaven has to be so large. It's for the women's closets!

But can you imagine if we get new eyes that can see the whole spectrum? You're going to be able to see the sounds coming off the piano. Right now we can only hear them. Imagine seeing the sounds. What if we get new ears that can hear the whole spectrum? You're going to be able to hear the colors, or smell them, or taste them!

We've only got five senses folks. Maybe there's more. But if God just took these five and expanded them to the max, we would spend forever walking around heaven going, "Wow! Did you smell that? Here, lick that! Wow!"[7]

"No eye has seen, no ear has heard, and no mind has imagined what God has prepared for those who love Him." What an absolutely unimaginable mind-blowing existence with God that we have to look forward to at the Rapture. I can't wait to get there, how about you? No wonder Jesus and Paul said, "Don't let your hearts be troubled," and "Comfort or encourage one another with these words."

Oh, but it gets even better. The **third benefit** for the Christian at the Rapture is **We Get a New Mission**. As if getting new bodies and going to heaven at the Rapture isn't awesome enough, the Bible also says that after the Rapture, at the end of the 7-year Tribulation, we get to *come back to earth* with Jesus at His Second Coming *and* we get to be a part of the 1,000 year Millennial Reign. This is where He rules and reigns on earth and ushers in an amazing time of peace and prosperity to the whole planet. Now, one of the reasons why it's so peaceful and wonderful is because satan is bound during that time!

Revelation 20:1-4 "And I saw an angel coming down out of heaven, having the key to the Abyss and holding in his hand a great chain. He seized the dragon, that ancient serpent, who is the devil, or satan, and bound him for a thousand years. He threw him into the Abyss, and locked and sealed it over him, to keep him from deceiving the nations anymore until the thousand years were ended."

So, according to the Bible, after the 7-year Tribulation is over, during the Millennial Kingdom, satan is actually bound for 1,000 years where he can't mess with us, or touch us, or anybody else on earth! How many of you would say that's going to be a wonderful existence? To finally have our greatest archenemy *bound*! Where he can't incite evil and suffering and all the other rotten things like he does today! That's going to be pretty awesome!

But once again, that's still just the tip of the iceberg. For some reason, just like with heaven, we Christians seemed to be ill equipped in our understanding of the Millennial Kingdom, the place where we're headed after the Second Coming of Jesus Christ! So let's take a look at the characteristics of this time-frame and see just exactly what we're headed for.

CHARACTERISTICS OF MILLENNIAL KINGDOM

- The government will be a Theocracy, with the Messiah, Jesus Christ, ruling and reigning as King in Jerusalem.
- The Twelve disciples will rule over the 12 tribes of Israel and there will be other smaller subdivisions of authority awarded for faithfulness.
- Judges will be raised up and will demonstrate the Theocratic power of Christ to rule with inflexible righteousness and justice.
- War will be but a relic of the past.
- Jerusalem, known for war, bloodshed, and international tensions, will at last become the city of peace and the capitol of the world.
- There will be religious peace with Jews and Gentiles worshipping the Lord together.
- There will be a just economy for everyone and no longer will wealth be monopolized by only a few privileged families.
- Nature will cooperate with man again and productivity will return. Earthquakes, tornadoes, floods, etc., will be absent.
- Our work will no longer be in vain and our children will no longer be doomed to misfortune. Work will continue throughout the Millennium for God designed work for us as a source of provision. But in the Millennium, our work will yield multiple gains much more than what we need for survival, which means we will have enough resources for nice vacations, leisure and fun.[8]

Now, that sounds like a pretty wonderful place to be! Are you looking forward to being there? I am! Yet, it gets even better! Let me share with you a couple more aspects of the Millennial Kingdom and you tell me if this isn't mind-blowing!

One, the Bible says that things will return to Garden of Eden like conditions and people will live a **Long, Full, Rich Life**.

Isaiah 65:20 "Never again will there be in it an infant who lives but a few days, or an old man who does not live out his years; he who dies at a hundred will be thought a mere youth."

During the Millennial Kingdom, righteous people, those who were redeemed during the 7-Year Tribulation, not the Church, because we've already received our new Resurrected Bodies at the Rapture prior to the 7-year Tribulation, but those people with natural bodies who enter the Millennial Kingdom, will reach their full life. They will live *as long as the trees*. Longevity of life, like in the Garden of Eden, will be restored. By the time a person reaches 100 years old they will just be entering the *prime* of their life instead of their twilight. Someone in their 60's will be considered a youth not a retiree!

But that's not all. The Bible also says the Millennial Kingdom will also be a time where we will have **Peace with Nature**. Check this out!

Isaiah 11:6-9 "The wolf will live with the lamb, the leopard will lie down with the goat, the calf and the lion and the yearling together; and a little child will lead them. The cow will feed with the bear, their young will lie down together, and the lion will eat straw like the ox. The infant will play near the hole of the cobra, and the young child put his hand into the viper's nest. They will neither harm nor destroy on all my holy mountain, for the earth will be full of the knowledge of the LORD as the waters cover the sea."

The Bible clearly states that in the Millennium, all wild animals will be tamed. Not just my vicious wiener dogs, but *all* wild animals. It will be "Domesticated Africa." Even the leopard will be tamed like a goat. Isn't that awesome? That's not only possible, to be at peace with nature, but one day, the Bible says the *whole earth* is going to be like that in the Millennial Kingdom. The wolf, the lamb, the leopard, the goat, the calf, the lion, the cow, the bear, the cobra, all of nature will lie down together, and a little child will lead them. What a place to be! Amen?

So guess what? That's where we're going after the Rapture occurs! We're coming back at the end of the 7-year Tribulation with Jesus for the Millennial Kingdom! One man stated about that time-frame:

"Under the direction of Jesus Christ, the resurrected believers of the Church will provide the leadership necessary to create a just society for mankind. The *greatest adventure* we could ever imagine awaits us in the reality of the Kingdom of Christ."[9]

Again, no wonder Jesus and Paul said, "Don't let your hearts be troubled," and "Comfort or encourage one another with these words." This is going to be awesome after the Rapture!

And if you love Jesus, you're going to get something even more awesome than that at the Rapture. The **fourth benefit** for the Christian at the Rapture is **We Get a New Relationship** with Jesus. In other words, no more of this invisible stuff. One day, we shall see Him as He is in all His glory and splendor. This is what John states:

1 John 3:2-3 "But we know that when He appears, we shall be like Him, for we shall see Him as He is. Everyone who has this hope in Him purifies himself, just as He is pure."

Again, get your life right! Jesus could come back at any moment and hopefully He'll find you living a good godly life, pure like Him, because you love Him and want to be a good example to others when you share the Gospel as we saw before. But as you just read, the Bible clearly states that we will actually get to see Jesus personally and after all He's done for us, I sure hope we're able to give Him a hug and say thank you from the bottom of our hearts!

But this is something we get to experience at the Rapture! It makes you want to bust out in praise! In fact, when it comes to the appearing of Jesus, the Bible declares that all of heaven busts loose! Let's take a look at the response of heaven concerning the Second Coming of Jesus when He comes back at the end of the 7-year Tribulation to set up the Millennial Kingdom.

Revelation 19:1-9 "After this I heard what sounded like the roar of a great multitude in heaven shouting: 'Hallelujah! Salvation and glory and power belong to our God, for true and just are His judgments. He has condemned the great prostitute who corrupted the earth by her adulteries. He has avenged on her the blood of His servants.' And again they shouted: 'Hallelujah! The smoke from her goes up for ever and ever.' The twenty-four elders and the four living creatures fell down and worshiped God, who was seated on the throne. And they cried: 'Amen, Hallelujah!' Then a voice came from the throne, saying: 'Praise our God, all you His servants, you who fear Him, both small and great!' Then I heard what sounded like a great multitude, like the roar of rushing waters and like loud peals of thunder, shouting: 'Hallelujah! For our Lord God Almighty reigns. Let us rejoice and be glad and give Him glory! For the wedding of the Lamb has come, and His bride has made herself ready.' Fine linen, bright and clean, was given her to wear. (Fine linen stands for the righteous acts of the saints.) Then the angel said to me, 'Write: 'Blessed are those who are invited to the wedding supper of the Lamb!' And he added, 'These are the true words of God.'"

Now, I'm kind of thinking that *all of heaven* is just a little bit excited about the Return of Jesus Christ, how about you? Slightly! What a Praise Service! Hallelujah, Hallelujah, praise God, give Him glory! Why? Because this is awesome news! Jesus Christ is coming back to put an end to evil and suffering once and for all, and He's going to set up His Millennial Kingdom and for those who belong to Him we get to be a part of the greatest celebration of all time called *the Marriage Supper of the Lamb*! It's going to be awesome!

We get to be with our King Jesus forever! The One Who has *saved us* and *rescued us* from the *dominion of darkness*! He has *defeated death*, *hell*, and the *grave* and He's coming back to *get us* before the 7-year Tribulation begins and *throw us* an amazing *wedding party*! That's something to get excited about!

So guess what? That's what we get to be a part of when the Rapture occurs! Our Lord Jesus Christ, you know, the One we say we love, is coming back to *get us* His Bride! Our King, our Heavenly Commander, our Prince of Peace is coming back for us! We get to see our King face to face and what a King He is, as this man shares:

"The Bible says my King is a seven way King. He's the King of the Jews, He's the King of Israel, He's the King of Righteousness, He's the King of the ages, He's the King of Heaven, He's the King of Glory, He's the King of Kings and He's the Lord of Lords!

He's my King, - do you know Him?

My King is a sovereign King. He's enduringly strong, He's entirely sincere, He's eternally steadfast, He's immortally graceful, He's imperially powerful, He's impartially merciful.

Do you know Him?

He's the greatest phenomenon that has ever crossed the horizon of this world!
He's God's son, He's the sinners Savior, He's the centerpiece of civilization,
He's unique! He's unparalleled, He's unprecedented,

He's the loftiest idea in literature, He's the highest personality in philosophy,
He's the supreme problem in higher criticism, He's the fundamental doctrine of
true theology, He's the miracle of the age,

He is - yes He is, the superlative of everything good that you choose to call Him,
He's the only one Who is qualified to be an all sufficient Savior;

Do you know Him?

He supplies strength for the weak, He's available for the tempted and the tried,
He sympathizes and He saves, He strengthens and sustains, He guards and He
guides, He heals the sick, He cleansed the lepers,

He forgives sinners, He discharges debtors, He delivers the captives, He defends
the feeble, He blesses the young, He serves the unfortunate, He regards the
aged, He rewards the diligent and He beautifies the meek.

Do you know Him?

My King is the key to knowledge: The wellspring of wisdom; the doorway of
deliverance; the pathway of peace; the roadway of righteousness; the highway of
holiness, and the gateway of glory!

His office is manifold: His promise is sure. His light is matchless. His goodness
is limitless. His mercy is everlasting. His reign is Righteous. His yoke is easy,
and His burden is light.

I wish I could describe Him for you, but He's indescribable! He's
Incomprehensible! He's invincible! He's Irresistible!

You can't get Him out of your mind or off your hands! You can't out-live Him
and you can't live without Him! Death couldn't handle Him, and the grave
couldn't hold Him!

That's my King, That's my King, That's my King, and He's the kingdom and the power and the glory – Forever and ever and ever and ever and ever! AMEN!!!

Do you know Him?"[10]

This is why I truly believe that Jesus and Paul said about the Rapture, "Don't let your hearts be troubled," and "Comfort or encourage one another with these words." When the Rapture happens, it's going to be awesome! I get a New Body, a New Home, a New Mission, and a New Relationship with Jesus. I get to see Him face to face. No more problems, no more pain, no more trials, no more having to deal with this wicked world system, and I get to spend eternity with My King Jesus Who has defeated them all! That's why it's called *the blessed hope*!

Remember, the Rapture is Imminent, it could occur at any moment, maybe even while you're reading this book. Which means, all these things we just talked about are about to take place. It's time to get excited just like all of Heaven! What a journey to look forward to, amen?

Don't let your hearts be troubled, encourage one another with these words, comfort one another. One of these days, maybe even today, that's going to be us, the Christian. As one man stated: "It's going to be a stupendous eternal destiny!"[11]

Part II

The Timing of the Rapture

Chapter Four

The Jewish Wedding Ceremony

Naturally, that all leads to the next question concerning the Rapture. WHEN? To answer that, we're now going to look at the **fourth thing** to avoid being deceived and that is **What is the Timing of the Rapture**? This is unfortunately where a lot of the confusion and division seems to come in over the Biblical teaching of the Rapture. As one researcher stated:

"The timing of the Rapture is one of the most controversial and often debated issues in eschatology. The Bible teaches that at some point in the future Jesus will come, and the bodies of all deceased Church age believers will be resurrected and all living believers will be Raptured to meet the Lord in the air. The truth of the Rapture is agreed upon by most Christians, but the same is not true when it comes to the timing of the Rapture. Simply stated, the key issue is this: Will the Church go through any or all of the seven-year tribulation before the Rapture occurs? Or to put it another way – when will the believing be leaving?

This question is much more than just a theological, ivory tower debate. There is a great deal at stake depending on which view is Biblical. Think about it. If the Rapture occurs in our lifetime, your future will be very different depending on which of these views is correct. Will you be here to see the Antichrist? Will you be forced to choose whether to take his mark on your right hand or forehead? Will you witness the carnage of the wrath of God poured out on the whole world? Or will you be in heaven during this time experiencing a glorious fellowship and intimacy with the Lamb and His sheep? Will you and I be here for none, half, three-fourths or all of the tribulation? It's an important and sobering question."[1]

This is precisely why we're producing this book. We already observed several passages in the Bible that clearly teach about a literal Rapture, but those particular passages don't tell us exactly *when* the Rapture occurs, only that it does.

In fact, I can clearly see the rationale as to *why* God wouldn't tell us the *exact* time of the Rapture. It goes back to what we saw earlier. If we knew exactly when, then we're back into a similar scenario with the other positions on the Rapture, the mid-trib, pre-wrath, or post-trib. If you know the exact time, then you have a tendency to goof off, and get worldly and lazy, and procrastinate in sharing the Gospel. So God says, "I'm not going to tell you exactly when. You just need to be ready at *all times* and make the most of *what time* you have left!" Again, Imminency is important.

However, even though the Bible doesn't give us the exact day or hour of the Rapture, I think there's one thing we can be confident of in the Bible, and that is that the Rapture must occur *before* the 7-Year Tribulation begins. This is what's called the Pre-Tribulation Rapture position. The Church is rescued, Raptured, just prior to the 7-year Tribulation.

The **first evidence** the Rapture takes place *prior* to the 7-year Tribulation is in **The Jewish Wedding Ceremony**. Believe it or not, tucked away in the ancient traditions of the Jewish Wedding Ceremony, we find an interesting parallel of the Rapture of the Church, the Bride of Christ, and Jesus Christ coming to get her. In fact, even at the birth of Jesus we see how He's always been planning on coming back and getting His Bride.

Matthew 2:11 "On coming to the house, they saw the child with his mother Mary, and they bowed down and worshiped Him. Then they opened their treasures and presented Him with gifts of gold and of incense and of myrrh."

Now, I'm sure most of us are very familiar with this passage of Scripture concerning the wise men and the gifts they brought to Jesus after His birth. But what most people miss about this passage is the *purpose* of these gifts and how they signify another reason why Jesus was being born into this world in the first place. It's found in the phrase there; Gold, Incense, and Myrrh. This is what most people miss. I'll never forget the first time I came across this nugget in an old Jewish Custom and Mannerism book that I have. In this particular book, there's a section dealing with the Jewish Customs and Mannerisms for Marriage. In one part it talks about the items that a Bride and Groom would adorn themselves with just prior to their marriage ceremony. Now can you guess what three items the Groom would adorn himself with when it was time to *go get his bride*? That's right; Gold, Incense, and Myrrh.[2]

Granted some would say that the Gold was used to aid in his flight to Egypt, for monetary reasons, and the Frankincense and Myrrh were symbolic of His death to come. It could be; I'm not discounting that. But I do find it interesting that *it just so happens* that the Bible also talks about us being the *Bride of Christ* and here we see Jesus being given the *exact three items* that a *Groom* adorns Himself with when it was time to go get his bride. I don't think that's by chance.

It also makes me wonder if this is not what the myriad of angels that appeared to the shepherds were *also* rejoicing over, that the time had finally come for their Lord and ours to *go get His Bride*. They're busting out in praise, just like all of heaven in Revelation 19 when Jesus comes back at His Second Coming! Why? Because Jesus has come to get His Bride and His Bride is going to the Father's House, not the 7-year Tribulation!

In fact, if you continue to study the Jewish Customs and Mannerisms you're going to see this wonderful truth all over the place. So much so, that I believe that Jesus went to *great lengths* to make sure we received this point. This is seen when we compare our relationship with Him in the Bible to the **Seven Phases** of a Jewish Marriage Ceremony.

The **first phase** of a Jewish Marriage Ceremony is called the **"Shiddukhin" or the "Match."** You see, unlike today, Jewish marriages were arranged by the fathers. What the father would do is get a person to be the "matchmaker" and go find a bride for his son. Guess what? That's exactly what the Bible says Jesus did for you and I.

John 15:16 "You did not choose Me, but I chose you."

John 6:37;44 "All that the Father gives Me will come to Me...No one can come to Me unless the Father who sent Me draws him."

Now, it appears to me that God the Father is the One Who matched us with Jesus, how about you? In fact, if you keep thinking about it, you'll see that's exactly what we're doing when we get saved. We're accepting Jesus' love proposal to be "matched" or married to Him forever.

Now sometimes this "Match" occurred when both were children, and sometimes it occurred a year before the marriage itself. But often the bride and groom did not even meet until their wedding day, which is just like you and I. We're waiting for our marriage in great expectation! Peter puts it this way:

1 Peter 1:8 "Though you have not seen him, you love him; and even though you do not see him now, you believe in him and are filled with an inexpressible and glorious joy."

Why? Because our Wedding Day approaches and we can't wait to see Jesus for the very first time!

The **second phase** in a Jewish marriage ceremony was called the **"Mohar"** or the **"Bride Price."** Right after the "match" was made, a mohar or bride price was hashed out between both parties over the value of the Bride. Again, that's exactly what the Bible says Jesus did for you and I. In fact, *the Bride price He paid was extremely high*!

1 Corinthians 6:19,20 "You are not your own; you were bought at a price."

1 Peter 1:18,19 "For you know that it was not with perishable things such as silver or gold that you were redeemed…but with the precious blood of Christ."

Now, I'd say that's a pretty high bride price to pay, don't you think? Furthermore, if Jesus paid *that big of a price* for us, then I'd say He must love us an awful lot, how about you?

The **third phase** in a Jewish marriage ceremony was called the **"Mattan"** or the **"love gifts."** In this phase, the groom would offer the bride gifts *even though he didn't have to*. He simply did it as an expression of his love for her. Now guess what? That's exactly what the Bible said Jesus did for you and I. He gave us some awesome love gifts! Check it out for yourself:

ETERNAL LIFE: **John 10:27-28** "My sheep listen to My voice; I know them, and they follow Me. I give them eternal life, and they shall never perish; no one can snatch them out of My hand."

PEACE: **John 14:27** "Peace I leave with you; My peace I give you. I do not give to you as the world gives. Do not let your hearts be troubled and do not be afraid."

FORGIVENESS: **1 John 1:9** "If we confess our sins, He is faithful and just and will forgive us our sins and purify us from all unrighteousness."

JOY: **John 15:11** "I have told you this so that My joy may be in you and that your joy may be complete."

I'd say those are some pretty awesome "love gifts," how about you? Now what you have to keep in mind is that these "love gifts" are voluntary. Jesus didn't have to give them. Therefore since He did give them, I'd say He sure must love us an awful lot, how about you?

The **fourth phase** in a Jewish marriage ceremony was called the **"Shiluhim"** or the **"dowry."** Now in this phase, the Father of the bride would give her gifts. The purpose of these gifts was to help equip her for her new life with the groom.

Once again, guess what? That's exactly what the Bible says *God the Father* has done for you and I. Listen to how He equipped us:

THE SPIRIT TO LIVE FOR HIM: **John 14:16-17** "And I will ask the Father, and He will give you another Counselor to be with you forever – the Spirit of truth."

SPIRITUAL GIFTS TO SERVE HIM: **Romans 12:6** "We have different gifts, according to the grace given us."

AN ENGAGEMENT RING TO REMEMBER HIM: **2 Corinthians 1:21-22** "Now it is God who makes both us and you stand firm in Christ. He anointed us, set his seal of ownership on us, and put his Spirit in our hearts as a deposit, guaranteeing what is to come."

The word "deposit" is actually the Greek word for "*engagement ring.*" Therefore, the Bible says that God gives us the Holy Spirit as a reminder or pledge that one day we'll be with Him forever, *just like the reminder of an engagement ring*. What a gift, huh?

The **fifth phase** in a Jewish marriage ceremony was called the **"Ketubah"** or the **"marriage contract."** In this phase, the marriage was legally formalized by a written marriage contract called the ketubah. It recorded the bride price, the promises of the groom, and the rights of the bride.

So guess what? That's exactly what the Bible says God has done for you and I. How? By giving us the *New Contract* or covenant stated by Jesus Himself.

1 Corinthians 11:25 "In the same way, after supper He took the cup, saying, "This cup is the new covenant in My blood; do this, whenever you drink it, in remembrance of Me."

Whether you realize it or not, every time we Christians take communion, it's a reminder of our "marriage contract" with Jesus. So if Jesus signed our marriage contract with *His own blood* then I'd say it's pretty secure, how about you?

The **sixth phase** in a Jewish marriage ceremony was called the **"kiddushin"** or the **"betrothal."** It was here that *after the marriage contract was signed* the couple became what was called betrothed. A betrothed couple was, for all legal purposes, considered to be married. This is why it was big news when Mary became pregnant and Joseph reacted the way he did. They were legally married alright, betrothed, but they hadn't consummated the marriage yet. It "appeared" Mary had cheated on him. But of course, Jesus, the child, was born of the Holy Spirit.

Furthermore, the Betrothal period was a time of Preparation. Even though they were legally married, the couple still didn't live together. Why? Because they still had to go and make preparations for their new life together.

For instance, the Bride had to demonstrate her *purity* during this time. She underwent what was called a Mikvah, a ritual cleansing bath. Now we all know Who of course has cleansed us from our sins. That's right! Jesus!

1 John 1:9 "If we confess our sins, He is faithful and just and will forgive us our sins and purify us from all unrighteousness."

But the Bride also had to demonstrate that she was *faithful* in that she was not pregnant. She would often wear a veil whenever she stepped out of her house to indicate that she was "out of circulation", i.e., set apart for marriage to a particular man. This let other men know she is "spoken for." She is no longer available because she has been bought with a price. She is set apart and consecrated to her bridegroom *and* she will *resist* any other offers as she waits for her one true love who has bought and paid for her. She is his and his alone. In Hebrew, she is called a "mkudeshet," meaning one who is betrothed, sanctified, dedicated to another.

This is how we the Church, the Bride of Christ, are supposed to be *right now* as we await our Lord's Return. We are to show ourselves pure from *sin*, *worldliness*, *false teachers*, etc. This is why Paul stated the following:

2 Corinthians 11:2 "I am jealous for you with a godly jealousy. I promised you to one husband, to Christ, so that I might present you as a pure virgin to Him."

Now the groom, he also had his preparations to make as well. First of all, he was exempt for one year from military service to, "Bring happiness to his wife."

Deuteronomy 24:5 "If a man has recently married, he must not be sent to war or have any other duty laid on him. For one year he is to be free to stay at home and bring happiness to the wife he has married."

The Jewish sages also said he had to "Harvest a vineyard." In other words, he basically prove he could "bring home the bacon," if you will. But the groom ALSO had to go back to his father's house and start building an addition to the father's house called the bridal chamber. It was here that the couple would consummate their marriage and settle down and live together as a family.

Now guess what? That's exactly what the Bible says Jesus is doing *right now* for you and I. Let's go back to this passage on the Rapture of the Church, now in this context.

John 14:1-3 "Do not let your hearts be troubled. Trust in God; trust also in Me. In My Father's house are many rooms; if it were not so, I would have told you. I am going there to prepare a place for you. And if I go and prepare a place for you, I will come back and take you to be with Me that you also may be where I am."

Think about this. If God took 6 days to create the heavens and the earth in all its majesty, then can you imagine how incredible our bridal chamber is going to be if Jesus has been working on it for 2,000 years?

The **seventh stage** in the Jewish wedding ceremony was the **"nissuin"** or **"the taking."** Now once the chamber was completed, the Father would inspect it and tell the son, "Okay, go get your bride." You can see the wisdom in this, why *the father* was the one to make *the final decision*. I mean, think about it. If it was up to the son, he's all excited, he would just build some shack or lean-to and go off and get his bride! But the Father knew this had to be a special place and built and furnished just right.

So one day, when our Heavenly Father feels our Bridal Chamber is just right, He's going to tell His Son Jesus to *go get your bride*!

Now the neat romantic thing about this was the Jewish bride had no idea when her groom was coming. *It could be at any time*. Therefore, she always had to be ready for his sudden arrival. Typically, this "abduction" would occur in the middle of the night, when the Jewish brides were "stolen" away. The Jews had a special understanding of a woman's heart. What a thrill it was for her to be "abducted" and carried off into the night, not by a stranger but by one who loved her so much that he paid such a high bride price for her. *Very romantic*!

And when he did, he would *take* or *abduct* her and whisk her away to the Father's house. But *right before he got there*, the groom and his attendants would make their way by torchlight through the dark streets of the town to the house of the bride. They would catch her totally off guard. This is why she always had to have a "lamp" and "oil" to be ready to go. Don't fall asleep, always be expecting! It could happen anytime! Then upon arrival at the bride's house, the groom's party would announce their arrival with a shout, "Behold, the bridegroom cometh!" and blow the shofar, the traditional "trumpet" made from a ram's horn.

Now, guess what? That's exactly what the Bible says we need to be ready for! Why? Because Jesus could come at any moment and abduct us, His Bride, the Church. You better be ready! Don't be sleeping! It's called the Rapture!

1 Thessalonians 4:16-18 "For the Lord himself will come down from heaven, with a loud command, with the voice of the archangel and with the trumpet call of God, and the dead in Christ will rise first. After that, we who are still alive and are left will be caught up together with them in the clouds to meet the Lord in the air. And so we will be with the Lord forever. Therefore encourage each other with these words."

You bet it's an encouragement! Because as we saw, the words "caught up" is where we get our word "Rapture" from. What it literally means is a "catching or snatching away" just like an *abduction* with a bride. Do you think that's by chance? No way! Yes, we don't know the day nor the hour, but after 2000 years, you'd think Jesus is getting pretty close to finishing that Bridal Chamber, amen? We better get ready!

Now once the couple returned to the father's house, they would consummate the marriage and celebrate their wedding feast *for the next seven days* (during which the bride remained closeted in her bridal chamber). And so it is that we too, the Bible says, are whisked away and closeted in our Bridal Chamber, during the 7 year Tribulation. We're up in heaven at the Father's house enjoying our Wedding Day while the unbelieving world is unfortunately undergoing His Wrath.

Then after the Marriage Supper, Jewish tradition records for us that this is when the bride and groom are presented to the world as "man and wife." This also just happens to correspond to the time when Jesus returns to earth at the end of the 7-year Tribulation accompanied by His Bride "dressed in fine linen, white and clean."

Revelation 19:11-14 "I saw heaven standing open and there before me was a white horse, whose rider is called Faithful and True. With justice he judges and makes war. His eyes are like blazing fire, and on His head are many crowns. He has a Name written on Him that no one knows but He Himself. He is dressed in a robe dipped in blood, and His Name is the Word of God. The armies of heaven were following Him, riding on white horses and dressed in fine linen, white and clean."

That is, the clothing of the Church, the Bride of Christ. Now when you stir all this together, this is why Jesus repeatedly says *you need to be ready* for His *abduction*. Why? Because one day, it's going to be too late! The offer to become a Bride of Christ isn't always going to be there. You need to respond *now* if you're not saved!

If you think about it, the Bible really is a *Divine Romance Book*. It's a *Cosmic Love Story* of how God has made a way for us to enter into a beautiful, loving, intimate, personal relationship with Him, a Bride-like relationship with Him, through Jesus Christ! It's awesome!

But the bad news is, one day, as Jesus said, if you don't respond to this wonderful truth, His Love Proposal, His Wedding Invitation, you're going to be shut out, and the door is going to be closed to the *Marriage Supper of the Lamb*. One day you might find yourself *left behind*. So the question is, "Are you ready?" Jesus is coming back, and He's coming back for His Bride just like He said He would. He's building the Bridal Chamber as we speak, and when He's done, the Father is going to give His permission, "Son, go get your Bride." When He does, Jesus is going to snatch her, the Church, and abduct us, just like in a Jewish Marriage Ceremony.

Therefore the point is this. You better make sure you're ready to go. You better make sure you're really a Bride of Christ. Please, be prepared before it's too late. Receive the greatest Wedding Present of all, the gift of eternal life, *now*!

Chapter Five

The Unknown Hour

The **second evidence** the Rapture takes place *prior* to the 7-year Tribulation is in **The Unknown Hour**. As we've already seen, the Pre-Trib Rapture is imminent, it can happen at any time, there's no prophetic event that needs to occur before it can take place. We also saw the Apostle Paul comforting and reassuring the Thessalonica Church to not worry about being in the 7-year Tribulation or missing the Rapture because the Rapture occurs *before* the "Day of the Lord" which occurs *during* the 7-year Tribulation.

Therefore, since that "Day" obviously hasn't happened yet, and it happens during the 7-year Tribulation and the Rapture happens before that, the Rapture could happen at any time. It's imminent. Thus we need to be ready at all times. This is why the Scripture tells us repeatedly to be waiting, expecting, being patient, alert, living self-controlled lives, in light of this imminent event.

Philippians 3:20 "But our citizenship is in heaven. And we eagerly await a Savior from there, the Lord Jesus Christ."

Colossians 3:4 "When Christ, who is your life, appears, then you also will appear with Him in glory."

1 Thessalonians 1:10 "And to wait for his Son from heaven, whom He raised from the dead – Jesus, Who rescues us from the coming wrath."

1 Timothy 6:14 "To keep this command without spot or blame until the appearing of our Lord Jesus Christ."

James 5:8 "You too, be patient and stand firm, because the Lord's coming is near."

1 Thessalonians 5:6 "So then, let us not be like others, who are asleep, but let us be alert and self-controlled."

Titus 2:13 "While we wait for the blessed hope – the glorious appearing of our great God and Savior, Jesus Christ."

Revelation 3:3 "Remember, therefore, what you have received and heard; obey it, and repent. But if you do not wake up, I will come like a thief, and you will not know at what time I will come to you."

These verses clearly indicate that Jesus' arrival will occur when nobody expects it. You always need to be ready. When it happens, it's going to be sudden, surprising, and at an unknown time. In fact, that's what the word Rapture implies, "To remove suddenly or a sudden snatching or a sudden catching away, to seize, to carry off." It's a surprising quick departure. Again, that's why the Bible repeatedly says, be ready! Don't goof off, don't get lazy, and make sure you're really saved in the first place. This is not a game. You don't want to miss the sudden departure or sudden snatching away.

This is also why the Rapture and the Second Coming are two distinct events. The Rapture could happen at any moment with no prophetic signs needing to happen before its fulfillment. However, the Second Coming of Jesus is clearly preceded by many events, which occur *during* the 7-year Tribulation. Such as:

- The Rise of the Antichrist (Revelation 12:13-17; Zechariah 13:7-9)
- A Treaty with Israel (Daniel 9:27)
- The Rebuilding of the Jewish Temple (Matthew 24:15; 2 Thessalonians 2:3-4; Revelation 11:1-2)
- The Plagues and Judgments and Persecutions Destroying Most of the World's Population (Revelation 6-18)[1]

All these events and many more occur during the 7-year Tribulation. All precede the Second Coming, which means, the Second Coming, unlike the Rapture, *can become* a calculated event *if* you're *in* the 7-year Tribulation.

For instance, in Revelation 12:6 we see that the Jewish people will have to wait upon the Lord for 1,260 days, starting when the Antichrist stands in the Temple of God and declares himself to be God as mentioned in 2 Thessalonians 2:4.

Revelation 12:6 "The woman fled into the desert to a place prepared for her by God, where she might be taken care of for 1,260 days."

2 Thessalonians 2:4 "He will oppose and will exalt himself over everything that is called God or is worshiped, so that he sets himself up in God's temple, proclaiming himself to be God."

This event will take place at the midway-point of the 7-year Tribulation. It's called the abomination of desolation.

Daniel 9:27 "He will confirm a covenant with many for one 'seven.' In the middle of the 'seven' he will put an end to sacrifice and offering. And on a wing of the temple he will set up an abomination that causes desolation, until the end that is decreed is poured out on him."

When the Jewish people flee into the wilderness, they know that all they have to do is wait out those 1,260 days.[2] They're at the halfway point.

Matthew 24:15-16 "So when you see standing in the holy place 'the abomination that causes desolation,' spoken of through the prophet Daniel – let the reader understand – then let those who are in Judea flee to the mountains."

So as you can see, the Second Coming clearly becomes a calculated "known" event. Furthermore, some would even say you could predict the general time frame of the Second Coming as far back as the beginning of the 7-year Tribulation when the Antichrist makes a treaty or covenant with the nation of Israel already mentioned in Daniel 9:27. The Tribulation period is a 7-year period, the final week of Daniel's 70th week prophecy, so just add another 1,260 days for the first half to the already mentioned second half, which was calculated as 1,260 days, and you get a total of 2,520 days for the whole thing.

But wait a second. Doesn't this create a contradiction in Scripture? I thought Jesus said when referring to His Second Coming in Matthew 24 that no one would "know" the day or hour of His Second Coming.

Matthew 24:36 "No one knows about that day or hour, not even the angels in heaven, nor the Son, but only the Father."

Matthew 24:42 "Therefore keep watch, because you do not know on what day your Lord will come."

Matthew 24:44 "So you also must be ready, because the Son of Man will come at an hour when you do not expect Him."

Matthew 24:50 "The master of that servant will come on a day when he does not expect him and at an hour he is not aware of."

Matthew 25:13 "Therefore keep watch, because you do not know the day or the hour."

All of these verses are talking about the Second Coming of Jesus, so which is it? Will we "know" when His Second Coming happens or not? Well, first of all, the events mentioned in Matthew 24 (wars, rumors of wars, earthquakes, pestilences, signs in the sky, abomination of desolation, martyrdom, etc.) as "signs" of His Coming are meant just for that. They are "signs" for those in the 7-year Tribulation to "know" when He was coming back. Jesus gave those signs in response to the Disciples question to Him, "Tell us when this will happen and what will be the sign of Your coming." These "signs" do indeed give them the ability to know the *general time period* of the "beginning" of the Second Coming, with the "Sign" of the Son of Man. But they do not give them *the exact day or hour* of the "remaining events" that "follow" the Second Coming, that is, the actual establishing of the kingdom and judgment. One researcher puts it this way:

"The time period of the Second Coming will be known, it has to be known. It has to be known because of all the sequence of events. The abomination of desolation will be an historical event. The tremendous worldwide conflicts, the wars, the rumors of wars, the nation rising against nation, kingdom against kingdom, the famines, the pestilences, the descriptions of Revelation 6 to 18 where the fresh water is devastated and the salt water is devastated and the sea is turned to blood and where the day is set off its normal cycle and daylight is shortened and there's a greater amount of darkness, and all of those events that are very observable will indicate that it is the general period and the general time of the Second Coming.

But the day and the hour will not be known. That will come with suddenness in an unexpected way. We know that the Coming of the Son of Man is immediately after the Tribulation. But how immediately the establishment of the kingdom and judgment that follows, we don't know.

To approach it another way, remember this: That both Daniel in the Old Testament and John in the New Testament writing in Revelation tell us that the Great Tribulation, the second half of the 7-year Tribulation, is a period of three and a half years, 42 months, 1,260 days. We find that in Daniel 7:25, 9:27, and 12:7. We find it in Revelation 11 verses 2 and 3, in Revelation Chapter 12 verse 14 and Revelation 13 verse 5.

So, there are all those indicators, very clearly, that say the second half is a three-and-a-half-year period. It starts with the abomination of desolation in verse 15, the antichrist setting up his self-worship. So that's very observable.

Immediately after, says verse 29, comes the "sign" of the Son of Man in heaven. Now, how immediately after He *comes and establishes His Kingdom*, we don't know. There's some latitude in that. There's a period of time in there.

Daniel gives us a hint of this latitude because in Daniel 12:11 where he speaks of a period of testing and tribulation (after the abomination of desolation, the halfway point of the 7-year Tribulation) of 1,290 days, he adds another 30 days on the end.

And then in Daniel 12:12, he speaks of 1,335 days – he adds another 45, making a total of 75 days. So Daniel sees a three-and-a-half-year period, 42 months, 1,260 days, and then he sees another period, which is not described as to its content of 75 days.

It's at least a 75-day interval we see, *but it might even be more than that.* We don't really know because we don't know specifically to what Daniel refers. But there's a time period in there that is *undefined.*

Therefore, there will be all these "signs" leading up to the "sign" of the Son of Man in heaven, the beginning of His Coming, and then "some time" following that, Jesus will establish His Kingdom and judge. No man knows that. It is hidden from men probably because they would dawdle themselves away thinking that in that last and final moment they might take the steps to make things right just in the nick of time.

Therefore God doesn't tell them the exact day or hour."[3]

So the people who are in the 7-year Tribulation will have "signs" to give them the ability to know the "Sign of the Son of Man," the beginning of the Second Coming, but they will not know the exact day or hour of the remaining events that follow the Second Coming, the actual establishing of Jesus' kingdom and judgment. No contradiction there at all.

Either way, the point is this. The Second Coming, the beginning of it, can become a "calculated event" if you're in the 7-year Tribulation. Yet the Rapture remains an "unknown event" *only* if it takes place "prior" to the 7-year Tribulation. Once a person is *in* the 7-year Tribulation, events become calculable.

Therefore, the only way for these two viewpoints to be true, a known event, the Sign of the Son of Man, the beginning part of Jesus Second Coming, and an unknown event, the Rapture of the Church, is to separate these two distinct events. One, the Rapture of the Church, which comes before the 7-year tribulation at an unknown time, and two, the Second Coming of Jesus, which takes place at the end of the 7-year Tribulation, a known time.

This is why the Scripture clearly presents the Rapture and the Second Coming as two distinct events. Here are just 20 differences:

The Rapture	The Second Coming
Christ comes in the air	Christ comes to the earth
Christ comes for His saints	Christ come with His saints
Believers are taken away	Unbelievers are taken away
Christ claims His bride	Christ comes with His bride
Christ gathers His own	Angels gather the elect
Christ comes to reward	Christ comes to judge
There are no signs. It is imminent	Many signs precede it
Revealed only in New Testament	Revealed in both Old and New Testaments
Mystery	Foretold
The Mount of Olives is unchanged	Mount of Olives is divided

The Rapture	The Second Coming
It is a time of blessing and comfort	It is a time of destruction and judgment
Involves believers only	Involves Israel and the Gentile nations
Will occur in a moment the blink of an eye	Will be visible to the entire world
Tribulation begins	Millennium begins
The Lord takes believers to heaven	Believers return from heaven
Living believers obtain glorified bodies	Elect remain in same bodies
Believers go to the Father's House	The Elect stay on earth
Satan remains free	Satan is bound
False Prophet & Antichrist at large	False Prophet & Antichrist thrown into Lake of Fire
Unbelievers remain on earth	Unbelievers go to hell[4]

So as you can see, the Rapture and the Second Coming are clearly two distinct separate events. One is known and the other is unknown and thus they must happen at different times. The Rapture could happen at any moment without warning. The Second Coming is preceded by many signs and can be calculated.

Only the Pre-trib position allows for the Rapture to remain an unknown hour. Remember, if I find myself *in* the 7-year Tribulation then the "unknown" event becomes a "known event" because I can "calculate" it, based on the signs given during that 7-year period.

This is precisely what the other positions on the Rapture do. For instance, if I believed the Rapture was going to occur at the midway-point of the 7-year Tribulation, the mid-trib position, or ¾ the way through the Tribulation, the Pre-wrath position, or all the way to the end with the Post-Trib position, then the Rapture becomes a *known event*.

Just like the nation of Israel, to whom Matthew 24 is addressed, now all I have to do is pay attention to all the "signs" that take place during the 7-year Tribulation that's mentioned in the Book of Revelation, Matthew 24 and elsewhere, like the Seal Judgments, the Trumpet Judgements, the Bowl Judgments, the Antichrist, all that stuff, and calculate accordingly. All of those positions *destroy* the possibility for the Rapture to be an *unknown event*.

Therefore, the Rapture *has* to occur *before* the 7-year Tribulation and its seven years of signs to calculate the event! If you're in it, you can calculate it. The Pre-Trib position is the only position that says there is no heads up warning, and thus you better *get ready* and *be ready* at *all times*! It cannot be known. Be ready now!

Chapter Six

The Absence of the Church

The **third evidence** the Rapture takes place *prior* to the 7-year Tribulation is in **The Absence of the Church**. You see, you'd think if the Church of Jesus Christ really was going to be thrust into the worst time in the history of mankind, the 7-year Tribulation, as stated by Jesus, then you'd find the Church all over the place during that time frame. However, a study of the Scripture reveals that there's a complete absence of the Church, which just so happens to support the Pre-Trib position.

The **first way** we see the Absence of the Church in the 7-year Tribulation is with the **Outline of Revelation**. You see, it just so happens that the Book of Revelation is naturally outlined in a way that promotes the Pre-Trib Rapture.

"THE THINGS WHICH YOU HAVE SEEN"
Chapter 1 – John's Vision of Jesus

"THE THINGS THAT ARE NOW"
Chapters 2-3 – The 7 Churches of Asia Minor

"THE THINGS WHICH WILL TAKE PLACE LATER"
Chapters 4-19 – The Tribulation (Daniel's 70th Week)
Chapter 20 – The Millennial Reign of Christ
Chapters 21-22 – The New Heavens and New Earth[1]

Notice how Chapters 2-3 clearly deal with the Church prior to the future events that will take place in the 7-year Tribulation. However, the Church ceases to become a topic at all during those future events. The point is this. There is so much information and so many chapters devoted to that horrible time frame in the Book of Revelation, one would think that if the Church was going to be in there, they'd be an object of focus once in a while like they were in Chapters 2-3. However, it's not. It would appear by the Book of Revelations' own outline that the reason why the Church ceases to become a topic of discussion during the horrible 7-year Tribulation is because the Church is not going to be a part of the horrible 7-year Tribulation. The Church ceases to become a topic because they have ceased to be on the planet at that time. Their future is elsewhere, therefore, there's nothing to discuss. Do you really think the manner in which the Book of Revelation is outlined is by chance?

By the way, this is not some nifty outline that Pre-Trib scholars have put together themselves just to support their own position on the Rapture. It is actually given to us by God in the very first Chapter of the Book of Revelation.

Revelation 1:19 "Write, therefore, what you have seen, what is now and what will take place later."

The **second way** we see the Absence of the Church in the 7-year Tribulation is with the **Omission of the Word Church**. The Book of Revelation is one of the biggest prophetic sources of information concerning the tragic events of the 7-year Tribulation, Daniel's final week of his 70th week prophecy. In its pages we are given massive amounts of detailed information in regards to this horrible time frame and therefore, again, you'd think if the Church of Jesus Christ was going to be a part of this time frame, then the "word" Church would repeatedly be in there. However, it's not. The word "Church" is mentioned repeatedly in Chapters 1-3, but it is never mentioned as being on the earth in Chapters 4-18, the chapters that deal with the 7-year Tribulation period. Is this by chance? Again, I think not. The word "Church" is absent because the Church is absent! They left at the Rapture prior to the 7-year Tribulation. You can see this absence for yourself with the following chart:

The Use of the Word "Church" in Revelation

Rev 1-3	Rev 4-18	Rev 20-22
"Church" 19 times	"Church" 0 times	"Church" 1 time[2]

Think about it. If the Church was going to experience any or all of the coming horrible 7-year Tribulation, then you'd not only expect a heads up warning from Jesus "for" the Church, but also a serious in-depth, lengthy and detailed presentation "to" the Church on how to handle it, conduct themselves, tips on trying to somehow survive, etc.. However, we see none of that.

Yet, throughout the other books of the New Testament we see a plethora of detailed information given to the Church on how to conduct themselves at this time, how to live in this world at this time, deal with persecution etc., but no instructions let alone mentioning the Church at all during the "time" of the 7-year Tribulation. It seriously begs the question, "Why?" Could it be the reason why the Church is not given instructions let alone mentioned at all during the 7-year Tribulation is because the Church is nowhere to be found during the 7-year Tribulation and thus there is no need for instructions to be given? I think so. So does this researcher:

"It is remarkable, that in the key section dealing with the 7-year Tribulation in the Bible, Revelation 4-18, there is an absolute silence about the Church. And that silence is deafening. The Greek word for "Church" ekklesia occurs 20 times in the book of Revelation. In Revelation 1-3 the Church is specifically mentioned 19 times where Jesus addresses seven letters to seven specific Churches in Asia Minor: Ephesus, Smyrna, Pergamum, Thyatira, Sardis, Philadelphia, and Laodicea. In these letters the Lord gives detailed instructions and admonitions to the Churches.

But then, suddenly, beginning in Revelation 4, John shifts from in-depth messages to the Church, to total silence about the Church for 15 chapters. Incredibly, the Church is never mentioned once in Revelation 4-18. This absolute silence is striking and unexplainable if the Church continues on earth during the Tribulation.

In Revelation 4:1 the Apostle John, who is a member of the Church, is called up to heaven and projected into the future in a kind of spiritual time machine. In the subsequent 15 chapters, from Revelation 4-18, John looks down on earth as the events of the tribulation unfold. But the Church does not appear again until Chapter 19 where she is pictured as a bride, beautifully adorned for her husband, who returns to earth with her glorious Bridegroom at the Second Coming.

Revelation 19:7 "Let us rejoice and be glad and give Him glory! For the wedding of the Lamb has come, and his bride has made herself ready."

This clearly indicates that the Bride has already been in heaven for some time since she has "made herself ready." The Church is then referred to again specifically by the word ekklesia in Revelation 22:16 for the final time. The place of the Church in the Book of Revelation, is compelling evidence that the Church will not be present on earth during the tribulation."[3]

Another key book in the Bible that details the horrible events of the 7-year Tribulation is not just the Book of Revelation but the Book of Matthew, specifically Chapter 24. Now even though the word "Church" is not mentioned in there either, some would erroneously say these events apply to the Church and thus the Church is in the 7-year Tribulation. However, a quick look at the facts again reveals that the Church is absent there as well.[4]

First of all, as with Revelation 4-18, the word "Church" is not mentioned at all in Matthew 24. Not once. Nada, Nothing. Why? Because the context in Matthew 24 clearly reveals it has nothing to do with the Church. The Church does not even come into existence until Acts Chapter 2. Rather, Matthew 24 is dealing with the Jewish people who are one of the primary reasons why there is a 7-year Tribulation in the first place.

Furthermore, we know Matthew 24 cannot be referring to the Church because Jesus starts the Chapter off by saying that the Jewish Temple will be torn down to the ground and destroyed, which did happen in 70 AD. But then a few verses later He says a rebuilt Jewish Temple comes back into existence with Jewish people apparently worshipping at it again. We see this with His reference to the Abomination of Desolation in the Book of Daniel where as we saw, the Antichrist goes up into that Temple and declares himself to be god halfway into the 7-year Tribulation.

The point is this. The Jewish Temple being destroyed or rebuilt has no significance for the Church. Jesus says the Church doesn't need a manmade Temple because we have become the Temple of God by the indwelling Holy Spirit.

1 Corinthians 3:16 "Don't you know that you yourselves are God's temple and that God's Spirit lives in you?"

So the Church is only concerned about "being" God's temple, not a Jewish Temple. However, a manmade Jewish Temple being destroyed and rebuilt is a *very* significant issue for the Jewish people to whom this Chapter is addressed.

Furthermore, Jesus also tells the people during that time frame to "flee to the mountains."

Matthew 24:16 "Then let those who are in Judea flee to the mountains."

Notice He says, "those in Judea." Where's that? Israel! This is not the Church nor can it be the Church. Think about it. Only a small minute fraction of the Church, i.e. Christians live in Israel. If this were referring to the Church it would make this command to flee absolutely meaningless. Secondly, the command to flee is, "to the mountains." Most scholars believe the place referred to here is the ancient rock city of Petra. Question: "Can the whole Church fit into Petra?" I think not. However, the remnant of the Jewish People can.

Next we see Jesus mentioning that those people of that time are apparently "keeping the Sabbath Day."

Matthew 24:20 "Pray that your flight will not take place in winter or on the Sabbath."

Question: "Does the Church observe a traditional Jewish Saturday Sabbath?" No. But the Jewish people do even to this day! We Christians not only worship on Sunday in honor of the Resurrection of Jesus Christ, but we are never given the command to worship on the Jewish Sabbath day. Why? Because we have the Lord of the Sabbath Himself, Jesus Christ. We have the "reality" not the "shadow." This is why the Bible says the following when referring to the Church and the Jewish Sabbath:

Colossians 2:16-17 "Therefore do not let anyone judge you by what you eat or drink, or with regard to a religious festival, a New Moon celebration or a Sabbath day. These are a shadow of the things that were to come; the reality, however, is found in Christ."

Technically, we are free to worship Jesus any day we want as New Testament Christians. However, traditionally we typically come together "the first day of the week" (Sunday) in honor of the Resurrection of Jesus.

Acts 20:7 "On the first day of the week we came together to break bread."

Therefore, the point is this. How could Jesus be talking about the Church in Matthew 24 when He says these people need to "pray that their flight doesn't take place on the Sabbath" if the Church doesn't worship on the Sabbath? Could it be He's referring to the Jewish people who still *do* to this day worship on the Sabbath? I think so.

Furthermore, the Chapter starts out with the Apostles asking Jesus what are the signs of His coming.

Matthew 24:3 "As Jesus was sitting on the Mount of Olives, the disciples came to Him privately. 'Tell us,' they said, 'when will this happen, and what will be the sign of Your coming and of the end of the age?'"

This "coming" He's referring to is not the Rapture but the Second Coming of Jesus which occurs at the end of the 7-year Tribulation. This is why the events that follow, the "signs" of His Second Coming, are all signs that take place *during* the 7-year Tribulation. This can easily be demonstrated by paralleling the events of the Olivet Discourse, Matthew 24 and the parallel passage in Luke 21, with Revelation 6, the beginning point of the 7-year Tribulation.

Olivet Discourse & Revelation 6

Signs of His Coming	**First Six Seals**
24:4-5: False Christs	6:1-2: White Horse (Antichrist)
24:6-7: War	6:3-4: Red Horse (Global War)
24:7: Famine	6:5-6: Black Horse (Global Famine)
24:9: Death	6:7-8: Pale Horse (Global Death)
24:9-13: Martyrdom	6:9-11: 5th Seal Altar of Souls (Global Martyrdom)
Luke 21:11: Signs in the Sky	6:12-17 6th Seal (Signs in the Sky)[5]

As we've already seen, the Church is not mentioned once and is clearly absent during these horrible events mentioned in Revelation Chapters 6-18. They will not be a part of the 7-year Tribulation. So why would the events of Matthew

24 be speaking of the Church when these events parallel perfectly the events in Revelation Chapter 6 that occur *during* the 7-year Tribulation?

In addition, this would also mean that the following often misquoted passages of Scripture in Matthew 24, that some would say is referring to the Rapture of the Church, *cannot* be referring to the Church as well. The whole Chapter of Matthew 24 is referring to Israel, not the Church.

Matthew 24:31 "And He will send his angels with a loud trumpet call, and they will gather His elect from the four winds, from one end of the heavens to the other."

Matthew 24:40-41 "Two men will be in the field; one will be taken and the other left. Two women will be grinding with a hand mill; one will be taken and the other left."

Unfortunately, many people will misquote these passages as Rapture passages when they are not. One, we've already demonstrated that Matthew 24 has nothing to do with the Church, but rather Israel. Therefore, whatever is happening in these passages is happening to Israel. Secondly, when you compare these passages in Matthew 24, that some say refer to the Rapture of the Church, to the undisputed passage in 1 Thessalonians 4, that clearly does deal with the Rapture of the Church, it reveals to us that it *cannot* be the same event.

1 Thessalonians 4:15-18 "According to the Lord's own word, we tell you that we who are still alive, who are left till the coming of the Lord, will certainly not precede those who have fallen asleep. For the Lord Himself will come down from heaven, with a loud command, with the voice of the archangel and with the trumpet call of God, and the dead in Christ will rise first. After that, we who are still alive and are left will be caught up together with them in the clouds to meet the Lord in the air. And so we will be with the Lord forever. Therefore encourage each other with these words."

Now contrast this with the events of Matthew 24:

- Where does 1 Thessalonians 4 mention the darkening of the sun (Matt. 24:29)

- Where does 1 Thessalonians 4 mention the moon not giving its light (Matt. 24:29)

- Where does 1 Thessalonians 4 mention the stars falling from the sky (Matt. 24:29)

- Where does 1 Thessalonians 4 mention the powers of the heavens being shaken (Matt. 24:29)

- Where does 1 Thessalonians 4 mention all the tribes of the earth mourning (Matt. 24:30)

- Where does 1 Thessalonians 4 mention all the world seeing the coming of the Son of Man (Matt. 24:30)

- Where does 1 Thessalonians 4 mention God sending forth angels (Matt. 24:31)

- In Matthew 24 the Son of Man comes on the clouds, while in 1 Thessalonians 4 the ascending believers are in the clouds.

- In Matthew 24 the angels gather the elect, while in 1 Thessalonians 4 the Lord Himself gathers the believers. Also, 1 Thessalonians 4 only speaks of the "voice" of the archangel.

- In Matthew 24 nothing is said about a resurrection, while in 1 Thessalonians 4 it is the central point.

- In Matthew 24 the order of ascent is absent while in 1 Thessalonians 4 it is another central point.

- In Matthew 24 the elect are gathered after Christ's arrival to earth, while in 1 Thessalonians 4 the believers are gathered in the air and taken to heaven.[6]

Clearly these are two distinct, different events dealing with two very distinct, different groups of people. So what are the passages of Matthew 24 dealing with in regards to angels coming and gathering the "elect" with one person being taken while another is left? Simple. They're talking about the angel harvest at the end of the 7-year Tribulation where the "elect" or Israel and any "believing" Gentiles who have not died during the 7-year Tribulation are "gathered" to enter the Millennial Kingdom. The "others" are the unbelieving unredeemed who are cast into hell. Obviously, they don't get to be a part of the

Millennial Kingdom. We see this angel "harvest" in Revelation 14, the "pulling" of the Wheat and Tares of Matthew 13, and in the "separation" of the "Sheep and Goats" in Matthew 25.

Revelation 14:14-16 "I looked, and there before me was a white cloud, and seated on the cloud was one 'like a son of man' with a crown of gold on His head and a sharp sickle in His hand. Then another angel came out of the temple and called in a loud voice to him who was sitting on the cloud, 'Take your sickle and reap, because the time to reap has come, for the harvest of the earth is ripe.' So he who was seated on the cloud swung his sickle over the earth, and the earth was harvested."

Matthew 13:36-43 "Then He left the crowd and went into the house. His disciples came to Him and said, 'Explain to us the parable of the weeds in the field.' He answered, 'The one who sowed the good seed is the Son of Man. The field is the world, and the good seed stands for the sons of the kingdom. The weeds are the sons of the evil one, and the enemy who sows them is the devil. The harvest is the end of the age, and the harvesters are angels. As the weeds are pulled up and burned in the fire, so it will be at the end of the age. The Son of Man will send out his angels, and they will weed out of his kingdom everything that causes sin and all who do evil. They will throw them into the fiery furnace, where there will be weeping and gnashing of teeth. Then the righteous will shine like the sun in the kingdom of their Father. He who has ears, let him hear.'"

Matthew 25:31-34,41,46 "When the Son of Man comes in His glory, and all the angels with Him, He will sit on His throne in heavenly glory. All the nations will be gathered before Him, and He will separate the people one from another as a shepherd separates the sheep from the goats. He will put the sheep on his right and the goats on his left. Then the King will say to those on his right, 'Come, you who are blessed by my Father; take your inheritance, the kingdom prepared for you since the creation of the world.' Then he will say to those on His left, 'Depart from me, you who are cursed, into the eternal fire prepared for the devil and his angels.' Then they will go away to eternal punishment, but the righteous to eternal life."

In other words, as one researcher stated:

"It is done. The goats are destroyed, the tares are destroyed, and the good are kept, the sheep and the wheat."[7]

Or as Matthew in Chapter 24 says, "the elect." Still another researcher states the following:

"It is quite clear that since the Church is not mentioned in Matthew 24, then verse 31 cannot be a reference to the Rapture of the Church. Instead, as one studies the context, it becomes quite clear that our Lord speaks of an end time regathering of elect Israel in order to return them to the land for the Millennium. Instead of using El Al airlines, the Lord will use angelic carriers to transport His people back to their land."[8]

So, as you can see, these events in the Book of Revelation, let alone Matthew 24 are not dealing with the Church at all. They are dealing with Israel. They are dealing with events that happen during the 7-year Tribulation, and the end of the 7-year Tribulation, just prior to the Millennial Kingdom, including the angel harvest of the elect at that time, not the Church. The Church is not mentioned at all in these passages because the Church was removed at the Rapture and became absent just prior to the 7-year Tribulation.

Chapter Seven

The Location of the Church

Many people who disagree with the Pre-tribulation Rapture of the Church say in regards to the location of the Church, "Well, that's easy to answer. The location of the Church is *in* the 7-year Tribulation." For supposed proof they cite the word "saint" and attribute it to the "Church." Now the word "saint" does appear during the events mentioned in the Book of Revelation concerning the 7-year Tribulation, however, a quick look at the facts reveals that it cannot be referring to the Church.

First of all, the word "saint" in the Bible simply means, "holy one." And when you look at the Scripture, Old and New Testaments, you'll see that there are *many different kinds of people* being referred to as a "saint" or "holy one." There are Old Testament saints, New Testament saints, future Tribulation saints, and even saints in the Millennial Kingdom. So just because you see the word "saint" doesn't mean it's referring to you and I today, the "Church Age Saint." There are all kinds of "holy ones" throughout the Bible. Rather, what determines the "identity" of the word "saint" and to whom it's referring is its "context." Just as it is said that the three most important things in Real Estate is location, location, location, so it is with correct Bible interpretation; context, context, context.

For example, take the one English word, "cool." I can use it in many different ways. Even though it's spelled the exact same way, with the exact same letters, the context determines its meaning. For instance, what if I were to state the three following sentences:

- "Wow! That outfit you have on is cool!"
- "Hey, is everything okay? Your attitude towards me is kind of cool."
- "Brrrr. The weather outside is cool."

Now, notice how all three times, the word "cool" was spelled the exact same way with the exact same letters, but each one had a *totally different meaning*. What determined the *correct meaning* was the "context" in which it occurred. So it is with the word "saint." Is it referring to an Old Testament saint, a New Testament saint, a 7-year Tribulation saint, or a Millennial saint? Context determines the correct meaning.

Therefore, that's how we are to rightly interpret "saint" and it's usage during the horrible events of the 7-year Tribulation. For instance, take these passages:

Revelation 13:7 "He was given power to make war against the saints and to conquer them. And he was given authority over every tribe, people, language and nation."

Revelation 13:10 "If anyone is to go into captivity, into captivity he will go. If anyone is to be killed with the sword, with the sword he will be killed. This calls for patient endurance and faithfulness on the part of the saints."

Revelation 17:6 "I saw that the woman was drunk with the blood of the saints, the blood of those who bore testimony to Jesus."

Many people who disagree with the Pre-Tribulation Rapture position will oftentimes cite these verses along with others and say, "See, the Church is in the 7-year Tribulation because it says saint." Really? Just who are these "saints" mentioned here? Remember; context, context, context. Certainly these are not Old Testament saints because that time frame has already passed. Secondly, it can't be referring to the Millennial Kingdom saints because that's still in the future. Likewise I would say neither can it be referring to the New Testament Church Age saints because as we've already seen, there is strong evidence that the New Testament Church left at the Rapture of the Church prior to these events in the 7-year Tribulation and we still have a long ways to go on that evidence. Therefore, that only leaves one other option. These passages must be referring to the Tribulation saints who get saved "after" the Rapture "during" the 7-year Tribulation.

First of all, we know that people can and will get saved during the 7-year Tribulation due to the powerful evangelism campaign going on in the world through the 144,000 male Jewish evangelists, the two witnesses and the angel that flies through the sky declaring the eternal gospel.

Revelation 7:4,9 "Then I heard the number of those who were sealed: 144,000 from all the tribes of Israel. After this I looked and there before me was a great multitude that no one could count, from every nation, tribe, people and language, standing before the throne and in front of the Lamb. They were wearing white robes and were holding palm branches in their hands."

Revelation 11:3 "And I will give power to my two witnesses, and they will prophesy for 1,260 days, clothed in sackcloth."

Revelation 14:6 "Then I saw another angel flying in midair, and he had the eternal gospel to proclaim to those who live on the earth – to every nation, tribe, language and people."

Therefore, the Tribulation saints, those who get saved "during" the 7-year Tribulation, are the "saints" who the above passages are referring to. The lesson is they should've gotten saved "before" the Rapture occurred prior to the 7-year Tribulation. Yes, you finally got saved; praise God for that, but now you're in a heap of trouble. This is because the Book of Revelation clearly states that most of the people who get saved during that horrible time frame will be horribly murdered and martyred and even have their heads chopped off.

Revelation 6:9-10 "When He opened the fifth seal, I saw under the altar the souls of those who had been slain because of the word of God and the testimony they had maintained. They called out in a loud voice, 'How long, Sovereign Lord, holy and true, until you judge the inhabitants of the earth and avenge our blood?'"

Revelation 20:4 "And I saw the souls of those who had been beheaded because of their testimony for Jesus and because of the word of God. They had not worshiped the beast or his image and had not received his mark on their foreheads or their hands."

Therefore, the point is this. Get saved now before it's too late! You don't want to be there! But I think it's clear when you do the homework, just because you see the word "saint" in the Book of Revelation, doesn't mean at all that it refers to you and I today, the "Church Age Saint." Rather, it's referring to those who made a huge horrible mistake and procrastinated too long in getting saved. Context determines its meaning.

Furthermore, not only do we *not see* the Church, let alone the word "Church" mentioned during the horrible events that occur during the 7-year Tribulation, which includes the usage of the word "saint" not being applicable to the New Testament Church in the Book of Revelation, but there is powerful evidence that we *do see* the *location* of the Church in the Book of Revelation. And surprise, surprise, they're nowhere on earth during the 7-year Tribulation. Rather they just so happen to be *in heaven*, which just so happens to be the location where we Christians go after the Rapture.

The **first evidence** of the Church going up into heaven after the Rapture prior to the 7-year Tribulation is the phrase, "**Come Up Here.**"

Revelation 4:1 "After this I looked, and there before me was a door standing open in heaven. And the voice I had first heard speaking to me like a trumpet said, 'Come up here, and I will show you what must take place after this.'"

So here we see right after Chapters 1-3 where in the Book of Revelation the "word" Church is repeatedly mentioned again and again 19 times, the very next phrase in Chapter 4 begins with a command to "Come up here." The "here" or locale is clearly defined by the words, "a door standing open in *heaven*." From here on out, the Church is not mentioned again until the *end* of the 7-year tribulation with the Return of Jesus Christ at the Second Coming. The focus now switches to the Jewish people and God's wrath being poured out on the Gentile nations.

Now, even though this command is being given to the Apostle John, who by the way is a part of the Church, many would believe that this is a prophetic reference to the Rapture of the Church before all the horrible events of the 7-year Tribulation begin in Chapter 6. Why? Because, first of all, the phrase, "Come up here" just happens to be the exact same phrase used in Revelation 11 that speaks of the two witnesses who are killed in the middle of the 7-year Tribulation who are then "bodily" resurrected and ascend into "heaven" as well.

Revelation 11:12 "Then they heard a loud voice from heaven saying to them, 'Come up here.' And they went up to heaven in a cloud, while their enemies looked on."

The second clue that Revelation 4:1 is referring to the Rapture of the Church is found in the next phrase, "a door standing open in heaven." It just so happens that we don't see another "door opening in heaven" until the end of the 7-year Tribulation where this time the armies of heaven, including the Church, are let out at the Second Coming of Jesus.

Revelation 19:11,14 "I saw heaven standing open and there before me was a white horse, whose rider is called Faithful and True. With justice He judges and makes war. The armies of heaven were following Him, riding on white horses and dressed in fine linen, white and clean."

Notice the phrase there, "Dressed in fine linen, white and clean." This is a clear reference to the Church as Revelation 19 reveals.

Revelation 19:7,8 "His bride has made herself ready. Fine linen, bright and clean, was given her to wear. (Fine linen stands for the righteous acts of the saints.)"

The "Bride of Christ" "her" "the Church" is given "fine linen" which is the "righteous acts of the saints." This is clearly a reference to the Church at the end of the 7-year Tribulation coming back with Jesus at His Second Coming. Heaven opens up to receive the Church. Heaven opens up again to let the Church back out.

So according to the Scripture, it would appear that the Church goes into heaven at Revelation 4, prior to the 7-year Tribulation, and then comes out again in Revelation 19 at the end of the 7-year Tribulation. This clearly fits the timeline of a Pre-tribulation Rapture scenario. Again, this is why the Church is mentioned all throughout Chapters 1-3 but then "disappears" until the Second Coming of Jesus at the end of the 7-year Tribulation. The obvious question to me is, "Do you really think this order of events in the Book of Revelation is by chance?" I think not, especially when you examine the alternative.

You see, if the Church really was to be around during this horrible time frame in the 7-year Tribulation, then one would expect a different command to be given. Not, "Come up here" but, "Stay down there," or "Good luck in the midst of all that," or "Boy, wait until you see what's coming next and what you're going to have to go through," or "See you in seven years," or even, "Have fun trying to survive now." But rather, what we see is the command, just like at the Rapture, "Come *up* here" and the Church disappears and is absent until the

Second Coming. I don't think that's by chance. It fits perfectly with the Pre-Tribulation Rapture scenario.

Furthermore, it also needs to be noted that the Church will be busy during the 7-year Tribulation while in heaven, and none of it has anything to do with experiencing God's wrath as this researcher states:

"While the 7-year Tribulation is occurring, the Bible records the Church will be busy with three events. None of the three have to do with suffering on a world being destroyed.

The first event the Raptured Church will participate in is a judgment by God – the Judgment of the Just. This judgment on works is not to determine eternal destiny, but to determine degrees of reward (2 Cor.5:10; Rev.19:6-9).

The second event is the Marriage Supper of the Lamb. This feast celebrates the spiritual marriage of Christ's Bride – the Church – to her Savior. (Rev.19:7-9).

The third event follows the Marriage Supper of the Lamb and is the Church's preparation to follow the King of Kings into the Battle of Armageddon at the conclusion of the Tribulation. This event is the Second Coming of Jesus Christ (Zech. 14:1-21; Matt. 24:29-31; Mk. 13:24-27; Lk. 21:25-27; Rev. 19:11-21). Revelation 19:14 identifies the Church in their "fine linen, white and clean," which was given to them during the first event – the Judgment of the Just. The Church and angelic forces follow the King of Kings into His Second Coming to the earth, but only Jesus Himself will engage in battle and with mere words defeats the nations in siege against Jerusalem."[1]

Speaking of what the Church is "wearing," this brings us to the **second evidence** of the Church going up into heaven at the Rapture prior to the 7-year Tribulation, and that is the phrase, "**The 24 Elders**." It just so happens we see a "group of people" clearly being mentioned "in heaven" while the horrible events are unfolding "on earth" during the 7-year Tribulation. That group is the Twenty-Four Elders.[2]

Revelation 4:4 "Surrounding the throne were twenty-four other thrones, and seated on them were twenty-four elders. They were dressed in white and had crowns of gold on their heads."

Revelation 4:10-11 "The twenty-four elders fall down before Him who sits on the throne, and worship Him who lives for ever and ever. They lay their crowns before the throne and say: 'You are worthy, our Lord and God, to receive glory and honor and power, for You created all things, and by Your will they were created and have their being.'"

They are also mentioned in Revelation Chapters 5, 7, 11, and 14 and in all occurrences they are clearly located in heaven. So the natural, logical question is, "Who are these 24 Elders in heaven?" Well, once again, a quick look at the context reveals the answer. It's the Church!

Now, some would say that the 24 Elders refer to Angels, or Israel, and even all the redeemed Israel and the Church. But I think the context clearly reveals it can only be the Church. We see that in various ways.

The **first evidence** the 24 Elders is referring to the Church is the **Timing**. Now, notice how the initial introduction of these 24 Elders just happens to be right after the command to "Come up here" is given. We already saw this command refers to the Church being Raptured just prior to the 7-year Tribulation. Therefore, based on the order of the introduction of the 24 Elders following the Rapture, this tells us the Church gets Raptured and then gets a new identity, the 24 Elders.

The **second evidence** the 24 Elders is referring to the Church is the **Location**. Again, as was stated above, notice just where these 24 Elders happen to be. In heaven! As one researcher states:

"Are they on earth getting ready for the tribulation? No! They are in heaven worshiping Him who sits on the throne and the Lamb. From their first mention in Revelation 4:4, the 24 elders are in heaven, judged, rewarded and enthroned. If the elders represent the Church, this is another indication that the Church must be Raptured to heaven before the first judgment of the tribulation is unleashed in Revelation 6:1.

The only place you find the Church in Revelation 4-18 is in heaven as the twenty-four elders who are seated on thrones, dressed in white, crowned with crowns worshiping the Lamb."[3]

Speaking of which, the **third evidence** the 24 Elders is referring to the Church is the **Crowns**. First of all, crowns are never promised to angels, nor are angels ever seen wearing them. Yet the Bible says the Church will receive rewards/crowns at the Rapture and the Judgment Seat of Christ.

2 Timothy 4:8 "Now there is in store for me the crown of righteousness, which the Lord, the righteous Judge, will award to me on that day – and not only to me, but also to all who have longed for his appearing."

1 Peter 5:4 "And when the Chief Shepherd appears, you will receive the crown of glory that will never fade away."

This timing of receiving the crowns would also mean that the 24 Elders (the Church) couldn't receive their crowns unless the Rapture has *already* taken place. Another indication of the Pre-Tribulation Rapture.

Furthermore, the crowns also shows us that the 24 Elders cannot be referring to Israel because Old Testament believers will not be resurrected and rewarded until after the tribulation is over.

Daniel 12:1-2 "At that time Michael, the great prince who protects your people, will arise. There will be a time of distress such as has not happened from the beginning of nations until then. But at that time your people – everyone whose name is found written in the book – will be delivered. Multitudes who sleep in the dust of the earth will awake: some to everlasting life, others to shame and everlasting contempt."

The **fourth evidence** the 24 Elders is referring to the Church is the **Title**. Now, the word "Elder" comes from the Greek word "presbuteros" and this just happens to be used in the New Testament to refer to "Church" leadership.

Titus 1:5 "The reason I left you in Crete was that you might straighten out what was left unfinished and appoint elders in every town, as I directed you."

1 Peter 5:1-2 "To the elders among you, I appeal as a fellow elder, a witness of Christ's sufferings and one who also will share in the glory to be revealed: Be shepherds of God's flock that is under your care, serving as overseers – not because you must, but because you are willing, as God wants you to be."

The word "Elder" or "Presbuteros" is also where the Church word "Presbyterian" comes from. It's clearly a term used of "Church" issues. By the way, this is also why nowhere in the Bible are angels ever addressed as, or considered "Elders." This is a term applied only to human beings.

The **fifth evidence** the 24 Elders is referring to the Church is the **Number**. I think the other question that has to be asked about the 24 Elders is,

"Why is there exactly 24? Why not 32 or 15 or 3 or even 178? Why are these Elders numbered as 24?" Well, a quick look in the Old Testament reveals the answer as this researcher shares:

"The Levitical priesthood in the Old Testament numbered in the thousands (1 Chron 24). Since all of the priests could not worship in the temple at the same time the priesthood was divided into 24 groups, and a representative of each group served in the temple on a rotating basis every two weeks. While the nation of Israel was a kingdom of priests (Ex 19:6), only Aaron's sons were allowed to enter God's presence. However, all believers in the Church are priests unto God."[4]

1 Peter 2:5,9 "You also, like living stones, are being built into a spiritual house to be a holy priesthood, offering spiritual sacrifices acceptable to God through Jesus Christ. But you are a chosen people, a royal priesthood, a holy nation, a people belonging to God, that you may declare the praises of him who called you out of darkness into his wonderful light."

Therefore, these 24 Elders are not indicative of Israel but rather they represent the entire New Testament Church of Jesus Christ.

The **sixth evidence** the 24 Elders is referring to the Church is the **Position**. Notice how these 24 Elders are positioned. Not on a couch. Not a day bed. Not even a lazyboy. Of all things they are seated upon, it's *thrones*. Now here's what's important about this positon or placement. Sitting on thrones or being "enthroned with Christ" is a clear promise to the Church!

Revelation 3:21 "To him who overcomes, I will give the right to sit with Me on My throne, just as I overcame and sat down with My Father on His throne."

The Elders and the Church get to sit in the same position. I don't think that's by chance. I think they're one and the same.

The **seventh evidence** the 24 Elders is referring to the Church is the **Distinction**. How anyone can say the 24 Elders are angels is beyond me when the Bible draws a clear distinction between the two, even in the exact same verse.

Revelation 5:11 "Then I looked and heard the voice of many angels, numbering thousands upon thousands, and ten thousand times ten thousand. They encircled the throne and the living creatures and the elders."

How can angels be the Elders when they're clearly two distinct entities in the exact same passage?

The **eighth evidence** the 24 Elders is referring to the Church is the **Redemption**. If there's one thing clear in the Scripture, it's that Jesus died for people, not angels. He gave His life and died on the cross to "purchase" or "redeem" human beings unto Himself, not angelic beings. This just happens to be how the 24 Elders describe themselves. They are people who have been purchased or redeemed and they bring this truth out with the new song they get to sing.

Revelation 5:9 "And they sang a new song: 'You are worthy to take the scroll and to open its seals, because you were slain, and with your blood you purchased men for God from every tribe and language and people and nation.'"

"Purchasing" or "redeeming" people is clearly a word used to refer to the salvation of the Church, not angels. Paul also mentions that elsewhere:

Galatians 3:13-14 "Christ redeemed us from the curse of the law by becoming a curse for us, for it is written: 'Cursed is everyone who is hung on a tree.' He redeemed us in order that the blessing given to Abraham might come to the Gentiles through Christ Jesus, so that by faith we might receive the promise of the Spirit."

Why do the Elders sing a song of "redemption"? Because the Elders are synonymous with the Church who has also been "redeemed."

The **ninth evidence** the 24 Elders is referring to the Church is the **Clothing**. A quick look at the clothing that these 24 Elders are wearing clearly reveals we're also dealing with the Church. They are "dressed in white." This just happens to be the same clothing of the redeemed in the "Church Age."

Revelation 3:5 "He who overcomes will, like them, be dressed in white. I will never blot out his name from the book of life, but will acknowledge his name before My Father and His angels."

Revelation 3:18 "I counsel you to buy from Me gold refined in the fire, so you can become rich; and white clothes to wear, so you can cover your shameful nakedness; and salve to put on your eyes, so you can see."

Revelation 4:4 "Surrounding the throne were twenty-four other thrones, and seated on them were twenty-four elders. They were dressed in white and had crowns of gold on their heads."

Revelation 19:7,8 "His bride has made herself ready. Fine linen, bright and clean, was given her to wear." (Fine linen stands for the righteous acts of the saints.)"

So as you can see, the Church is seen in "white" garments "before" the Rapture happens (Revelation 3) and then is seen again with them after the Rapture happens "in heaven" (24 elders in Revelation 4) and then still has them on after "leaving heaven" and returning to earth with Jesus at His second Coming (Revelation 19).

Also, this "clothing" issue not only helps to identify the 24 Elders as the Church, but it also helps to draw a clear distinction between those who get saved now (Church Age Saints) and depart this world at the Rapture of the Church just prior to the 7-year Tribulation, and those who procrastinate and get saved after the Rapture during the 7-year Tribulation (Tribulation Saints) as this researcher points out:

"That brings up another interesting distinction in Revelation. Have you ever noticed the difference in the clothing of those that stand before the Throne of God in Revelation? Whenever we see those that are martyred in the Tribulation they are clothed in white robes that had to be washed before they could stand before the Throne.

However, there is a second group of people, (New Testament Church) present from the very beginning of Chapter 4 that wear the white raiment of the priesthood of heaven. This is the very same raiment worn by the Lord Jesus Christ.

The martyrs (Tribulation Saints) are clothed in white robes which are STOLE in Greek, Revelation 6:11, 7:9-14. The Church (The 24 Elders) are clothed in the white linen raiment of the priesthood which are HIMATION in Greek, Revelation 3:5, 3:18, 4:4."[5]

Isn't it interesting that you see two totally different garments for two totally different groups of people? Those who get saved now before the 7-year

Tribulation, and those who procrastinate and get saved later. Once again, I think the lesson is clear. Get saved now!

So as you can see, it is not only clear that the 24 Elders is speaking of the Church, but since they are nowhere on earth during the horrible 7-year Tribulation, but rather enjoying and worshipping Jesus in heaven, there is no way you can place the Church in the horrible events of the 7-year Tribulation. They are absent, enjoying God's blessings, due to the Rapture of the Church that took place prior to the 7-year Tribulation.

Chapter Eight

The Promises to the Church

As if what we've seen so far isn't abundantly clear enough that the Church is absent from the earth during the 7-year Tribulation, we even have evidence from the Bible and Jesus Himself that the Church, His Bride, would be nowhere around during that horrible time frame. In fact, God has made bold blanketed promises to that fact.

The **first promise** from God that His Church will not be around during the 7-year Tribulation is **The Church is Kept from that Hour.**[1] This is the promise made by Jesus Himself in the Book of Revelation to the faithful Church of Philadelphia who had endured some serious hardships while still on earth.

Revelation 3:10 "Since you have kept My command to endure patiently, I will also keep you from the hour of trial that is going to come upon the whole world to test those who live on the earth."

First of all, even though this passage is speaking directly to the Philadelphian Church at that time, it is clearly speaking to all of Christ's Church of all time. Otherwise you would have to say that all the words of encouragement and warnings to the Seven Churches of the Book of Revelation are not applicable to us today. That would not only be ridiculous, but it would be about as ridiculous as saying, "The Book of Romans (or any other Book in the New Testament for that matter) was addressed to the Romans at that time and therefore it has no application to me today. Not so. As with the other Epistles in the New Testament, yes, even though they were written to a specific Church at a specific time, the spiritual truths are applicable to all the Churches of all time, including you and I today.

So, if you look at the context of this passage in Revelation 3, you'll see that this Church was faithful to keep God's Word, they didn't deny Jesus' Name, and they put up with some serious persecution from non-believers. Obviously, they were true Born Again Christians. Therefore, Jesus promises these faithful Christians that although they have had it rough here on earth for a little while defending Him and standing up for Him and not giving up, He will at least reward them by "keeping them" or "sparing them" from "the hour of trial that is going to come upon the whole world to test those who live on the earth."

Now, notice the "timing" of this promise. It is given to the Church "prior" to Revelation Chapter 4 where we already saw that the Church is "taken" up into heaven "prior" to the 7-year Tribulation beginning in Revelation Chapter 6. So this promise "to be kept from" this "hour of trial" just happens to also fit the timing of the order of events in the Book of Revelation concerning the Rapture.

Also, notice the distinction of two different groups of people here: the Church that gets "kept from the trial" that is coming upon the whole world, and those who get "tested while still being on the earth." These are clearly two distinct, different groups of people and thus, as one researcher admits, "What is that if not the Rapture?"[2] I would agree for several more reasons.

First of all, the phrase "hour of trial" is the Greek words "hora peirasmos" which simply means "time of testing" or "season of testing." It's not specifically "one hour" but rather a specific "period" or "season of time" when those who are not of the Church, who are still on the earth, will be tested.

Second, notice the context of the testing, "the whole world." This period of testing will come upon the whole planet at the same time. Therefore, this cannot be speaking of some "localized event" in Philadelphia, of some earthquake or some atrocity or some other disaster or even more persecution than they were already experiencing in some future time. And neither can it be speaking of any "local event" in any other part of the world outside of Philadelphia. Rather it has to be speaking of some "global event" that affects the "whole world" and not just for an "hour" or some other short period of time but rather a "sustained" period of time, literally an "extended season." If this time frame is not clearly speaking of the 7-year Tribulation, then I don't know what is. That "period of testing" will affect the whole world, those who remain on the earth, and last for a season or period of time, that of seven years.

Besides, the promise here to the Church is not an "exemption" from "general trials" for they were already undergoing trials and Jesus makes it clear that we Christians will experience general trials while still here on earth, especially when we live for Him and preach His truth.

Matthew 5:11-12 "Blessed are you when people insult you, persecute you and falsely say all kinds of evil against you because of Me. Rejoice and be glad, because great is your reward in heaven, for in the same way they persecuted the prophets who were before you."

John 16:33 "I have told you these things, so that in Me you may have peace. In this world you will have trouble. But take heart! I have overcome the world."

Therefore, this promise from Jesus in Revelation 3:10, to be "kept from this time of trials" cannot be speaking of general localized troubles that all Christians face throughout all of Church history that He clearly warned about. Rather, it has to be speaking of a promise to be exempt from the 7-year Tribulation, the specific time period of testing that is coming upon the whole world as described in Revelation 6-18. It has to be. Otherwise this isn't much of an encouraging promise from Jesus. "You're going through a 'general trial' now but I'm going to reward your faithfulness by keeping you from 'one general trial' later in the future." It makes no sense. However, a promise to never be put under "God's wrath" and have to endure the "worst time in the history of mankind non-stop for seven years of hell on earth", that would encourage a Christian in their general trials!

Third, notice that this promise from Jesus is a promise to be "completely taken out of" this extended period of testing. This is important because there are those that say the Church is *in* the 7-year Tribulation and yet God "preserves them through it." The problem is that's not at all what the word means and once again it negates the encouragement of the promise.

The phrase, "keep you from" is a very explicit term. It is the Greek words, "tereo ek" which means, "keeping out of" or "keeping separated from" or "keeping safe from." Therefore, if this "keeping from" is in fact referring to the 7-year Tribulation which I think it clearly is as mentioned for the reasons above, then this clearly shows us that we the Church are *evacuated* out of the 7-year Tribulation, not *protected* through it as some would say. Rather, common sense tells us that the only way to be "kept from," "separated from", "kept out of" the 7-year Tribulation is to be "removed from it" before it ever begins! Sounds like a Pre-Tribulation Rapture to me!

In fact, if that isn't clear enough that the Church has to be "removed" before the 7-year Tribulation begins in this promise, then let's take a look at some other common sense analogies that apply "tereo ek" and you tell me if that's not what it clearly entails.

The War Analogy: "The Second World War was a time of trial and trouble for much of the world. Suppose you lived on earth prior to this great war, and you were given this promise: 'You will be kept from the trial of World War II.' This means that you would not face any of the bullets or bombs or battles of the war.

Perhaps you would be located in a part of the world not directly involved in the conflict. You could still be in the world, but protected from the war. But suppose you were given this promise: "You will be kept from the TIME of World War II."

For this to be fulfilled you could not be on earth during the entire period of years from 1941 to 1945. To be exempt from *the time* is to be absent at the time when the event takes place."[3]

The Test Analogy: "Let's suppose that I announce an exam will occur on such and such a day at the regular class time. Then suppose I say, 'I want to make a promise to students whose grade average for the semester so far is A. The promise is: I will keep you from the exam.'

Now I could keep my promise to those A students this way: I would tell them to come to the exam, pass out the exam to everyone, and give the A students a sheet containing the answers. They would take the exam and yet in reality be kept from the exam. They would live through the time but not suffer the trial. This is Post-Tribulationism: protection while enduring.

But if I said to the class, 'I am giving an exam next week. I want to make a promise to all the A students. I will keep you from the hour of the exam.' They would understand clearly that to be kept for the hour of the test exempts them from being present during that hour. This is Pre-Tribulationism, and this is the meaning of the promise of Revelation 3:10.

And the promise came from the risen Savior who Himself is the deliverer of the wrath to come. Thank God, we will be kept from the hour of testing."[4]

The Miscellaneous Analogy: "To be *kept out of* jail means that the person will not be behind bars. To be *kept out of* the swimming pool means that the person is exempt from getting wet. To be *kept out of* the army means that the person was not allowed in the army, and thus he was exempt from serving in the army. If a basketball player was *kept out of* the entire ball game, it means that he did not get to play at all. He did not see any action. If a sign on a person's property said, "KEEP OUT!" then this means that the person did not want you on his property at all. He did not want your presence there at all.

Moses was *kept out of* the Promised Land, which means that he did not enter at all. To be KEPT OUT OF "the hour of trial" that will come upon all the world means that the person will not enter that time at all. He will be exempt from that time. He will not be present on earth during that time."[5]

So, as you can see, even with common sense analogies, it is clear that Jesus' promise to "keep His Church from" the "hour of trial" coming on the "whole world" is a complete removal and evacuation from the 7-year Tribulation and definitely *not* a preservation through it as Post-Tribulationalism, Pre-Wrath, and Mid-Tribulationists promote. That would be a clear denial of what the words "tereo ek" means.

Besides, if Jesus had truly meant to say that His Church would be "preserved through" the 7-year tribulation then He would have used the Greek preposition "dia" which does carry with it that meaning. However, He deliberately chose "tereo ek" which clearly means "an evacuation from."

Furthermore, if the other positions want to say that Revelation 3:10 is a promise of "protection" for believers "through" the tribulation, then how do they explain Revelation 6 and 7 which presents millions of believers being "martyred" during the tribulation?

Revelation 6:9-11 "When he opened the fifth seal, I saw under the altar the souls of those who had been slain because of the word of God and the testimony they had maintained. They called out in a loud voice, 'How long, Sovereign Lord, holy and true, until You judge the inhabitants of the earth and avenge our blood?' Then each of them was given a white robe, and they were told to wait a little longer, until the number of their fellow servants and brothers who were to be killed as they had been was completed."

Revelation 7:9,13-15 "After this I looked and there before me was a great multitude that no one could count, from every nation, tribe, people and language, standing before the throne and in front of the Lamb. They were wearing white robes and were holding palm branches in their hands. Then one of the elders asked me, 'These in white robes – who are they, and where did they come from?' I answered, 'Sir, you know.' And he said, 'These are they who have come out of the great tribulation; they have washed their robes and made them white in the blood of the Lamb.'"

As has already been outlined earlier, the Pre-Tribulationalist would simply respond that these "martyred people" are referring to the Tribulation Saints who get saved "after" the Rapture and thus there is no contradiction with the promise in Revelation 3:10 to be "kept from." You have two different groups of people here. However, the other positions clearly have a contradiction on their hands. These people are *not* being preserved. They're being killed. Could it be because their position is wrong? I think the answer is obvious, as this researcher states:

"Indeed, the first century believers that made up the assembly in Philadelphia never lived to see the time of trouble that this verse describes. 'The hour of testing' spoken of by the Lord would not be fulfilled for some two thousand years, and yet the Lord was true to His promise to the Philadelphian believers even as He is true to this same promise with respect to Church Age believers living today.

There is coming a day when the entire world will be on trial. God will be the awesome Judge and all those who dwell on the earth will endure this time of terrible testing. It will be a time that will involve the terrible plagues and judgments described graphically in Revelation 4-18.

But in Revelation 3:10 the Lord promised His Church Age believers that they would be exempt from the hour of trial or trouble that would come upon all the world. He did not promise to keep us *through* this time or to keep us *in* this time, but He promised to keep us *out* of this time. He will keep us out of this time by removing us from the earth prior to the 7-year tribulation."[6]

The **second promise** from God that His Church will not be around during the 7-year Tribulation is **The Church is Kept from His Wrath**.[7] And if there's one promise that's clear in the Bible, it's got to be this one; "The Church is no longer under the Wrath of God." This is an important distinction to make because some people who disagree with the Pre-Tribulational Rapture position will invariably state something like this in regards to the Church not being in the 7-year Tribulation, "Oh yeah? The Bible says Christians are guaranteed to go through "tribulation" therefore how can you say they won't be in the *7-year* Tribulation?" Or as one researcher states:

"Many people strongly object to the notion that the Church will be Raptured to heaven to escape the time of tribulation on earth. They think this is a form of Christian escapism. After all, they argue, who are we to think that of all the generations of believers who have lived that we are somehow so special that we will be rescued from the coming time of trouble and tribulation."[8]

To me, the answer to this objection is simple. The 7-year Tribulation isn't the same thing as general tribulation. As was already stated prior along with Scriptural examples, it is clear that yes, we the Church will experience and are even promised general trials and persecution. However, the 7-year Tribulation is a specific outpouring of God's "wrath" not just everyday trials or general tribulation. In fact, it's two completely different Greek words.

General tribulation is the Greek word, "thlipsis" which refers to "pressure, oppression, affliction, distress, troubles, or trials." However, God's "wrath" in the Greek is the word "orge" which means "anger, violent emotion, wrath, or indignation." So yes, we are clearly promised to experience "general tribulation" "thlipsis," or "trials, troubles, and affliction", no disagreement there. However, "wrath" or "orge" is referring to God's "anger or indignation" and the Scripture is clear, Jesus set His Church free from that.

Romans 5:8-11 "But God demonstrates His own love for us in this: While we were still sinners, Christ died for us. Since we have now been justified by His blood, how much more shall we be saved from God's wrath through Him! For if, when we were God's enemies, we were reconciled to Him through the death of His Son, how much more, having been reconciled, shall we be saved through His life! Not only is this so, but we also rejoice in God through our Lord Jesus Christ, through whom we have now received reconciliation."

1 Thessalonians 1:10 "And to wait for His Son from heaven, whom He raised from the dead – Jesus, Who rescues us from the coming wrath."

1 Thessalonians 5:9-11 "For God did not appoint us to suffer wrath but to receive salvation through our Lord Jesus Christ. He died for us so that, whether we are awake or asleep, we may live together with Him. Therefore encourage one another and build each other up, just as in fact you are doing."

These Scriptures make it abundantly clear that while yes we the Church may experience "thlipsis" or "general tribulation" on earth here today, we will *never* experience God's "orge" or His "wrath" including the future time of "wrath" being poured out on earth during the 7-year Tribulation.

That's why we see the specific phrase there, "*the* coming wrath." Not just "wrath" but "*the* coming wrath." Wrath has the definite article in front of it in that passage which points to the specific time of wrath coming in the future, the Day of the Lord, or the 7-year Tribulation.

By the way, this "wrath" here is not referring to the "wrath of hell" as some would say because the Thessalonians already knew that. That's the barebones message of the Gospel. Besides, the context of 1 Thessalonians 5 is clearly talking about the wrath of the 7-year Tribulation, the Day of the Lord, not the wrath of hell. Therefore, the wrath spoken of that we are delivered from is clearly the 7-year Tribulation.

This is also why we saw in the first promise that the Church was to be "kept from" the 7-year Tribulation because the 7-year Tribulation is a time of God's "wrath" and this second promise shows us clearly that we are "saved," "rescued," and "not appointed" unto that time frame. Total consistency.

In fact, it also fits the consistent timing of Paul's encouragement to the Thessalonian Church. In Chapter 1 he says, "Jesus rescued us from God's wrath," and then in Chapter 3 he talks about the Rapture and being "caught up together with them in the clouds to meet the Lord in the air and so we will be with the Lord forever" before the 7-year Tribulation. Then in Chapter 5 he reiterates it again, "Therefore encourage one another with these words" the truth that we are not "appointed to suffer under God's wrath" during the 7-year Tribulation. Again, total consistency. It's a natural, seamless and logical flow.

Furthermore, focus on the words there, "rejoice" and encourage." Paul says to "rejoice" about this truth that we are "saved" from the wrath of God and to "encourage" one another with it. Why? Because being "saved" from God's wrath and "rescued" from God's wrath, and no longer being "appointed" to suffer under God's wrath including the time when it's poured out during the 7-year Tribulation is something to get excited over.

Which by the way, is a serious problem for those who disagree with the Pre-Tribulational Rapture position. If I am going to have to suffer under God's wrath for 3½ years, 5½ years or all 7 years of the 7-year Tribulation as the Mid-Trib, Pre-Wrath or Post-Trib position espouses, then what's so comforting about that? This is hell on earth. This is the worst time in the history of mankind as Jesus states. Why and how could I rejoice in that? This command to "encourage" makes no sense *unless* you are promised to be "saved," and "rescued," and "not appointed" unto that horrible time frame. One man states this:

"Believers in every generation have faced trouble. Some have faced terrible persecution and even martyrdom. Jesus Himself told His disciples, 'In the world you have tribulation' (John 16:33b). Acts 14:22b the Apostle Paul said, 'Through many tribulations we must enter the kingdom of God.' Let me make it very clear that I *do not* believe that Christians are somehow exempt from the troubles of this life – even serious trouble. A cursory reading of the Bible would prove this point. True believers get ill, have family problems, deal with emotional stress, face persecution, lose their jobs, and die. We live in a fallen, sin-cursed world. But there is a vast difference between the troubles and tribulations of this life that we all face and the wrath of God poured on a godless, sinful planet in the final years of this age. It's the difference between tribulation (with a little 't') and *THE* Tribulation (with the definite article and a big 'T')."[9]

This is also why we see two totally different groups of people being talked about in the letters to the Thessalonica Church concerning the Rapture, as this man shares:

"In 1 Thessalonians 5:1-5 the interplay between the different audiences is critical. Notice the pronouns that are in italics.

'Now as to the times and the epochs, brethren, *you* have no need of anything to be written to *you*. For *you yourselves* know full well that the Day of the Lord will come just like a thief in the night. While *they* are saying, 'Peace and safety!' then destruction will come upon *them* suddenly like birth pangs upon a woman with child; and *they* shall not escape. But *you*, brethren, are not in darkness, that that day should overtake *you* like a thief; for *you* are all sons of light and sons of the day. *We* are not of night nor of darkness.'

Notice the dramatic change in this setting between *you* and *we* (the believers) in the first and second person, and *they* and *them* (the unbelievers) in the third person. It's striking. The wording indicates that when the tribulation comes there will be two groups of people each exclusive of the other. One group will be Raptured, and the other will face destruction. The Day of the Lord will come upon *them*, and *they* shall not escape (5:3).

Then in 5:4 there's a sudden contrast: 'But *you* are not in the darkness.' *They* stand in sharp contrast to the believers in vv. 4-11 who will escape. This clear distinction between the unbelievers, who will not escape, and the believers, who will escape, is another strong indication that believers are exempt from the wrath of the Day of the Lord."[10]

In fact, if you think about it, how could there *not* be two groups of people being mentioned here? If there wasn't, it wouldn't make sense for another important reason. How could God have His Church, the Bride of Christ be under His wrath when He clearly gave us His Son to rescue us from His wrath? God's wrath is horrible! Would our Heavenly Husband brutally beat His Bride before He receives her? What kind of a loving Husband is that? Is He a wife beater? Also, we the Church are called the Body of Christ. If there are not two groups of people here, does this mean Jesus also beats up His own Body before He comes back? I thought He was already "beaten" for our sake on the cross to save us from wrath? I think the answer is obvious as these gentlemen concur:

"One is forced to ask, how could the Lamb of God die and rise again to save the Church from wrath and then allow her to pass through the wrath that He shall pour upon those who reject Him? Such inconsistency might be possible in the thinking of men, but not in the acts of the Son of God."[11]

"God's wrath will be unlike anything the world has ever seen. And we are forced to ask the question – why would God leave His Bride on earth during this time? It makes no sense. Christ is not intending to bring His Bride to heaven bruised, battered, bleeding, and badly damaged by the dreadful persecutions of the Antichrist, which will come upon the world during the Tribulation. Rather, He has promised to take His Church home in timely fashion, so that she will be kept from the hour of Tribulation in the world."[12]

Now, there are those that would say, "I agree with you that the Church or Bride of Christ is not appointed unto God's wrath, but the 7-year Tribulation is not a time that is full of God's wrath." Or in other words, "It doesn't last all 7 years." Really? Well, this is where the other Rapture positions begin to creatively dance around this Biblical truth. They know the Bible is clear that the Church is "not appointed" unto God's wrath, so in order to "squeeze" the Church into the 7-year tribulation, they have to somehow, someway "make it look like" God's wrath doesn't occur during the whole time period, and/or come up with some other inventive scenario. For instance:

- **Post-Tribulationists** – They believe the Church will be left here on earth to go through this entire terrible time of devastation but that God will "protect" His people during that time.

- **Pre-Wrath** – They agree that Church age believers will be spared from the wrath of God but they limit the time of God's wrath to the final part of the 7-year Tribulation. According to them, all the destruction in the first three-fourths of the 7-year Tribulation is due to the wrath of man and the wrath of satan and therefore the Church isn't Raptured out until after that when they say the wrath of God begins.

- **Mid-Tribulationists** – They argue that God's wrath is not poured out until the last half of the 7-year Tribulation and that Christians will be caught up just before the wrath of God begins in that second half.

In response to the Post-Tribulationalist position, we already saw that there will be no "sparing" at all during this time because the Bible is clear that millions of Tribulation saints will be martyred in the 7-year Tribulation. Also, the Tribulation Saints are not the same identity as the Church Age Saints. That's why God *did* promise His Church Age Saints that they would be "saved," "rescued," and not be "appointed" to *any* of that time during the 7-year Tribulation, unlike what the Post-Tribulationalists would have you and I believe, that we are in *all* of it. Wrong. *All* 7 years is an outpouring of His wrath, therefore we escape it *all*.

Furthermore, to answer the creative dancing around of God's wrath in the 7-year Tribulation by the Pre-wrath position and the Mid-Tribulationalist position, *all* 19 judgments mentioned in Revelation Chapters 6-18 are God's wrath, not just some of them. Also, the seal judgments, which are opened at the very *beginning* of the 7-year Tribulation, are brought forth not by man or satan, but by the Lamb Himself, the Lord Jesus Christ.

Revelation 6:1-2 "I watched as the Lamb opened the first of the seven seals. Then I heard one of the four living creatures say in a voice like thunder, 'Come!' I looked, and there before me was a white horse! Its rider held a bow, and he was given a crown, and he rode out as a conqueror bent on conquest."

As you can see from the very beginning point of the 7-year Tribulation, the Lamb, Jesus (God), is opening the seals from His throne and the order is given for judgment to begin. This is not coming from man or satan, but God Himself, and at the very beginning of the 7-year Tribulation. To say this is coming from man or satan is an abomination. God is the One giving the order for His wrath to begin and it continues all the way to the end of the 7-year period. See for yourself:

Revelation 6:16-17 "They called to the mountains and the rocks, 'Fall on us and hide us from the face of him who sits on the throne and from the wrath of the Lamb! For the great day of their wrath has come, and who can stand?"

NOTE: Even though the word "wrath" is not found in Revelation until 6:16-17, the famine, sword, pestilence, and wild beasts in the first four seal judgments are often associated with God's wrath in other places in the Bible. See (Jer 14:12; 15:2; 24:10; 29:17; Ezek 5:12, 17; 14:21). Also, the verb "has come" doesn't even mean the "wrath" started just then. It's in the Greek aorist tense which speaks of a past event. This means the "wrath" has already been going on and these people in this text are just now acknowledging it.

Revelation 11:18 "The nations were angry; and Your wrath has come."

Revelation 14:10 "He, too, will drink of the wine of God's fury, which has been poured full strength into the cup of His wrath."

Revelation 14:19 "The angel swung his sickle on the earth, gathered its grapes and threw them into the great winepress of God's wrath."

Revelation 15:1 "I saw in heaven another great and marvelous sign: seven angels with the seven last plagues – last, because with them God's wrath is completed."

Revelation 15:7 "Then one of the four living creatures gave to the seven angels seven golden bowls filled with the wrath of God, who lives for ever and ever."

Revelation 16:1 "Then I heard a loud voice from the temple saying to the seven angels, 'Go, pour out the seven bowls of God's wrath on the earth.'"

Revelation 16:19 "The great city split into three parts, and the cities of the nations collapsed. God remembered Babylon the Great and gave her the cup filled with the wine of the fury of His wrath."

Sounds to me like somebody needs to stop "dancing around" the Scriptures and let them speak for themselves, which by the way is how we're supposed to rightly interpret the Bible. But as you can see, even by God's own Word, His wrath is going to be poured out during the *entire* 7-year Tribulation. Therefore, not only is the Pre-Tribulational Rapture position the only position that *agrees* with the Bible, but this would mean the other positions and their versions of God's wrath are a *lie*. Which is precisely why God has told us the *truth* when He promised that His Church would be, "saved, "rescued," and not "appointed" unto that time-frame at all whatsoever, as this man concludes:

"The nature of the *entire* seven year tribulation period is one of pounding judgment from God Himself against a rebellious world. The judgment of God begins with the first seal that is opened in Revelation 6:1 and continues all the way until the Second Coming in Revelation 19:11-21. God Himself and the Lamb are the source of this wrath against the world from start to finish.

Most Americans are well aware of what happened on December 7, 1941. It was 'a day that will live in infamy.' The Japanese bombed Pearl Harbor inflicting heavy casualties on the U.S. Navy and crippling our Pacific fleet. Most people also know what happened on December 8, 1941. President Franklin D. Roosevelt called on Congress to make a formal declaration of war against Japan and the axis powers of Germany and Italy.

However, most people probably *don't* know what happened on December 9, 1941. President Roosevelt issued an order calling all the U.S. Ambassadors home from Japan, Germany, and Italy. Before he unleashed the full wrath of the American military machine on these nations, he wanted to make sure that no American civilians were in harm's way. The wrath of America was for her enemies, not her own people.

In the same way, before God declares war on this godless world at the beginning of the tribulation, unleashing His unmitigated wrath, He will call His ambassadors home (2Cor 5:20). God's wrath is not for the citizens of His heavenly kingdom."[13]

Chapter Nine

The Removal of the Church

The **first evidence** of the Removal of the Church prior to the 7-year Tribulation is with the **Thessalonian Believers**. It just so happens that the Apostle Paul clearly mentions another event that must take place before the Antichrist can be revealed during the 7-year Tribulation. That event is the "removal of the restrainer." Let's take a look at that very important passage.

2 Thessalonains 2:1-8 "Concerning the coming of our Lord Jesus Christ and our being gathered to Him, we ask you, brothers, not to become easily unsettled or alarmed by some prophecy, report or letter supposed to have come from us, saying that the Day of the Lord has already come. Don't let anyone deceive you in any way, for that day will not come until the rebellion occurs and the man of lawlessness is revealed, the man doomed to destruction. He will oppose and will exalt himself over everything that is called God or is worshiped, so that he sets himself up in God's temple, proclaiming himself to be God. Don't you remember that when I was with you I used to tell you these things? And now you know what is holding him back, so that he may be revealed at the proper time. For the secret power of lawlessness is already at work; but the one who now holds it back will continue to do so till he is taken out of the way. And then the lawless one will be revealed, whom the Lord Jesus will overthrow with the breath of His mouth and destroy by the splendor of His coming."

Now, as we saw before concerning this passage, the Apostle Paul is *comforting* and *reassuring* the Thessalonians from a misconception going around at that time by some false teachers saying these Christians missed the Rapture because the Day of the Lord had already come. But Paul says, "No! No! No! No!" Christians are *not* going to be around during that time and he's very emphatic about it.

First of all, we know this because the Bible says that the Day of the Lord is all about God's judgment and bringing people low. It's a time when He pours out His wrath, and anger, and desolation, and vengeance, and destruction. It's terrible. It's a time of gloominess and darkness and distress and trouble, and refers to the cataclysmic final judgment of God on the wicked, not the Church! That's why Paul says "Don't be deceived" *And* you should know better! "Don't you remember I already told you this?" In essence, "Why are you falling for this? You know you can't be there! I already went over this with you guys. Christians are nowhere around in the 7-year Tribulation! We left at the Rapture, prior to the 7-year Tribulation!" So, "Don't freak out and listen to these False teachers!" he says.

Again, if the Thessalonians thought that the Rapture came "after" the 7-year Tribulation started, and they received a letter saying that the Day of the Lord had already started which occurs during the 7-year Tribulation, then would they not be excited beyond words? Of course! They would have been hopeful that the Rapture was at the door because the 7-year Tribulation had already begun! They would not have been troubled or fearful. They would have been excited!

Yet that's precisely the point. The Apostle Paul is writing to alleviate their *fears* and *troubled hearts* concerning the fake letter that said the Day of the Lord had already begun and thus they were in the Tribulation. This *lie* is what freaked them out because they *knew* the Rapture occurred *before* this horrible time frame. This is why Paul says *comfort* or *encourage* one another with these words. You're not going to be here during that time. Calm down. The Rapture occurs before all that!

Then, as if that wasn't clear enough, that the Church is not going to be in the 7-year Tribulation, the Apostle Paul then goes on to give the Thessalonian believers *another* evidence that the Church will be nowhere around during the 7-year Tribulation. That's in the phrases, "the one who now holds it back" and "will continue to do so *until* he is taken out of the way."

So that's the $64,000 question. Who is the one "holding all this back," and who is the "one taken out of the way" so that all these events "can" happen, that is, the 7-year Tribulation and the revealing of the Antichrist? Well actually, throughout Church history there have been many suggestions as to who this is. For instance, some have said it is:

- The Roman Empire
- The Jewish State
- The Apostle Paul
- The Preaching of the Gospel
- Human Government
- satan
- Elijah
- Some unknown heavenly being
- Michael the archangel
- The Holy Spirit
- The Church[1]

As you can see, the opinions on the "restrainer's" identity vary greatly. However, I believe a careful study of these passages will reveal the identity of this "one" who is "holding all this back." First of all, the phrase there, "holds it back" is "katecho" in the Greek and it simply means, "to restrain, to hold back, or to hinder the course or progress of." Secondly, it is preceded by the word "now" as in "now holds it back" which is the Greek word "arti" and it means, "right now, at this very time, at this very moment." Third, the word "one" as in "the one who now holds it back" is referred to in both the neuter and masculine. Fourth, the phrase "taken out of the way" are the Greek words "ginomai meso" which means, "to arise from the midst" or "be made or finished from among."

So you put all this together in the context and I think you can begin to narrow it down. Whoever this "one" is must be "removable," and must be also at the same time "powerful enough to hold back" or "restrain evil" and the "appearance of the Antichrist" *right now*. To me, that would leave you with only one option and that is the Holy Spirit's presence in the Church today.

Think about it. Are we not the "salt and light" of the earth, maintaining God's righteous decrees which "restrains" evil from marching forward without total restraint? Also, is not our presence here on earth "preventing" the appearance of the Antichrist? I mean, wouldn't we be the very first ones pointing him out to the world, blowing the whistle, ruining his plans and warning everyone not to fall for his lies and deceptions? Of course!

Therefore, once we the Church "arise from the midst" and are "taken out of the way" before this time period begins, the 7-year Tribulation, then there's nothing "holding back" the Antichrist from "appearing" and his "evil plans" and "evil in general" from spreading "unrestrained." It truly becomes, "the worst time in the history of mankind" as Jesus forewarns and as this man shares:

"Second Thessalonians 2:3-8 outlines and describes in broad terms three important ages that take us from the Present Age to Eternity.

The Present Age (Before the Rapture)	The Age of Restraint
The Tribulation Age (After the Rapture)	The Age of Rebellion
The Messianic Age (After the 2nd Coming)	The Age of Revelation

Amazingly, this Present Age in which we live is described as the time or age of Restraint. There is something or someone who is restraining or holding back the full blast of evil that is to come when the Antichrist is unleashed. If this evil world we live in now is described as time of restraint what in the world will it be like when the restraint is removed? What will this world be like when all restraint against the Antichrist and his wickedness is taken out of the way? It will be like removing a dam from a lake – evil will overflow this world swamping everything in its path."[2]

In other words, you don't want to be around during that time frame. Furthermore, the Holy Spirit's presence in the Church is the only explanation that also answers the identity of the "one" as being "both" neuter and masculine at the same time. In the Bible the word for Spirit is "pneuma" which is neuter, and yet at the same time the Bible consistently refers to the Holy Spirit in the masculine. Case closed. The "one" who is both neuter and masculine at the same time is the Holy Spirit's presence in the Church today.

Now, notice I didn't say this identity was "just" the Holy Spirit Himself but the Holy Spirit's presence in the Church today. That's because the Holy Spirit is God who is omnipresent and thus cannot be removed from the earth completely. Secondly, we also know, as has already been mentioned, that millions of people will be saved during the 7-year Tribulation which require the Holy Spirit to still be functioning on the earth convicting them of the need for salvation. Therefore it has to be the Holy Spirit's "restraining influence" in the Church today. His ministry on earth at that time will simply revert back to the way it was in the Old Testament before the Church was in existence, as these men state:

"The one who holds back the onslaught of satan, is the restraining influence of God the Holy Spirit, Who presently restrains evil through the Church. In Acts 2, the Holy Spirit came to earth in a new capacity that He had not fulfilled before. He was present on earth before that time, but now He came to fulfill a new ministry.

The Spirit was present during creation according to Genesis 1:2, and was on earth all during Old Testament times to convict sinners and uniquely empower certain ones of God's people. But on the day of Pentecost He came to earth with a new ministry – to indwell each individual believer and the Church as a whole.

And the presence of the Spirit in all believers individually and corporately is the means God uses in this age to restrain evil. That restraining influence will be here as long as the Church is here. The return of the Holy Spirit to heaven will not be a complete withdrawal from earth, but a return in the sense that He came at the very beginning of the Church age."

"The removal of the Holy Spirit does not have to be an all or nothing proposition. I believe His being 'taken out of the way' will only be a degree of removal. Before the Church Age, people were able to find salvation, which obviously meant the Holy Spirit was at work on earth. When the outpouring of the Holy Spirit occurred at Pentecost, we didn't have a second Holy Spirit come to earth. His removal at the Rapture will only be a reversal or ending of the Pentecostal outpouring."

"For when the Church is removed at the Rapture, the Holy Spirit goes with the Church insofar as His restraining power is concerned. His work in this Age of Grace will be ended. Henceforth, during the 7-year Tribulation, the Holy Spirit will still be here on earth, of course – for how can you get rid of God? But He will not be indwelling believers as He does now. Rather, He will revert to His Old Testament ministry of 'coming upon' special people."[3]

So that only leaves us with one final question. When then will the Church and thus the Holy Spirit's "restraining" influence be removed from the earth? Well, I think the answer is obvious once again based on the context. It has to be "before" the 7-year Tribulation begins.

We already saw that the whole context of this passage is dealing with the Day of the Lord, the 7-year Tribulation, and the manifestation of the Antichrist. Paul already alleviated the "fears" of the Thessalonica Church from the *lie* that was going around that they were in the Day of the Lord, hence the 7-year Tribulation, and thus "encouraged" them that the Church was *not* going to be anywhere around during that time frame. So the Church, the "restraining influence" has to be removed prior to this event, the 7-year Tribulation.

Also, the manifestation of the Antichrist is also foretold in Daniel 9:27 which is the very event that starts the 7-year Tribulation.

Daniel 9:27-28 "He will confirm a covenant with many for one 'seven.' In the middle of the 'seven' he will put an end to sacrifice and offering. And on a wing of the temple he will set up an abomination that causes desolation, until the end that is decreed is poured out on him."

This "one seven" that the Antichrist makes a covenant with the people of Israel is the final week of Daniel's 70th week prophecy concerning Israel and the Gentile nations, not the Church. The Church doesn't even come into existence until literally centuries later. Lord willing, we'll get to that in much greater detail in just a little bit. Furthermore, this "week" or "seven" is why we have a 7-year Tribulation in the first place.

But as you can see, the original manifestation of the Antichrist "begins" at the "beginning" of the 7-year Tribulation with the peace treaty with Israel and the Church is nowhere to be found during this time frame. Later in the "middle" of the seven, halfway into the 7-year Tribulation, the Antichrist commits the "abomination that causes desolation" by declaring himself to be god in the rebuilt Jewish temple. This just so happens to fit the exact time frame of the Pre-Tribulational Rapture of the Church mentioned by Paul in 2 Thessalonians 2.

One – The Rapture of the Church prior to the Beginning

2 Thessalonians 2:1-2 "Concerning the coming of our Lord Jesus Christ and our being gathered to Him, we ask you, brothers, not to become easily unsettled or alarmed by some prophecy, report or letter supposed to have come from us, saying that the Day of the Lord has already come." (Paul reassures that the Church is gone prior to the 7-year Tribulation)

Daniel 9:27 "He will confirm a covenant with many for one 'seven.'" (The Church is not mentioned in this "seven," because it deals with Israel and the Gentile nations)

Two – The Revealing of the Antichrist in the Beginning

2 Thessalonians 2:3 "Don't let anyone deceive you in any way, for that day will not come until the rebellion occurs and the man of lawlessness is revealed, the man doomed to destruction."

Daniel 9:27 "He will confirm a covenant with many for one 'seven.'"

Three – The Abomination of the Antichrist in the Middle

2 Thessalonians 2:4 "He will oppose and will exalt himself over everything that is called God or is worshiped, so that he sets himself up in God's temple, proclaiming himself to be God.

Daniel 9:28 "In the middle of the 'seven' he will put an end to sacrifice and offering. And on a wing of the temple he will set up an abomination that causes desolation, until the end that is decreed is poured out on him."

So as you can see, according to Daniel's and Paul's timeline, the Antichrist is revealed "first" when he makes a treaty or "covenant" with the people of Israel at the beginning of the 7-year Tribulation, the final week of Daniel's 70th week prophecy. Then in the "middle" of that time period he declares himself to be god in the rebuilt Jewish temple, i.e. the abomination of desolation. Therefore, the "one" holding him back from doing these things must be "taken out of the way" before the 70th week or the 7-year Tribulation begins. Only the Pre-Tribulational Rapture position fits this Biblical timeline, as these researchers also conclude:

"The Church must be removed before the man of sin is revealed. The man of sin will be revealed when he makes a treaty with Israel (Dan. 9:27), and this will mark the beginning of Daniel's 70th week. Thus the Church must be removed prior to the beginning of Daniel's 70th week (prior to the 7 year Tribulation)."

"Because the revealing of the Antichrist coincides with the beginning of the 7-year Tribulation starting with his peace treaty with Israel (Daniel 9:27), then the Restrainer has to be removed before the Tribulation. Therefore, the Rapture and the removal of the Church must coincide, and at the beginning of the seven years."

"Trying to identify antichrist is just a waste of time because he will not be revealed until after the Rapture (2 Thessalonians 2:1-12). Only after the Rapture of the Church will the identity of the antichrist be revealed. In other words, you don't want to know who he is. If you ever do figure out who he is, you have been left behind!"[4]

The **second evidence** of the Removal of the Church prior to the 7-year Tribulation is with **Previous Believers**. Some people scoff at the idea of a Rapture of the Church because they just can't see how God could "spare" some people from a time of His judgment while others "have" to be "in" it. They claim its "unfair" for some to escape God's judgment, like the Rapture of the Church from the 7-year Tribulation, while others have to suffer "through" it. However, again, we shouldn't be surprised by this merciful gesture from God. He's done it many times throughout the Bible.

THE SPARING OF NOAH & LOT

If you take a look at the accounts of both Noah and Lot, I think you can clearly see that they and their immediate families were not only "spared" from God's judgment, but the people around them had an opportunity to join them in God's rescue, however, they unfortunately rejected His merciful offer and therefore suffered the consequences.

Genesis 7:7 "And Noah and his sons and his wife and his sons' wives entered the ark to escape the waters of the flood."

Genesis 19:23-25,29 "By the time Lot reached Zoar, the sun had risen over the land. Then the LORD rained down burning sulfur on Sodom and Gomorrah – from the LORD out of the heavens. Thus He overthrew those cities and the entire plain, including all those living in the cities – and also the vegetation in the land. So when God destroyed the cities of the plain, He remembered Abraham, and He brought Lot out of the catastrophe that overthrew the cities where Lot had lived."

So here we see Noah and his family "escaped" the waters of the flood and Lot (along with his two daughters as mentioned in Genesis 19) were "brought out" of that time of catastrophe. In fact, all of them were not only "spared" from the judgment, but the very judgments themselves did not "start" until they were "safe." The flood didn't come until Noah and his family entered the "safety" of the ark. Likewise the fire didn't come down and destroy Sodom and Gomorrah until Lot and his daughters were "safely" led away.

So it will be with the Rapture of the Church. We will "escape" and be "spared" from the 7-year Tribulation, and it is only when the Church is "brought out" and led "safely into heaven" that the time of judgment, the 7-year Tribulation will begin.

However, some would say Noah and Lot are actually examples of God "preserving" His people "through" His time of judgment and thus become examples of how God will "preserve" the Church "through" the 7-year Tribulation. Yet, we've already seen a multitude of examples as to why the Church will not be around during the 7-year Tribulation. However, let's take a closer look at these passages and see if there's really a "preserving" going on here.

First, notice how Noah and His family are "above" the waters not "in" the waters with the rest of the world "glub glubbing it" during this time of judgment. Noah was not holding his breath trying to survive or "preserve" his life "under" the water. He's "out of the water" "above it all." That's not a picture of "preserving," that's a picture of "escaping" just like the text says.

Secondly, if God had really meant for Noah and his family to be preserved "in" this time of judgment "under" the water, then I think He would have instructed Noah to build a "submarine" to be "submerged in" so he could trudge "through it" like everyone else. However, God told Noah to build an "ark" so that you and your family would "float" "escape" and be "rescued" "above" the waters and "spared" from the judgment "below."

Similarly Lot and his two daughters were "led out" of the place of judgment and not told to build a shelter "in the midst" of the judgment. A shelter "in" would be "preserving" but a "leading out" is clearly a "sparing."

Still other examples of "certain people" being "spared" from a time of God's judgment would be Israel's escape from Egypt as mentioned in both Old and New Testaments:

Hebrews 11:29 "By faith the people passed through the Red Sea as on dry land; but when the Egyptians tried to do so, they were drowned."

As well as the deliverance of Rahab in Jericho as is also mentioned in the Old Testament and the New Testament Book of Hebrews:

Hebrews 11:31 "By faith the prostitute Rahab, because she welcomed the spies, was not killed with those who were disobedient."

It is clear that there is nothing "unfair" going on here and that God will indeed spare "certain people" before His judgment falls. Besides, His mercy is still being extended today; how dare you call Him "unfair." No one "has" to suffer though any of the next coming judgment, the 7-year Tribulation, if they would just respond to God's "rescue" call "today" through Jesus Christ.

However, just like it was in Noah's and Lot's day, if they resist, it's not God's fault, it's theirs. They will themselves be responsible for finding themselves in that horrible time of judgment. They had their way out, but they rejected it. In essence, they are the ones responsible for being left behind. The similarities are being repeated, as this man shares:

"God wouldn't destroy the wicked in Noah's day until Noah and his family were all safely aboard the ark. Not one drop of rain fell until Noah and his family were on the ark and God had shut the door. Afterwards, the rains fell and the wicked were utterly destroyed. The same is true of Lot and his family. No judgment could fall upon Sodom, until Lot and his family were removed. Likewise, the Church will be Translated (Raptured) away from this sin-cursed world before the 7-year Tribulation."[5]

However, the Rapture of the Church is not just a "sparing" from God's judgment like the above Biblical examples. It is a complete "removal" from God's judgment. Yet, once again, unfortunately, some people will also scoff at the idea of the Rapture of the Church prior to the 7-year Tribulation because they say it cannot be found elsewhere in the Bible. Therefore, they say it's not wise to build a doctrine off of it, let alone place your hopes in it. Really? Actually, even a cursory reading of the Bible, including the very first book of the Bible, the Book of Genesis, shows that this isn't the first time we see God "completely" rescuing "certain people" from a horrible time frame, including His judgment on the whole planet, like the 7-year Tribulation will be. Let's take a look at another Biblical example.

THE RAPTURE OF ENOCH

Enoch lived in this world before the time of Noah's Flood and the Bible mentions something that happened to him that was very unique.

Genesis 5:21-24 "When Enoch had lived 65 years, he became the father of Methuselah. And after he became the father of Methuselah, Enoch walked with God 300 years and had other sons and daughters. Altogether, Enoch lived 365 years. Enoch walked with God; then he was no more, because God took him away."

First of all, if you look at all of Genesis Chapter 5, before and after the account of Enoch, you will see that everyone else who was mentioned there, save Noah at the very end, died. Something "special" happened to Enoch. Secondly, the words "took him away," explain what was so "special." It is the Hebrew word "laqach" which means, "to carry away, to seize or take out of, to fetch or be removed." Third, the timing of this "fetching," "removing," or "seizing away" is "prior" to the Global Flood where God pours out His judgment upon this sinful wicked world the first time. Furthermore, we are given more details about the "special" account of Enoch in the New Testament book of Hebrews:

Hebrews 11:5 "By faith Enoch was taken from this life, so that he did not experience death; he could not be found, because God had taken him away. For before he was taken, he was commended as one who pleased God."

So here we see that Enoch was not just "taken" or "carried away," or "removed" but he was removed "without experiencing death." Sounds like a Rapture scenario to me! In fact, the word "taken" there in the New Testament is "metathesis" and it literally means, "a transfer from one place to another." No wonder he "could not be found." God had "Raptured" or "transferred Enoch to heaven" without experiencing death! That's just like the New Testament Rapture of the Church! In fact, God has suddenly "transferred people" more than once in the Scripture:

- Elijah went up by a whirlwind into heaven (2 Kings 2:11).
- Philip was Raptured (suddenly removed) from one place to another (Acts 8:39).
- Paul was Raptured to the third heaven (2 Cor. 12:2,4).
- The Lord Jesus was taken up to heaven at the ascension (Acts 1:1-2,9;Rev. 12:5).[6]

Therefore, as you can see, is it really an "odd" event for God to literally "transfer someone from one place to another" i.e. to heaven prior to Him pouring out His judgment upon our wicked and sinful world? I think not, as the Scripture clearly reveals, and as these researchers also state:

"Enoch was a man who never died. What happened to him was very unusual! But the amazing thing is that the Bible tells us that what happened to Enoch is going to happen again, perhaps very soon! And this time it will not happen to just one man, it will happen to many people. There will be a whole group of people who will never see death. There will be a whole group of people who will suddenly be removed from the earth and they will not be found by those who remain on the earth. This unusual future event is called The Rapture."

"While the Rapture of the Church is the first time that God will take a large group of people from earth to heaven without experiencing death, it will not have been the first time that God takes individuals to heaven in this way. A number of years ago I had a meal with one of the most well-known Reformed theologians in America. The purpose of our get-together was to discuss the issue of Bible prophecy. A number of times throughout our conversation he would stop in mid-sentence and make a comment about how absurd the whole concept of the Rapture was. He was not questioning the timing of the Rapture at this point, but the very idea and concept of a Rapture. Of course, my response was that even though he thought it ridiculous, the Bible teaches this strange event. In fact, the Rapture of the Church will not be the first Rapture in history."[7]

In other words, God choosing to "remove" and "take away" "certain groups of His people" prior to His pouring out of His judgment upon our wicked and sinful planet, is not at all at "odds" with the Scripture, both Old and New Testaments, nor is it "unfair" of Him to do so. As it was in the days of Noah and Lot, so it is today. You have a chance to "escape" through Jesus. He is willing to "remove you," "carry you away," and "transfer you to heaven" prior to His next outpouring of judgment upon this planet in the 7-year Tribulation, if only you would call upon the Name of Jesus today and be saved. The choice is yours.

But know this, if you choose to say no now, then just like the people found out the hard way in Noah and Lot's day, you of your own doing, not God, will have chosen to "remain" on earth and "suffer" the worst time in the history of mankind, the horrible 7-year Tribulation. The question is, "Are you ready for the Rapture?"

Chapter Ten

The Purpose of the Tribulation

It is amazing to me how many different ways and means and attempts people, who are against the Pre-Tribulational Rapture position, will try to "squeeze" the Church "into" the 7-year Tribulation. Even after all the evidence we've seen thus far to the contrary, they will still blindly persist. Even though I disagree I can understand why, because their whole position for the timing of the Rapture is completely "dependent" upon the Church being in that horrible time frame.

But the problem is, if the Church isn't in there, then why do you persist in trying to make it so? Is that how we're supposed to rightly interpret the Scripture? Is not the Bible to speak "out" to "us" what it has to say to "us," not the other way around, "us" speaking "into" the Bible what "we" want it to say? Yet, this is precisely what these other positions do concerning the timing of the Rapture.

One of the biggest indicators that this is exactly what they're doing is when you go back to the very core issue of the 7-year tribulation and that is its *purpose*. Believe it or not, the whole purpose of the 7-year Tribulation has nothing to do with the Church. No wonder it's nowhere to be found! It shouldn't be a surprise. Rather, it has to do with God fulfilling His promises to the Remnant of the Jewish people and the outpouring of His wrath upon the rebellious Gentile nations. Let's take a look at where the 7-year Tribulation all began in the Book of Daniel.

Daniel 9:20-27 "While I was speaking and praying, confessing my sin and the sin of my people Israel and making my request to the LORD my God for his holy hill – while I was still in prayer, Gabriel, the man I had seen in the earlier vision, came to me in swift flight about the time of the evening sacrifice. He instructed me and said to me, 'Daniel, I have now come to give you insight and understanding. As soon as you began to pray, an answer was given, which I have come to tell you, for you are highly esteemed. Therefore, consider the message and understand the vision: Seventy 'sevens' are decreed for your people and your holy city to finish transgression, to put an end to sin, to atone for wickedness, to bring in everlasting righteousness, to seal up vision and prophecy and to anoint the most holy. Know and understand this: From the issuing of the decree to restore and rebuild Jerusalem until the Anointed One, the ruler, comes, there will be seven 'sevens,' and sixty-two 'sevens.' It will be rebuilt with streets and a trench, but in times of trouble. After the sixty-two 'sevens,' the Anointed One will be cut off and will have nothing. The people of the ruler who will come will destroy the city and the sanctuary. The end will come like a flood: War will continue until the end, and desolations have been decreed. He will confirm a covenant with many for one 'seven.' In the middle of the 'seven' he will put an end to sacrifice and offering. And on a wing of the temple he will set up an abomination that causes desolation, until the end that is decreed is poured out on him.'"

If you've ever wondered why it's specifically a "7" year Tribulation and not 94 or 135 or even a 2 year Tribulation, here it is. This is where it all began. The 7-year Tribulation is the final "seven" of "Seventy sevens" also known as the 70th week prophecy of the Book of Daniel. (KJV translates "sevens" as "week" as in "seven" days in a week) And upon closer examination of this text, you will see clearly that this time frame has nothing to do with the Church.

The **first reason** the final week of Daniel's 70th week prophecy has nothing to do with the Church is the **Verbiage**. When you take a look at this letter and to whom it is addressed, you'll clearly see it's NOT the Church. It can't be the Church. Take a look for yourself.

- Verse 20 – "my sin and the sin of my people Israel" (Daniel & the people of Israel)
- Verse 20 - "making my request to the LORD my God for his holy hill" (Daniel & Jerusalem)
- Verse 22 – "Daniel, I have now come to give you" (Daniel a Jewish Person)

- Verse 24 – "Seventy 'sevens' are decreed for your people and your holy city" (The Jewish people & Jerusalem)
- Verse 25 – "From the issuing of the decree to restore and rebuild Jerusalem" (Jerusalem)
- Verse 26 – "The people of the ruler who will come will destroy the city and the sanctuary" (Jerusalem)
- Verse 27 – "And on a wing of the temple he will set up an abomination that causes desolation" (Rebuilt Temple in Jerusalem)

Question, "Where is the Church in any of this?" Answer: *Nowhere*! Why? Because the verbiage clearly reveals that it's all about the Jewish people and Jerusalem and their rebuilt Jewish Temple, *not* the Church. In fact, the text even clearly states right in the middle of it that the "Seventy sevens" including the final seven are "decreed" for *your people*, Daniel's people, the Jewish people, *not* the Church!

The **second reason** the final week of Daniel's 70th week prophecy has nothing to do with the Church is the **Timing**. The approximate date for when Daniel wrote this book containing this 70th week prophecy which includes the teaching of the 7-year Tribulation is between 536-530 B.C. Question, "Where was the Church when this book and Prophecy was written?" Answer: *Nowhere*! Why? Because the Church didn't even come into existence until Acts Chapter 2 which is almost 570 years later! So how could Daniel be referring to the Church in this passage dealing with the 7-year Tribulation, the final week of Daniel's 70th week prophecy, when the Church wasn't even in existence yet? Answer: "*He can't!*"

This is also why the Apostle Paul referred to the Church as an Old Testament "mystery." The people at that time had no knowledge of it.

Romans 16:25 "Now to Him Who is able to establish you by my gospel and the proclamation of Jesus Christ, according to the revelation of the mystery hidden for long ages past."

Ephesians 3:2-5 "Surely you have heard about the administration of God's grace that was given to me for you, that is, the mystery made known to me by revelation, as I have already written briefly. In reading this, then, you will be able to understand my insight into the mystery of Christ, which was not made known to men in other generations as it has now been revealed by the Spirit to God's holy apostles and prophets. This mystery is that through the gospel the Gentiles are heirs together with Israel, members together of one body, and sharers together in the promise in Christ Jesus."

Ephesians 5:32 "This is a profound mystery – but I am talking about Christ and the Church."

Colossians 1:25-27 "I have become its servant by the commission God gave me to present to you the word of God in its fullness – the mystery that has been kept hidden for ages and generations, but is now disclosed to the saints. To them God has chosen to make known among the Gentiles the glorious riches of this mystery, which is Christ in you, the hope of glory."

As you can see, the Church was a "mystery" to the Old Testament writers, which obviously would include Daniel. So again, how in the world could Daniel be referring to the Church in this passage dealing with the 7-year Tribulation, the final week of Daniel's 70th week prophecy, when the Church wasn't even in existence *and* he had *no knowledge* of it period? Answer: *"He can't!"*

The **third reason** the final week of Daniel's 70th week prophecy has nothing to do with the Church is the **Gap**. Now, if you look at this 70th week prophecy from Daniel, you'll also see that it is basically God explaining how He will bring about the consummation of history. And in that examination you will also notice that there is a noticeable gap, a large gap, between the 69th week and the final 70th week. The question is, "Why?" Answer: "This is where the mysterious period of the Church fits in." It makes total sense. Let me show you what I mean. Why was this vision given to Daniel in the first place? What's the reason for it? Well, we see that reason clearly stated in verse 24.

Daniel 9:23-26 "Therefore, consider the message and understand the vision: Seventy 'sevens' are decreed for your people and your holy city *to finish transgression, to put an end to sin, to atone for wickedness, to bring in everlasting righteousness, to seal up vision and prophecy and to anoint the most holy.* Know and understand this: From the issuing of the decree to restore and rebuild Jerusalem until the Anointed One, the ruler, comes, there will be seven 'sevens,' and sixty-two 'sevens.' It will be rebuilt with streets and a trench, but in times of trouble. After the sixty-two 'sevens,' the Anointed One will be cut off and will have nothing."

So here we see that there will be a "total" of 70 sevens until God basically wraps up history and fulfills the rest of His promises that He made to the Jewish people. However, after 62 sevens and 7 sevens for a total of 69 sevens have passed, after the decree that goes out to restore and rebuild Jerusalem from Daniel's time, the Anointed One or the Messiah will be "cut off." That's exactly what we see with Jesus' Triumphal entry into Jerusalem. History records for us the date when King Artexerxes issued that commandment to rebuild Jerusalem in 445 B.C. So if you take the 69 sevens or years mentioned above that needs to transpire before the Messiah is cut off, and times that by 7 for each year, you get a total of 483 years. To calculate the exact number of days you need to take the 483 years and times it by 360 (because the Jewish calendar only had 360 days for each year) then you get a grand total of 173,880 days.

So what happened 173,880 days after the decree to rebuild Jerusalem? Well that just happens to be the exact date Jesus made His Triumphal entry into Jerusalem where He was rejected or cut off from His people! That's not by chance! And neither is the "gap" that is presented in the next verse.

Daniel 9:27 "He will confirm a covenant with many for one 'seven.' In the middle of the 'seven' he will put an end to sacrifice and offering. And on a wing of the temple he will set up an abomination that causes desolation, until the end that is decreed is poured out on him."

Now, we've already seen many times this verse is dealing with the Last Days Antichrist who makes a covenant with the people of Israel which is the very event that triggers or starts the final "seven" or "week" of the 70th week prophecy, i.e. the 7-year Tribulation. Then halfway into that final seven, the "middle of the seven", the Antichrist goes up into the Jewish Temple and declares himself to be god, which is called the abomination of desolation.

First of all, we know this final "seven" is still future because the Jewish people had their Temple destroyed in 70 A.D., and thus in order for this passage to be fulfilled, there needs to be another rebuilt Jewish Temple which obviously hasn't happened yet. However, they are making plans for it right now as we speak, but it's not fully into existence yet.

So the question is, "What has been going on in this "gap" between the 69 weeks of this 70th week prophecy where the Messiah gets "cut off" until now, where we're awaiting this "final week" the 70th week to be unleashed when the Antichrist makes a covenant with the Jewish people and halfway into it desecrates their Temple? Simple. This is where the "mystery" of the Church fits in. God is focused on the Church Age Saints during this "mysterious gap" period, and when that purpose for the "gap" is completed, the Church is then removed at the Rapture, and then His focus goes back on the Jewish people to consummate the "final week," as these researchers state:

"During the Church Age, (the gap) God has had no specific program with the nation of Israel. Rather, in this day of grace, He has been calling both Jew and Gentile to faith in Jesus Christ as the Savior of the world. All who so believe in this day are members of the Body of Christ. But God has not entirely forsaken His people. He has one last cycle of discipline for Israel. That period of discipline will come during Daniel's seventieth week, the week of the 7-year Tribulation."[1]

"The Church Age began on the Day of Pentecost, in Acts chapter 2. The Church Age is thus nearly 2000 years in duration. How then can we explain this amazing "GAP" between the 69th week and the 70th week? It is as if God's clock for Israel has stopped, waiting to start ticking again at some future time. What has God been doing in the meantime? During this 2000 year gap God has been:

- Building His Church (Acts 2:47; 1 Cor. 3:6-9; 12:18; Eph. 2:21-22; 1 Pet. 2:5).
- Taking out of the nations a people for His Name (Acts 15:14).
- Bringing in the fullness of the Gentiles (Rom. 11:25).
- Placing believers into a living organism (1 Cor. 12:13).
- Saving a "showcase" that will eternally display His matchless grace (Eph. 2:7).
- Manifesting Himself through His Body which is upon the earth (1 Tim. 3:15-16).

Just as the Church had an abrupt *beginning* shortly after the conclusion of the 69th week (the coming of the Spirit on the day of Pentecost), so we should expect the Church to have an abrupt *removal* shortly before the beginning of the 70th week.

The Pre-Tribulation model harmonizes perfectly with Daniel's 70th week prophecy while at the same time recognizing the parenthetical and mysterious nature of the Church Age (mysterious in the sense that it was not revealed on the pages of the Old Testament). The Pre-Tribulation model best explains this 2000 year gap and also keeps us from mixing up the Church Age with prophetic Jewish history."[2]

In other words, it explains the whole thing, no contradictions, which is how we're supposed to rightly interpret the Scripture.

The **fourth reason** the final week of Daniel's 70th week prophecy has nothing to do with the Church is the **Audience**. Now we know this final week, the 7-year Tribulation, is going to be a horrific time or as Jesus says, "The worst time in the history of mankind." But who is the audience of that time frame? Who is it dealing with? Well, when you take a look at the Scriptures surrounding that horrible seven years, the audience is clearly not the Church.

The **first audience** the 7-year Tribulation deals with is **The Jewish People**. Not only did we already see by the context of Daniel Chapter 9 that all the 70th week prophecy including the final week of that prophecy, the 7-year Tribulation, is clearly dealing with Daniel, a Jewish person, all the Jewish people, Jerusalem, and the Jewish Temple, and not the Church, but other passages in the Bible concerning this final week clearly reveal this same audience as being the Jewish people. Let's take a look at just a few of them.

Deuteronomy 4:1,25,27-31 "Hear now, O Israel, the decrees and laws I am about to teach you. Follow them so that you may live and may go in and take possession of the land that the LORD, the God of your fathers, is giving you. After you have had children and grandchildren and have lived in the land a long time-if you then become corrupt and make any kind of idol, doing evil in the eyes of the LORD your God and provoking Him to anger, The LORD will scatter you among the peoples, and only a few of you will survive among the nations to which the LORD will drive you. There you will worship man-made gods of wood and stone, which cannot see or hear or eat or smell. But if from there you seek the LORD your God, you will find Him if you look for Him with all your heart and with all your soul. When you are in distress and all these things have happened to you, then in later days you will return to the LORD your God and obey Him. For the LORD your God is a merciful God; He will not abandon or destroy you or forget the covenant with your forefathers, which He confirmed to them by oath."

Clearly we see Moses here speaking to the audience of Israel and encouraging them that even though they will in the future unfortunately rebel against God whereupon He will then scatter them around the world, He will nonetheless, in the later days, have mercy on them and not totally abandon them and still fulfill the covenant He made with their forefathers, the patriarchs. Notice there is no Church here.

Now how about this passage:

Jeremiah 30:4-7 "These are the words the LORD spoke concerning Israel and Judah: This is what the LORD says: 'Cries of fear are heard – terror, not peace. Ask and see: Can a man bear children? Then why do I see every strong man with his hands on his stomach like a woman in labor, every face turned deathly pale? How awful that day will be! None will be like it. It will be a time of trouble for Jacob, but he will be saved out of it.'"

Notice once again to "whom" the Lord is speaking about this horrible time frame. It's Israel and Judah, not the Church! That's why God says it's going to be a "time of trouble for Jacob," not a "time of trouble for the Church." Again, this is why as we saw before that the New Testament Epistles to the Church were *not* writing to the Church about how to "survive" the seven year Tribulation. If the Church was going to experience any or all of the coming horrible 7-year Tribulation as some would say, then you'd not only expect a heads up warning "for" the Church to get ready for this "time of trouble," but also how to deal with it, like God does for Jacob or Israel. However, you see none of that.

Instead, throughout the New Testament we see a plethora of detailed information given to the Church on how to conduct themselves at this present time, how to live in this world now, deal with current persecution, etc., but no instructions let alone mentioning the Church at all during the "time of trouble" of the 7-year Tribulation. Why? Because the 7-year Tribulation, Daniel's final week of the 70th week prophecy, has nothing to do with the Church. It's a time of Jacob's trouble, not the Church's trouble. It's not "Paul's Doom" or "Peter's Demise" or even "Ananias' Agony." No! It's Jacob's trouble, a Jewish name, for a Jewish people, for a Jewish time, not the Church.

Also, notice that this tells us that God is not done with the Jewish people, even after this "time of trouble for Jacob." God once again shows His mercy towards them by once again reiterating that He will still eventually "save them."

Let's take a look at the next passage.

Ezekiel 20:30,34-38 "Therefore say to the house of Israel: 'This is what the Sovereign LORD says: I will bring you from the nations and gather you from the countries where you have been scattered – with a mighty hand and an outstretched arm and with outpoured wrath. I will bring you into the desert of the nations and there, face to face, I will execute judgment upon you. As I judged your fathers in the desert of the land of Egypt, so I will judge you, declares the Sovereign LORD. I will take note of you as you pass under My rod, and I will bring you into the bond of the covenant. I will purge you of those who revolt and rebel against Me. Although I will bring them out of the land where they are living, yet they will not enter the land of Israel. Then you will know that I am the LORD.'"

So who is the audience of this passage concerning the Last Days when God pours out His wrath? The "house of Israel" not the "Body of Christ" or the Church. In fact, it can't be because as we already saw, the Church is not appointed unto God's wrath, which is what the passage is clearly dealing with, so it cannot be the Church. Rather, it is a time of "suffering" and "wrath" and "judgment" as is defined by the text for the Jewish people who have rebelled against God Who will then cause them "to pass under the rod," the Shepherd's rod, and separate the true remnant of Israel from the counterfeit. No unsaved Jew will ever enter the promised Millennial Kingdom at the end of the 7-year Tribulation, which God promised to the Patriarchs. Again, God is showing His mercy even in the midst of His "purging" or "purification" of Israel, not the Church.

Now let's take a look at this one:

Daniel 12:1 "At that time Michael, the great prince who protects your people, will arise. There will be a time of distress such as has not happened from the beginning of nations until then. But at that time your people – everyone whose name is found written in the book-will be delivered."

Now it's already been established that the audience Daniel is writing to in the Book of Daniel is the Jewish people i.e. Israel. And he is clearly sharing that in the future, the Jewish people will be going through a "time of distress" such as has never happened from the beginnings of nations until then. This is clearly speaking of the final week of Daniel's 70th week prophecy. Notice once again, God shows His mercy towards the Jewish people. Your people Daniel, Israel, all those that are saved, will be delivered in that time. As you can see, this has nothing to do with the Church.

In fact, speaking of rescuing a remnant of Israel during the 7-year Tribulation, we also see a parallel passage of this event in the Book of Revelation that also mentions the Archangel Michael "protecting" the Jewish people during this time frame.

Revelation 12:1-9 "A great and wondrous sign appeared in heaven: a woman clothed with the sun, with the moon under her feet and a crown of twelve stars on her head. She was pregnant and cried out in pain as she was about to give birth. Then another sign appeared in heaven: an enormous red dragon with seven heads and ten horns and seven crowns on his heads. His tail swept a third of the stars out of the sky and flung them to the earth. The dragon stood in front of the woman who was about to give birth, so that he might devour her child the moment it was born. She gave birth to a son, a male child, who will rule all the nations with an iron scepter. And her child was snatched up to God and to his throne. The woman fled into the desert to a place prepared for her by God, where she might be taken care of for 1,260 days. And there was war in heaven. Michael and his angels fought against the dragon, and the dragon and his angels fought back. But he was not strong enough, and they lost their place in heaven. The great dragon was hurled down – that ancient serpent called the devil, or satan, who leads the whole world astray. He was hurled to the earth, and his angels with him."

The woman with the 12 stars on her head is the nation of Israel and the 12 tribes. She was pregnant or gave birth to the Messiah Jesus, who came from the lineage of the Jewish people. Then satan tried to kill Jesus but Jesus defeated satan on the cross and ascended to the right hand of the Father in heaven and will then return to rule the nations with an iron scepter. Then the woman, Israel, flees into the desert for half of the 7-year Tribulation, the 1,260 days, where she is protected by the Archangel Michael. Why? Because other passages tell us there's a horrible slaughter of the Jewish people going on at this time.

Zechariah 13:8-9 "In the whole land, declares the LORD, two-thirds will be struck down and perish; yet one-third will be left in it. This third I will bring into the fire; I will refine them like silver and test them like gold. They will call on My Name and I will answer them; I will say, They are My people, and they will say, The LORD is our God."

Here we see from the prophet Zechariah that the Jewish people are "refined' by God, (notice it's the Jewish people getting "refined" not the Church) and finally turn back to God. However, as you saw, it comes at a horrible price. 2/3rds of the Jewish people don't make it. They are struck down while only 1/3rd survive. This 1/3rd survives due to the protection of the Archangel Michael as mentioned above.

We also see in the Bible that the one responsible for hunting the Jewish people down and killing 2/3rds of them during the second half of the 7-year Tribulation, is none other than the Antichrist. This is what Jesus warned about *to the Jewish people* in Matthew 24.

Matthew 24:15-21 "So when you see standing in the holy place 'the abomination that causes desolation,' spoken of through the prophet Daniel – let the reader understand – then let those who are in Judea flee to the mountains. Let no one on the roof of his house go down to take anything out of the house. Let no one in the field go back to get his cloak. How dreadful it will be in those days for pregnant women and nursing mothers! Pray that your flight will not take place in winter or on the Sabbath. For then there will be great distress, unequaled from the beginning of the world until now – and never to be equaled again."

Now again, as we saw before, Matthew Chapter 24 has nothing to do with the Church, and I think you can clearly see why contextually. It is obviously dealing with the Jewish people in the second half of the 7-year Tribulation where they flee from the Antichrist after his abomination that causes desolation that takes place in the rebuilt Jewish Temple in the "middle" of the "seven." Jesus then tells them to "flee" quickly and not to delay nor even think about going back for anything so they can be a part of the 1/3rd that gets sovereignly protected by God, via the Archangel Michael, and not end up dead like the other 2/3rds.

But here's the point. Notice how *all these passages* concerning the 7-year Tribulation (and there's many more believe you me), the worst time in the history of mankind, the "day of distress", the "time of Jacob's trouble, are all talking about Israel, the Jewish people, NOT the Church! Why? Because the audience of the 7-year Tribulation has nothing to do with the Church. It's all about Israel.

It is a time when God "refines" Israel, "redeems" Israel, and "fulfills" all His promises He made to Israel, as far back as the time of the Patriarchs and King David. Right now they are under a "temporary" hardness until the Church Age is over, the "gap" or what's also called the "fullness of the Gentiles." When that time "comes in" or is "over," the Church is removed via the Rapture, and Israel becomes the object of God's focus again. This is what Paul states in the Book of Romans to the Church:

Romans.11:25-27 "I do not want you to be ignorant of this mystery, brothers, so that you may not be conceited: Israel has experienced a hardening in part until the full number of the Gentiles has come in. And so all Israel will be saved, as it is written: 'The deliverer will come from Zion; He will turn godlessness away from Jacob. And this is My covenant with them when I take away their sins."

So as you can see, God is not done with the Jewish people. Right now they are hardened "in part" to the truth, but once again, when the Church has departed, "the full number of the Gentiles has come in," God will once again "deliver" them and fulfill His "covenant" He made with them. And the 7-year Tribulation is the very instrument He uses to get the job done! It's the final week of Daniel's 70th week prophecy concerning the Jewish people, not the Church, as these researchers reiterate:

"Israel has moved into a period of blindness and estrangement from God until a point of time called the fullness of the Gentiles, or the Church Age. But God has not finally and completely cast away the Jewish people. The Tribulation, then, will be a time of the conversion of Israel. The 7-year Tribulation will, therefore, be a time of great spiritual revival. It will mark the conversion of Israel and great activity by Israel for the conversion of the world. It will bring the Jewish people to accept Jesus as Messiah.

This is why in the Book of Matthew, whose primary audience is the Jews, Jesus explains to his Jewish followers what life will be like during the Tribulation. Also, Revelation 12 describes picturesquely a woman who gives birth and has to flee due to persecution during the Tribulation. The context shows the woman is Israel. And again, the Battle of Armageddon is the world against Israel. Two-thirds of the Jewish people will be killed. These texts and others show that the Tribulation is meant for the redemption of the Jewish people.

Why are the Jews the object of persecution during the Tribulation? For one, satan hates the Jewish people for giving the world the Scriptures and the Messiah, as well as he wishes to thwart God's promises to the Jews.

Secondly, the Jews have to be so desperately brought low that they finally call out to their Messiah 'Blessed is he who comes in the name of the Lord' (Mat. 23:29; Lk.13:35). The Tribulation, then, is used for Israel's redemption which also results in the punishment of the wicked.

The Church does not fit into this scenario, and are left out of the purposes of the 7-year Tribulation. Therefore, they would need to be removed – caught up – before the 7-year Tribulation begins."[3]

"The 7-year Tribulation does not deal with the Church at all, but with the purification of Israel. It is not the 'time of the Church's trouble,' but the 'time of Jacob's trouble.' The emphasis of the Tribulation is primarily Jewish. This fact is borne out by Old Testament Scripture, by the Olivet Discourse of Christ, and by the book of Revelation itself.

It concerns 'Daniel's people,' the coming of 'false Messiahs,' the preaching of the 'gospel of the kingdom,' flight on the 'Sabbath,' the temple and the 'holy place,' the land of 'Judea,' the city of 'Jerusalem,' the twelve 'tribes of the children of Israel,' the 'song of Moses,' 'signs' in the heavens, the 'covenant' with the Beast, the 'sanctuary,' the 'sacrifice and the oblation' of the temple ritual.

These all speak of Israel and clearly demonstrate that the Tribulation is largely a time of God's dealing with His ancient people prior to their entrance into the promised kingdom. The many Old Testament prophecies yet to be fulfilled for Israel further indicate a future time when God will deal expressly with this nation."[4]

And might I add, *not the Church*. The Church is not a part of this audience anywhere. It is clearly the audience of the Jewish people.

The **second audience** the 7-year Tribulation deals with is **The Gentile Nations**. Now even though some will admit that the 7-year Tribulation is a time when God "redeems" and "saves" and "restores" a remnant of Israel, fulfilling His promises way back to the time of the Patriarchs and King David, they will still try to "squeeze" the Church into this time frame by saying that the "other people" mentioned in the 7-year Tribulation is the Church. I don't think so! In fact, a cursory reading of the texts during that time frame reveals who these people are, and it clearly isn't the Church. Rather, it's the Gentile Nations who are under God's wrath, or what the Bible calls, "the inhabitants of the earth."

Revelation 6:10 "They called out in a loud voice, 'How long, Sovereign Lord, holy and true, until you judge *the inhabitants of the earth* and avenge our blood?'"

Revelation 8:13 "As I watched, I heard an eagle that was flying in midair call out in a loud voice: 'Woe! Woe! Woe to *the inhabitants of the earth*, because of the trumpet blasts about to be sounded by the other three angels!'"

Revelation 11:10 "*The inhabitants of the earth* will gloat over them and will celebrate by sending each other gifts, because these two prophets had tormented those who live on the earth."

Revelation 13:8 "*All inhabitants of the earth* will worship the beast – all whose names have not been written in the book of life belonging to the Lamb that was slain from the creation of the world."

Revelation 13:12 "He exercised all the authority of the first beast on his behalf, and made *the earth and its inhabitants* worship the first beast, whose fatal wound had been healed."

Revelation 13:14 "Because of the signs he was given power to do on behalf of the first beast, he deceived *the inhabitants of the earth*. He ordered them to set up an image in honor of the beast who was wounded by the sword and yet lived.

Revelation 17:1-2 "One of the seven angels who had the seven bowls came and said to me, 'Come, I will show you the punishment of the great prostitute, who sits on many waters. With her the kings of the earth committed adultery and *the inhabitants of the earth* were intoxicated with the wine of her adulteries.'"

Revelation 17:8 "The beast, which you saw, once was, now is not, and will come up out of the Abyss and go to his destruction. *The inhabitants of the earth* whose names have not been written in the book of life from the creation of the world will be astonished when they see the beast, because he once was, now is not, and yet will come."

So as you can see, there is a specific phrase that is used in the Bible to describe the second audience of those who *will be* in the 7-year Tribulation. Those who are not of the Jewish People are simply referred to as, "the inhabitants of the earth." Now, notice it doesn't say the word Church, period. In fact, the word "Church" is nowhere to be found. This is an obvious and important point. Why? Because if these "inhabitants of the earth" were indeed referring to the Church, then why not simply call them so and be done with it?

Rather, as we saw before, although the "word" Church is mentioned repeatedly in Chapters 1-3, it is *never* mentioned as being on the earth in Chapters 4-18, the chapters that deal with the 7-year Tribulation. Is this by chance? Again, I think not. The word "Church" is absent because the Church is absent! They left at the Rapture prior to the 7-year Tribulation and went to "heaven." That's why those who are "left behind" are called, "the inhabitants of the earth." The Church is now "inhabitants of heaven."

Now lest you doubt there is a distinction being drawn here between the "inhabitants of the earth" and "the Church in heaven," we already saw that in

Revelation 3:10 the Church was promised to *not* be in the "hour" of the 7-year Tribulation. In that exact same passage, we see that those who are "left in that hour" are called, "the inhabitants of the earth."

Revelation 3:10 "Since you have kept my command to endure patiently, I will also keep you from the hour of trial that is going to come upon the whole world to test *those who live on the earth*."

It is mind boggling to me for someone to say that the Church is the same thing as, "the inhabitants of the earth" who are in the 7-year Tribulation, when in the exact same verse it clearly draws a distinction between the two! "You" the Church, and "those" who live on the earth. In fact, it's even clearer than that because the exact same word is used in the above passage, "those who live on earth" that's translated in the other passages as, "the inhabitants of the earth." They're both the same Greek word "katoikeo" which means "earth dwellers" as this researcher states:

"The Greek word 'katoikeo' means, 'those who have settled down upon the earth, who have identified themselves with it.' The word conveys the idea of permanency and complete identification with the world. As such it would hardly be suitable if it described or even included the members of the Church, who upon earth are strangers and pilgrims (Heb. 11:13) and whose citizenship is in heaven (Phil. 3:20)."[5]

So based on this verse alone, there is no way you can include the Church in this identity of the "inhabitants of the earth" who will be in the 7-year Tribulation. Rather, the Church is promised to be a "heaven dweller" not an "earth dweller." Otherwise, it would negate the promise of Revelation 3:10 wouldn't it? Or as this man puts it:

"If the Church is to pass through the 7-year Tribulation, then farewell blessed hope, then welcome the coffin, then thrice welcome the undertaker!"[6]

Not good news if they were one and the same! The good news is it's not! It's two separate identities. The Church has been promised to be a "heaven dweller" not an "earth dweller."

But as you can see, based upon the Scripture, The Church *cannot* be "the inhabitants of the earth." And neither can you have it both ways. If you try to persist, then you are creating a contradiction in the Scripture and God doesn't contradict Himself, which means you're wrong. The Church is not present during this time, as this man shares:

"It is evident that the Tribulation also concerns God's judgment upon Christ-rejecting Gentile nations. Babylon, which "made all nations drink of the wine of the wrath of her fornication" (Rev. 14:8), shall herself "be utterly burned with fire: for strong is the Lord God who judgeth her" (Rev. 18:8).

The "cities of the nations" shall fall, after which satan shall be bound "that he should deceive the nations no more, till the thousand years should be fulfilled" (Rev. 20:3).

God's judgment falls likewise upon the individual wicked, the kings of the earth, the great, the rich, and the mighty, every bondman and every free man (Rev. 6:15-17). It falls upon all who blaspheme the name of God and repent not to give Him glory (Rev. 16:9). Wicked men, godless nations, suffering Israel – these may all be found in Revelation 6-18.

But one looks in vain for the Church of Christ, which is His body, until he reaches the nineteenth chapter. There she is seen as the heavenly bride of Christ, and when He returns to earth to make His enemies His footstool, she is seen returning with Him (I Thess. 3:13)."[7]

So as you can see, there are clearly two groups of people that make up the audience during the 7-year Tribulation. The Jewish people, and the Gentile Nations who are also known as "the inhabitants of the earth." The Church is nowhere to be found because they left at the Rapture. God will be pouring out His wrath upon these inhabitants of the earth this time, which again, as we saw before, is another reason why it can't be the Church. The Church is not appointed unto God's wrath.

However, just like with the first audience, the Jewish people, God will also extend His mercy to this second audience, the Gentile Nations or "the inhabitants of the earth." They too will have an opportunity to be saved, but most of them will be slaughtered for it. As we saw before, this explains the identity of the Tribulation saints that is also *not* the Church. The Church leaves at the Rapture prior to when the 7-year Tribulation begins and these "saints" mentioned are the "Gentile Nations" who are left behind and get saved "after" the Rapture.

However, the lesson is they should've gotten saved "before" the Rapture of the Church so as to avoid the whole thing. Why? Because as we saw before, most of them will be horribly murdered and martyred and have their heads chopped off.

Revelation 6:9-10 "When He opened the fifth seal, I saw under the altar the souls of those who had been slain because of the word of God and the testimony they had maintained. They called out in a loud voice, 'How long, Sovereign Lord, holy and true, until you judge the inhabitants of the earth and avenge our blood?'"

Revelation 20:4 "And I saw the souls of those who had been beheaded because of their testimony for Jesus and because of the word of God. They had not worshiped the beast or his image and had not received his mark on their foreheads or their hands."

Therefore, the point is this. Get saved now before it's too late! You don't want to be there! You don't want to be a Tribulation Saint! You need to become a Church Age Saint *now* before it's too late and avoid the whole thing as this man shares:

"To clarify, the Tribulation Period will be a time when God pours out His wrath upon mankind for his wickedness; but the primary purpose of the Tribulation Period is to prepare Israel to receive her King, Jesus Christ.

The Book of The Revelation, therefore, announces an amazing multitude of 144,000 witnesses who represent the twelve tribes of Israel. These will have been converted during the days of the Tribulation and will have a profound effect upon the world.

The Tribulation will be a time of massive conversion of Gentile multitudes. The Book of Revelation says, 'After this I beheld, and, lo, a great multitude, which no man could number, of all nations, and kindreds, and people, and tongues, stood before the throne, and before the Lamb, clothed with white robes, and palms in their hands (Rev. 7:9).'

Amazing spiritual results occur when the world comes to the end of itself, realizing that nothing on earth is of any value. It then turns in great numbers to faith in Christ as Messiah, bringing in a time of evangelism that will be one of the largest and most effective in the history of the world. The anguish of the Tribulation produces a most salutary result. But a fearful time it will be!"[8]

In other words, you don't want to be there! If you won't accept Jesus now as your Lord and Savior when it's relatively easy to do so, then don't kid yourself into thinking you will when you see millions of people disappear and the Rapture and now your head is on the chopping block! Get saved *now*! Don't make the worst mistake of your life! Take the way out, the only way out through Jesus Christ *now*! Become a part of the Church *today* and leave at the Rapture with the rest of us prior to the horrible 7-year Tribulation. You don't want to be left behind during that time frame! Become a "heaven dweller" not "earth dweller." You have been warned!

Part III

The Objections to the Pre-Trib Rapture

Chapter Eleven

The Red Herring Objections

The **fifth thing** we're going to look to avoid being deceived is **What about the Objections of the Pre-Trib Rapture**? Believe it or not, even with the massive amount of Biblical evidence we've already seen that clearly supports a Pretribulational Rapture of the Church, some will still object to this teaching and instead throw up various accusations against it. So let's now take a look at some of those oft repeated accusations against the Pre-Trib position, and you tell me if they hold any weight.

The **first accusation** against the Pre-Trib position is that **The Pre-Trib Rapture is Not Found in the Bible**. Now, as amazing as it sounds, some people reject the whole idea of a Rapture of the Church period, because they say, "The word 'Rapture' is not found in the Bible." But as we saw at the very beginning of this book, the English word "Rapture" comes from the Latin noun "raptura" which is a translation of the New Testament Greek word "harpazo." "Harpazo" is used 14 times in the New Testament and the basic idea of the word is to, "remove suddenly or a sudden snatching or a sudden catching away, to seize, to carry off." Therefore, it's become the perfect illustrative word to describe the event, the Rapture, where God suddenly takes up or snatches away His Church from earth to heaven. Jesus comes in the clouds, He catches or snatches us away, the Church, from the earth, then we return to heaven with Him.

So while yes, the English word "Rapture" doesn't appear in our current English Bibles, the Greek word "harpazo" repeatedly does appear, 14 times, in the original Greek text, which is where we translated our English word, "Rapture" from, which means the same thing. So what's your point? There's no "conspiracy" going on here. There's no "monkeying around" with the Bible just to support a "Rapture Doctrine." It's right there in the text. It has to be retranslated into English because none of us speak the original Koine Greek which is what the New Testament was written in. For instance, how many of you can read the following passage? This is 1 Thessalonians 4:16-18 the Rapture passage, in the original Greek:

4:16 οτι αυτοσ ο κυριοσ εν κελευσματι εν φωνη αρχαγγελου και εν σαλπι γγι θεου καταβησεται απ ουρανου και οι νεκροι εν χριστω αναστησονται πρωτον **4:17** επειτα ημεισ οι ζωντεσ οι περιλειπομενοι αμα συν αυτοισ α ρπαγησομεθα εν νεφελαισ εισ απαντησιν του κυριου εισ αερα και ουτωσ παντοτε συν κυριω εσομεθα **4:18** ωστε παρακαλειτε αλληλουσ εν τοισ λο γοισ τουτοισ[1]

Do you see the word "Rapture" in here? I don't. How about the dead in Christ rising, or Jesus descending from heaven to meet us in the air? Nope. So are the cynics right? No. The word "Rapture" is nowhere to be found in this gobbledygook because none of us speak it let alone read it, that is Koine Greek. This is precisely why we have to have the newer translations we have today. Language changes over time and God wants all people of every language to know His word, the Bible. So as the languages change over time, the Bible is retranslated to keep up with the changes. Sometimes the words change from the "previous" translation because the "new" language it's being translated into has a "new word" but the "meaning" is still the same.

As was stated above, the New Testament was written in Koine Greek which was then translated into Latin, because Latin had supplanted the Greek language to become the dominant language of the day. It stayed this way for many centuries until eventually the English language became the new dominant language of the day, which is why we translated the Bible into the new English versions we use on up to today. Which means then, *technically* the word "Rapture" IS found in the Bible, if you go back to an earlier version of it, as this man shares:

"First of all, the word 'Rapture' *is* found in the Bible, if you have the Latin Vulgate produced by Jerome in the early 400's. The Vulgate was the main Bible of the medieval Western Church until the Reformation. It continues to this day as the primary Latin translation of the Roman Catholic Church.

Yet, later, it was Protestants who introduced the word 'Rapture' into the English language from the Latin. It should not be surprising to anyone, that an English word was developed from the Latin which we use today known as 'Rapture.'

In Europe, during the Middle Ages and Reformation periods, the theologians were from various countries and therefore spoke different native tongues. However, the single language of the Church, both Catholic and Protestant was Latin. In fact, many of the first books written and published in the American Colonies during the seventeenth century were in Latin.

For example, Cotton Mather's famous history of the American Colonies during the seventeenth century was written in Latin and called *Magnalia Christi Americana,* or *The Great Works of Christ in America.* Because it was done in Latin it could be read throughout Europe by the educated class.

Thus, it should not be surprising to anyone that many new words came into the English language from a Latin source, especially in the realm of theology. Rapture is just such a word."[2]

Furthermore, the logic of saying, "We shouldn't believe in the Rapture because the word 'Rapture' is not found in the Bible" is about as "illogical" as saying, "We shouldn't believe in the Bible, because the word "bible' doesn't appear in the Bible," which it doesn't by the way; did you know that? In fact, there's all kinds of "Biblical words" that we use to describe "Biblical doctrines" that *do not* appear in the Bible.

For instance, does this mean we should not believe in the "Trinity?" Did you know the "word" trinity doesn't appear in the Bible? Yet the "teaching" or "doctrine" of the Trinity does.

Or how about the word "Millennium?" It appears nowhere in the Bible. Do we therefore not believe in a literal Millennial Kingdom? Or do we simply acknowledge that the word "Millennium" is the English word translated from the Greek word in the Bible, "chilioi," which means 1,000 years which is what the English word "Millennium" means?

Or how about Lucifer? Are we going to also deny the existence of a literal satan because the word "Lucifer" doesn't appear in the original text? It doesn't by the way you know. Or do we simply acknowledge that "Lucifer" is a Latin word used to describe satan in the original text, just like the word "Rapture" is from a Latin word used to describe the "catching away" in the original Greek.

It is simply amazing to me that people would actually use this line of reasoning to try to deny the Biblical teaching of the Rapture, as this researcher states:

"It amazes me that some folks write to me, questioning the validity of the Rapture, simply because the word 'Rapture' doesn't appear in the Bible.

Their logic fails because there are a huge number of words that don't appear in the Bible. Because God's Word was originally written in Hebrew and Greek, one could truthfully say that no English words are in the Bible.

For the record, the word 'Rapture' comes from the Latin word 'rapturo,' which in turn was a translation of the Greek verb 'caught up' found in 1 Thessalonians 4:17. You can call it the Pre-Trib Rapture, the Pre-Trib Rapturo, or the Pre-Trib Caught Up – it's all the same thing.

The literal Rapture event is clearly taught. The Bible teaches that the Lord will descend from Heaven into the air, and take believers to Heaven to the place he has prepared for them. Just because a term is not used in a text, does not mean that the event is not there.

This objection is one of those empty 'red-herring' objections that simply has no substance. In fact, nowhere in the scriptures does the word 'Bible' appear, but that doesn't stop people from referring to the collective scriptures as the 'Holy Bible.'"[3]

The **second accusation** against the Pre-Trib position is that **The Rapture is Not a Secret Event**. My answer to that is, "Well, who said it was?" Certainly not those who support the Pre-Tribulational Rapture of the Church! Rather, this is just a continuation of the illogical fallacy that we just covered. It's another "red herring" argument thrown against the Pre-Trib Position as this man shares:

"Hardly a week goes by that I don't receive material opposing the Pre-Trib Rapture which is filled with all kinds of error, both Scriptural and historical. For example, I ran across an article entitled 'Origin of the Secret Rapture Theory.' The first sentence said, 'It may surprise and even shock you that neither the word 'Rapture' nor the teaching of a secret Rapture is mentioned in ANY Christian literature prior to 1830 – including the Bible!"[4]

What? We just dealt with that in great detail in the previous point exposing how illogical and fallacious a statement like that really is. Yet, here you are using it again! Really? It appears you just keep throwing it out there hoping that something will stick. It's shocking as this man states:

"I am shocked that anyone could pack so much error into a single sentence."[5]

I would agree whole heartedly. But this is what those who object to the Pre-Tribulational Rapture of the Church do. They keep repeating the same old red herring arguments, Scriptural and historical fallacies, and hope that something will stick.

However, notice they've added some things to the first red herring argument. Not that just the word "Rapture" is not found in the Bible, but that the word "Rapture" is not found in "any Christian literature prior to 1830." Really? A quick look at the historical facts reveals this is yet another falsehood:

"It is not hard to find out when English words were first introduced into the language. One needs only to check *The Oxford English Dictionary* (*OED*) and it will cite examples of the history of the usage of the word. The oldest word in the 'Rapture' family is 'rapt.' *OED* cites examples of 'rapt' occurring in 1400 in English literature. The earliest instances of 'Rapture' in secular English literature are cited as 1605, 1607, and 1608.

OED provides seven nuances of the word Rapture. The fourth entry is the Biblical one defined as 'The act of conveying a person from one place to another *esp.* to heaven; the fact of being so conveyed.' Two examples of this use are cited from the seventeenth century. The first by a writer named Ward in 1647 and the other by J. Edwards (not the American Jonathan) in 1693. It does not take long to realize that these examples are well before 1830."[6]

So much for that red herring argument! Oh, but wait, there's more! Notice again how these objectors to the Pre-Trib position of the Rapture of the Church have also added a "third" red herring to the equation. That's the teaser word there, "secret." Ooh! That sounds diabolical, doesn't it? What they do is say that we who teach a Pre-Tribulational Rapture of the Church are actually advocating a "secret Rapture" that is unbiblical or a "myth." Really? As another researcher states: "Apparently they enjoy fighting with another straw man."[7]

First of all, again, who said this event the Rapture was "secret"? Not those who teach the Pre-Trib position, as this man shares:

"Sorry, but this is another mistake, another myth. In all my reading of Pretribulationism and discussion with Pretribulationists, I have never, that I can recall, heard a Pre-Trib Rapturist use the nomenclature of 'secret' Rapture to describe our view. I have only heard the phrase 'secret' Rapture as a pejorative term used exclusively by Anti-Pretribulationists."[8]

This line of thinking is about as wild as someone accusing someone else who eats cheeseburgers as being a "secret" cheeseburger eater. What are you talking about? Of course they eat cheeseburgers. However they never said nor do they ever eat them in "secret." That accusation came from "you" not them. They're not trying to "hide" anything. It's crazy!

So it is with the "Secret Rapture" proponents. This teaching is coming from "them" not the "Pre-Tribulationalist." Yet you still have the audacity to say that "we" are the ones "deceiving" people and are "leading others astray" with this "secret" Rapture. What are you talking about? We didn't come up with it, you did! We're not hiding from anything!

Furthermore, while the Pre-Trib Rapture can take place at any instant (the doctrine of Imminency as we saw before) this is in no way saying it's some sort of a "secret." First of all, how can you say it's a "secret" when it's been recorded for us in the Bible for the last 2,000 years for anyone to read at any time in history? In fact, the Apostle Paul even stated that he was writing about the Rapture of the Church so that *no one* would be "ignorant" about it!

1 Thessalonians 4:13, 16-17 "Brothers, *we do not want you to be ignorant* about those who fall asleep, or to grieve like the rest of men, who have no hope. For the Lord Himself will come down from heaven, with a loud command, with the voice of the archangel and with the trumpet call of God, and the dead in Christ will rise first. After that, we who are still alive and are left will be caught up together with them in the clouds to meet the Lord in the air. And so we will be with the Lord forever."

Second, the Pre-Trib Rapture is clearly going to be a global event with global ramifications "felt" by the whole planet, as these researchers state:

"The Rapture of the Church (all born-again believers in Jesus Christ for salvation since the Church Age began at Pentecost) will be anything but a 'secret'. The world will instantly go into cataclysmic chaos at the moment that stunning event takes place. The imagination is hard-pressed to fathom the ramifications of what will happen when millions suddenly vanish.

The Rapture will be mystifying, and to some an inexplicable phenomenon, but it will not be a secret. It will happen before the eyes of a stupefied planet of left-behind earth-dwellers. This declaration that Jesus will call His Church to be with Him seems audacious to many. But, it didn't seem so to the Apostle Paul. He explains what will take place next, in that stupendous fraction of a second:

"For the Lord himself shall descend from heaven with a shout, with the voice of the archangel, and with the trump of God: and the dead in Christ shall rise first: Then we which are alive and remain shall be caught up together with them in the clouds, to meet the Lord in the air: and so shall we ever be with the Lord" (1 Thess. 4:16-17).

So, the Rapture will take place. Believers and the bodies of those who died during the Church Age will be "caught up" in one single moment of time. 'ALL,' not 'some,' will go instantly to be with Jesus, who will then take them into heaven, where He has been preparing their dwelling places since He ascended from the Mount of Olives.

The Pre-Trib view holds that it will be a stunning, sudden, and unannounced-to-the-world-at-large break-in upon business as usual on Planet Earth. The Rapture will cause all left on earth to wonder what has happened."[9]

"The world will most certainly take notice when the Rapture occurs. If the Statue of Liberty suddenly vanished from New York Harbor, ABC, NBC, CBS, and CNN would break from regular programming to cover this marvel. To have millions of people disappear without a trace, the media storm cannot be imagined. If one car or airplane crashed without a driver or pilot, it would be a major news item. After the Rapture, the media will have thousands of examples to choose from.

Think of the vital positions that Christians hold in the workplace. Many businesses will be paralyzed by the loss of key personnel; the economy will suffer a devastating blow; and millions of people, who had friends and family members Raptured, will be terrified. The Rapture will create a media event that will rival any breaking news event from the past. If you turned on your television, you would find 24-hour-coverage on every channel. The President would be calling emergency meeting after emergency meeting, and Churches would be filled to overflowing."[10]

So much for being a "secret", huh? Thirdly, how do you explain all the "pre-advertisement" of the Pre-Trib Rapture from Pre-Trib proponents? This is not us trying to "deceptively hide" something in "secret" as this man states:

"The idea that no one will pay any lasting attention to what would have to be a cataclysmic event seems hard to believe. This is especially true since so much information about the Pre-Trib Rapture has already been disseminated in the form of millions of books, radio or TV broadcasts, and even in the form of bumper stickers: 'In Case Of Rapture This Car Will Be Unmanned.'"[11]

Doesn't look like the proponents of the Pre-Trib Rapture are trying to "hide" any of this from anyone! If anything, we're trying to "make sure" it *does not* remain a "secret," which means the other position ARE, as this man states:

"I have a hard time understanding how these folks could think Pretribulationists preach a secret Rapture. We seem to be doing our very best to popularize the Rapture before it takes place. I doubt that, afterwards, with all the car wrecks, plane crashes, and missing persons reports, the Rapture will remain a secret occurrence.

The only people I know who are attempting to keep the Pre-Trib Rapture a secret are its critics. Pre-Wrath and Post-Trib folks have the national media and the liberal Churches as their allies in their ongoing effort to silence all knowledge of the 'blessed hope.'"[12]

So as you can see, the Pre-Trib position not only *does not* teach a "secret Rapture myth" but it's the other positions who are guilty of doing the very thing they accuse the Pre-Tribulationalists of doing. Yet, incredulously, some will *still* accuse the proponents of the Pre-Trib positions of teaching a "secret" Rapture by quoting this verse:

Revelation 1:7 "Look, He is coming with the clouds, and every eye will see Him, even those who pierced Him; and all the peoples of the earth will mourn because of Him. So shall it be! Amen."

What they say is, "See here? This verse tells us that 'every eye will see Jesus' when He comes back, yet the Pre-trib position is saying it's going to be a "secret event" because nobody knows when." Really? Well, *again*, first of all, no proponent of the Pre-Trib position is saying that the Pre-Trib Rapture is going to be a "secret event." How many times do we have to go through this?

Secondly, this passage is not talking about the Rapture of the Church, but rather the Second Coming of Jesus Christ. As we saw before, in great detail, these are two separate distinct events in the Bible. That is why "every eye will see Him," and "all the people of the earth will mourn" because this passage is referring to the Second Coming of Jesus at the end of the 7-year Tribulation, not the Rapture of the Church which takes place prior to the 7-year Tribulation.

In fact, speaking of the Second Coming, there *are* those who teach a "secret" or "partial" Rapture of the Church, but it's *not* from the Pre-Trib proponents. Rather it's the other positions on the Rapture who believe that the Church will be IN the 7-year Tribulation and that only a "few enlightened ones" will be taken out right before the Second Coming of Jesus at the end of the tribulation. This is clearly *not* the teachings of the Pre-Tribulational Rapture of the Church, so who's really "guilty" of teaching a so-called "secret" Rapture here?

No, it is clear that the Pre-Tribulational Rapture position does NOT teach a "secret Rapture myth." Why people continue to maintain this "myth" is beyond me. Maybe it's like the old saying, "If you repeat a lie loud enough, long enough, often enough, the people will believe it." Surely the Pre-Trib Rapture will be one of the most "eye-opening" events in all of human history as this man shares:

"Modern-day society has witnessed some rather distressing events over the past century. We've seen the assassination of world leaders, national and international wars, and disasters of every sort. All of these events have left deep scars on the psyche of humanity. However, I think these events will pale in comparison to the panic that will be caused by the Pre-Trib Rapture.

The Rapture will someday give a new meaning to the word 'shock.' For the U.S., the attack on Pearl Harbor and the September 11 terrorist attacks currently rank as the most startling events in our nation's history. When the Rapture takes place, I am convinced it will be 100 times more shocking than Pearl Harbor and September 11 combined.

In the past, no single event has managed to touch each individual on a personal level. For example, very few people in 1941 had even heard about Pearl Harbor, let alone knew someone involved in the incident. The attacks on the World Trade Center and the Pentagon fall into the same category. Everyone saw the calamity on television, but it's unlikely that more than 1% of the US population knew any of the victims who worked in the Twin Towers or the Pentagon, or who were aboard the commercial airliners hijacked by the terrorists.

On the other hand, after the Rapture takes place, everyone left behind will know someone who was mysteriously taken away. It could be a neighbor, a distant cousin, or a person's entire immediate family.

Some prophetic commentators have tried to predict that there will only be a few halfhearted questions like, 'Where did everybody go?' Simple logic dictates that the people who find themselves left behind will be absolutely terrified by what has taken place.

I can only guess at the level of interest the press, government, and public will pay to the Rapture, but I'm sure it will be immense. As a result of the catching away of the Bride, I believe many individuals will turn to Christ and become numbered with the Tribulation Saints."[13]

Once again, the lesson is, you should've gotten saved before the Pre-Tribulational Rapture took place. It's no "secret", it's real and you better be ready!

The **third accusation** against the Pre-Trib position is **The Pre-Trib Rapture is Not Mentioned in a Single Verse**. Really? How many red herrings are we going to throw out today anyway? Believe it or not, even after all this evidence supporting the Pre-Tribulational Rapture of the Church, there are still those who object to it by saying, "There's not a *single verse* in the whole Bible that says the Church will be Raptured out prior to the 7-year Tribulation." Excuse me? We already saw a clear deduction from the Bible of a Pre-Tribulational Rapture of the Church via the Absence of the Church, the Location of the Church, the Promises to the Church, the Removal of the Church, and even the Purpose of the 7-year Tribulation. How can you say the Bible doesn't teach a Pre-Tribulational Rapture with all this evidence?

But they say, "Ah! But that's not a *single verse*." Okay, so what you're *really* saying is that *no* Biblical doctrine can be defined or surmised from a *deduction* made from the Bible. It has to be an *exact* teaching from an *exact* verse. It think that's a pretty ludicrous statement to make, especially when you look at the facts, as this man states:

"Oftentimes, people who make the argument against the Pre-Trib Rapture will say, 'The Bible does not say anywhere that the Church will be Raptured before the Tribulation.' But, the Bible says many things indirectly that need to be inferred.

For example, nowhere in the Bible does it say that we are not to commit abortion. But if we read 'Thou shall not kill,' we can safely infer that since you would have to kill to abort, that God would be against abortion.

Nor, for example, does the Bible directly say: 'Baptism must be by immersion.' Most of the major doctrines of the Bible *are* confirmed by such direct unassailable statements, yet some are not. Many precious Biblical truths do not lie exposed on the immediate surface."[14]

In other words, it's perfectly normal and expected at times that one will have to "deduce" Biblical teachings from the Bible, without being able to "point to a single verse." There's nothing sneaky let alone inconsistent going on here with teaching of the Pre-Trib Rapture from Biblical deductions, as some would accuse.

However, with that stated, how about these "single" verses from the Bible that support a Pre-Tribulational Rapture of the Church?

Romans 5:9 "Since we have now been justified by His blood, how much more shall we be saved from God's wrath through Him!"

1 Thessalonians 1:10 "And to wait for His Son from heaven, whom He raised from the dead – Jesus, Who rescues us from the coming wrath."

1 Thessalonians 5:9 "For God did not appoint us to suffer wrath but to receive salvation through our Lord Jesus Christ."

As we saw before, the 7-year Tribulation is a time of God pouring out of His wrath, and therefore since we the Church are "saved from," "rescued from," and "not appointed to" God's wrath, how can the Church be in this time frame? The only way we can truly be "saved from," "rescued from" and "not appointed to" God's wrath is to be "out of it" which means "out of the 7-year Tribulation" which is what the Pre-Trib Rapture position teaches.

But some would still object by saying, "This really isn't *explicitly stating* in a single verse that the Church leaves prior to the 7-year Tribulation, it's only "deduced" from it." First of all, even though I disagree with that assumption, we just saw there's nothing wrong with that, even if it that really were the case.

However, what about this next verse? Maybe this one will be more *explicit* for you. Is the Church around during the 7-year Tribulation?

Revelation 3:10 "Since you have kept My command to endure patiently, I will also keep you from the hour of trial that is going to come upon the whole world to test those who live on the earth."

As we saw before, this is clearly a promise from Jesus *in a single verse* to His Church that they will *not* be in the "hour of trial" or the 7-year Tribulation that is "going to come upon the whole world." How do you get any more *explicit* than this? In fact, only the Pre-Trib position is consistent with this Promise made by Jesus to His Church concerning them being *totally absent* from the 7-year Tribulation. He promised to keep us the Church "out of this time" by removing us from the earth "prior" to the 7-year tribulation.

But even if you *still* didn't want to accept this verse as a *single verse* supporting the Pre-Trib position and still somehow twist it around and say it's deducing and therefore invalid in answering your accusation, would you look at what you're doing with your teaching on the Rapture! You're guilty of doing to same thing! Nowhere in the Bible does it directly say that the Church will go through the tribulation as you would maintain. Is this not hypocrisy as this researcher states:

"Critics of the Pre-Trib Rapture like to point to the fact that the Bible never refers to the Rapture of the Church as the 'Pre-Trib Rapture' yet on the same hand neither does the Bible refer to the Rapture as the 'Pre-Wrath, Mid-Trib, or Post-Trib Rapture' either.

This is yet again a 'red-herring' objection with no substance at all in it. As was covered in 1 Thessalonians 5:9 the Bible promises us that we are to not to be subjected to the wrath to come, which is the 7-year Tribulation period or 70th week of Daniel."[15]

Chapter Twelve

The Unfair Objections

The **fourth accusation** against the Pre-Trib position is **The Pre-Trib Rapture is Not Fair**. Now, even though the Rapture is called the "Blessed Hope" and for good reason (we the Church are rescued from God's wrath that is poured out in the 7-year Tribulation) some people would still object and say that the Pre-Trib Rapture, that "version" of the "Blessed Hope," is unfair. They say it's "not right" that some people get to be "spared" from this time frame of God's judgment while others "have" to be "in" it, as the Pre-Trib Rapture position states.

However, as we saw before, this is nothing new. God has "spared" certain people many times in the Bible like in the previously stated examples of Noah and his family, Lot and his daughters, the Israelites in Egypt, and even Rahab the prostitute. Again, this is why the Rapture is called the "Blessed Hope." Like Noah, Lot, the Israelites, and Rahab, we are recused from this time of judgment. There is great "hope" in that.

I also think part of the misunderstanding comes from the confusion over the Biblical word "tribulation." There is a "Tribulation" with a "capital T" if you will, and "tribulation" with a "small t." The objectors to the Pre-Trib position state that we the Church are guaranteed "tribulation" in the Bible and therefore we shouldn't expect to be "exempt" from the 7-year Tribulation.

However, the 7-year Tribulation is not the same thing as general tribulation. The 7-year Tribulation is a specific outpouring of God's "wrath" which the Church is *not* appointed unto, while general tribulation refers to everyday trials or general tribulation that the Church *is* appointed unto. As we saw before, it's actually two different Greek words. General tribulation is the Greek word, "thlipsis" which refers to "pressure, oppression, affliction, distress, troubles, or trials." This is what we are promised as the Church.

Romans 8:35 "Who shall separate us from the love of Christ? Shall *tribulation*, or distress, or persecution, or famine, or nakedness, or peril, or sword?"

Romans 12:12 "Rejoicing in hope; patient in *tribulation*; continuing instant in prayer."

2 Corinthians 1:4 "Who comforteth us in all our *tribulation*, that we may be able to comfort them which are in any trouble, by the comfort wherewith we ourselves are comforted of God."

2 Thessalonians 1:4 "So that we ourselves glory in you in the Churches of God for your patience and faith in all your persecutions and *tribulations* that ye endure."

These passages are just talking about "general tribulation" that the Church will go through. However, God's "wrath" in the Greek is the word "orge" which means "anger, violent emotion, wrath, or indignation." So yes, we are clearly promised as His Church to experience "general tribulation" "thlipsis," or "trials, troubles, and affliction," no disagreement there. However, "wrath" or "orge" is referring to God's "anger or indignation" and the Scripture is clear, Jesus set His Church free from that.

Romans 5:9 "Since we have now been justified by His blood, how much more shall we be saved from God's *wrath* through Him!"

1 Thessalonians 1:10 "And to wait for His Son from heaven, whom He raised from the dead – Jesus, Who rescues us from the coming *wrath*."

1 Thessalonians 5:9 "For God did not appoint us to suffer *wrath* but to receive salvation through our Lord Jesus Christ."

So as you can see, we the Church *will* go through general troubles in life, hard times, persecutions, privations, etc. general tribulation. However, we are *saved* from God's wrath through Jesus Christ, which includes the 7-year Tribulation. Why anyone would "resist' or "object" to this wonderful good news from the Bible is beyond me, especially when you see it repeated in other Biblical examples, again like Noah and Lot and the others. It's almost like these people who object to the Pre-Tribulational teaching of the Rapture where the Church will be "spared" from God's wrath, actually "want" to be in that time frame themselves, as this man shares:

"You would think the desire to go through the 7-year Tribulation would be as popular as the desire to jump into a pit filled with vipers and broken glass. As illogical as it may seem, there appears to be a large number of Christians that fully expect to get roughed up before Christ returns.

Many Christians argue strongly for the right to suffer persecution at the hands of the Antichrist and the one world government. These tribulation saint wannabees constantly harp, 'Because Jesus and His disciples suffered persecution, we should expect no better.' It's been my experience that people with the weakest faith are generally the ones that talk the boldest. When the slightest difficulty comes their way, they cry to high heaven.

I hate to be the bearer of good news, but the word of God clearly states that believers will escape the tribulation bloodbath.

'For God hath not appointed us to wrath, but to obtain salvation by our Lord Jesus Christ.' (1 Thessalonians 5:9).

'Because thou hast kept the word of my patience, I also will keep thee from the hour of temptation, which shall come upon all the world, to try them that dwell upon the earth' (Revelation 3:10).

In one regard, people who think the Church will go through the tribulation are somewhat correct. I believe a huge number of people – who are Christians in name only – will find themselves left behind. By having the Rapture before the 7-year Tribulation, all those who find themselves facing the wrath of God will be without an excuse."[1]

But that brings up another objection from these people who think there's something "unfair" going on with the Pre-Tribulational Rapture teaching. They say something like this, "Well hey, wait a minute. You said the Church is not appointed unto God's wrath, but you readily admit that there are people who are going be 'saved' during the 7-year Tribulation. Aren't these people 'under' God's wrath?"

Yes, they are. But these people are not the same identity as the Church to whom the promise to be "saved" from God's wrath was made. As we saw before, the people who get saved during the 7-year Tribulation are the Tribulation Saints, not the Church Age Saints. The Church Age Saints were a "mystery" to the Old Testament writers.

Ephesians 5:32 "This is a profound *mystery* – but I am talking about Christ and the Church."

Thus being a "mystery" to the Old Testament writers, like Daniel through whom we are given the purpose of the 7-year Tribulation, the Church is not so surprisingly *not* found in this horrible time frame. Why? Because they can't be. It was a mystery to the writers like Daniel! So how could he include them?

Furthermore, as was stated earlier, the "mystery" of the Church also explains the "mysterious gap" between Daniel's 69th week and the final 70th week, the 7-year Tribulation. What has been going on during this long time frame, this long interval? This is the "mystery" of the Church Age. It will last until the "fullness of the Gentiles" comes in or the Rapture of the Church. And just as the Church had an abrupt *beginning* in Acts Chapter 2 shortly after the conclusion of the 69th week, Jesus' triumphal entry, so the Church will likewise have an abrupt *removal* shortly before the beginning of the 70th week, the 7-year Tribulation.

God will then "refocus" His attention on the Jewish people to fulfill His promises He made way back to the Patriarchs and King David. This would also mean that the Church is *not* Israel today, nor a "replacement" for Israel, as some would falsely state. The Church and Israel are two distinct identities, as this man shares:

"God began the nation of Israel with Abraham in Genesis 12. He began the Church on the day of Pentecost in Acts 2. So if Israel and the Church had a separate beginning, then why couldn't they have a separate conclusion?

Scripture tells us that God has a very definite plan for Israel and He has a very definite plan for the Church. We are not Israel. We are not the new Israel. We do not receive the promises of Israel. They are still for Israel. If you have the Church receiving all the promises for Israel, then God was a liar, because God made promises to Israel which He is not keeping. And so there must be a distinction.

Who has God destined for His judgment in the 7-year Tribulation? Israel and the Gentile nations. God has not destined the Church for wrath. There is no point in the Church going through the 7-year Tribulation. All the wrath that God's judgment could pile on us, has already been piled on whom? Christ at the cross. To say that we go through the 7-year Tribulation is to depreciate the work of Christ on the cross and to assume that there needs to be more wrath that we must take ourselves. That is blasphemy.

God does not will our destruction, but our deliverance. He doesn't make us the subjects of His wrath. He has no point in putting us under punitive action and then sudden destruction. He cherishes no angry purposes toward His Church. We're His beloved bride.

Remember the story of the Old Testament where Israel is seen to be the wife of Jehovah, right? The whole book of Hosea, the whole thing is devoted to a historical allegory of the relationship between God and Israel. Israel is seen as God's wife. What kind of wife? Adulteress, untrue, a harlot. And the promise is that the harlot would be restored in the kingdom.

Now watch, beloved. Israel is a wife, but a harlot. The Church though is a bride and a virgin. Those are not the same. You got it? Those cannot be the same. The Church is a chaste virgin. That is the mystery. That is the new thing. The new thing is a Church presented to Christ sanctified without spot, without blemish, clean and pure.

That can't be Israel. Israel is still an adulteress wife, fooling around with other gods, committing spiritual adultery and doesn't get restored yet until the time comes for the trouble in the 7-year Tribulation.

Don't confuse the chaste virgin presented to Christ with Israel, an adulteress, wretched harlot unfaithful to God. The one that He wants to whip into believing is Israel. Wrath, you see, is the destiny of unbelievers.

When I think about the future, do you know what I think about? I think about the fact that Jesus is coming. And I'm not looking for the 7-year Tribulation and I'm not looking for the antichrist. I'm looking for Jesus Christ. He is coming and we want to be ready when He gets here. I hope you're ready."[2]

Why? Because when the 7-year Tribulation begins, the wrath of God will be poured out upon this wicked and rebellious planet, and you don't want to be here. The only way to escape it is to become a part of the Church today through Jesus Christ.

But as you can see, the Church is clearly not the same identity as Israel, let alone the Tribulation Saints who do get saved after the 7-year Tribulation begins. It is only the Church during this present time who is promised to be "saved" from the "wrath of God" during the 7-year Tribulation.

Again, God will demonstrate His mercy in the midst of His judgement during the 7-year Tribulation by giving others an opportunity to be saved from hell.

Revelation 14:6 "Then I saw another angel flying in midair, and he had the eternal gospel to proclaim to those who live on the earth – to every nation, tribe, language and people."

A Gospel does indeed go forth during this time frame. But these people are not the same as the Church. Praise God they at least got saved from the eternal torments of hell, but due to their disbelief and/or procrastination today, they were not included with the Church Age Saints and thus have no promise of being saved from the horrors of the 7-year Tribulation. Rather, as we saw more than once, their heads will literally be on the chopping block.

Revelation 20:4 "And I saw the souls of those who had been beheaded because of their testimony for Jesus and because of the word of God. They had not worshiped the beast or his image and had not received his mark on their foreheads or their hands."

So again, the point is this. Get saved now before it's too late! Be a part of the Church Age Saints now, not the Tribulation Saints in the 7-year Tribulation. Avoid the whole thing through Jesus, as this man shares:

"Picture this: You wake up one morning and turn on the news and hear a most disturbing bulletin. Millions of people from every corner of the world have mysteriously vanished. You find it hard to believe, but as news from around the world confirms this mass disappearance, a shiver of foreboding and trepidation runs through your body.

You feel vulnerable, unsure and perhaps alone. The realization that the Rapture Christians spoke of has happened hits you like a baseball bat. You feel nauseated as the blood drains from your face and a dread fear creeps into your stomach. A fear you know is going to remain for some years to come.

You are left on earth and you know that the prophecies have come to pass and now you must face the woeful times talked about in the Apocalypse along with all those others who refused to heed the warnings. You are part of those left behind. You drop to your knees and beg God and Jesus to forgive you and help you. The dark night of the soul has begun.

Huge amounts of people are going to become believers after the 7-year Tribulation begins when they realize they have been left behind. These people will go through a horrific experience for the next several years. It is going to be a literal hell on earth for all who find themselves ensnared in this demonic coliseum.

Those who accept Jesus as Lord in this present time will be gathered together when the Lord returns before the events of the 7-year Tribulation begin. Those who realize they are stuck in the web of this horrible time are the unwise who were not ready for His coming. They must now endure the savage testing that is to be their wont in the ensuing years of tyranny under the power of the Antichrist's global army.

If any are reading this before the Rapture of the Church and have not yet come to know the Lord Jesus as your Savior, now is your chance to pull back from the brink of the dark Abyss into which the world will soon be plunged.

Accept the free gift of eternal life made available to you by the finished work of the shedding of the blood of Jesus Christ. All you have to do is believe and ask, and it shall be given. As a born again believer of the Church of God and a member of the Body of Christ, you will indeed be 'rescued from the wrath to come.'"[3]

The **fifth accusation** against the Pre-Trib position is **The Pre-Trib Rapture Produces Laziness**. Not only do some people falsely state that the

"Blessed Hope" is "unfair" to other people who have had to suffer, as we just answered in great detail, but believe it or not, they will even go so far as to state that the Pre-Trib Rapture produces "laziness" as well. Or to put it into their own words, "Will not anticipation produce irresponsibility? If a person is constantly anticipating the return of Jesus Christ, will he not become so heavenly minded that he is no earthly good?" Excuse me? So basically what you're saying is that the "Blessed Hope" is really a promise to become a "Blessed Couch Potato!" Where do you get that from? Certainly not from the Scripture!

As we saw before, the Bible repeatedly encourages us, the Church, to be ready at all times for the sudden Return of Jesus Christ at the Rapture. This is called the Doctrine of Imminency. It's imminent, in that it can happen at any time. That's why the Bible tells us over and over again to be waiting, be expecting, be alert, patient, and living self-controlled lives in the meantime, in light of this imminent event. There's no "Couch Potatoing" going on here! See for yourselves:

Philippians 3:20 "But our citizenship is in heaven. And we *eagerly await* a Savior from there, the Lord Jesus Christ."

1 Thessalonians 1:10 "And to *wait* for his Son from heaven, whom He raised from the dead – Jesus, Who rescues us from the coming wrath."

1 Timothy 6:14 "To *keep this command* without spot or blame until the appearing of our Lord Jesus Christ."

James 5:8 "You too, *be patient* and *stand firm*, because the Lord's coming is near."

1 Thessalonians 5:6 "So then, let us not be like others, who are asleep, but let us *be alert* and *self-controlled*."

These verses clearly indicate that Jesus' arrival will come when nobody expects it *and therefore* we the Church need to *always* be ready for it. That is, *always* be busy doing what the Master told us to do in the meantime, *not being lazy* or sitting around doing nothing. In fact, this clear "activity" created by the teaching of the Pre-Trib Rapture is precisely what is "witnessed" by the example of the Church of Thessalonica to whom one of the major Rapture passages was written, as this researcher admits:

"The apostle Paul compliments his friends of Thessalonica and says that they were waiting for the return of Jesus Christ, the Son of God, to come from heaven (1 Thess.1:10). We have the word for it; their attitude was bright anticipation, watchful, waiting.

What was the result of this attitude? It was not laziness nor disinterest, not at all. Rather, the Church at Thessalonica became one of the classic Churches of the New Testament as a result of their anticipating the return of Christ. The apostle Paul says that they did a number of things that made them one of the great Churches of the early age of Christianity.

1) They received the Word in much affliction, with joy in the Holy Spirit (verse 6). Constantly conscious of the reality of heaven, these people had little confidence in the word of man. Correspondingly, they had ultimate confidence in the Word of God.

We may well remind ourselves that the Rapture of the Church will bring an abrupt end to the foolish, mindless, human discourse of this world. Grandiose schemes and vast human enterprises will be of little or no consequence when Jesus comes again. Our generation is greatly mistaken by living on philosophy and vain deceit rather than the Word of God. Our foolish generation is ruled by human philosophers who are already in the grave. This would never be if proper attention had been given to the Word of God.

2) They became followers of Christ. The path of life is a deep mystery to many as they wonder about the purpose of their life. For the dear Christians at Thessalonica, this was no problem. They should live for Christ, of course. Soon, they believed, He would come again and, therefore, every step taken in pursuit of His perfect will would be certified and validated by that coming.

A reminder here is also appropriate. The Rapture of the Church will not merely deliver a generation of living Christians who are caught up to be with Him. It will also vindicate the purpose for which every Christian has lived a godly life in all of the ages of the Church. His coming will be a testimony to this and all previous generations that the life committed to Christ was not that of a fool. The wisdom of consecration will certainly be forever certified when Jesus comes again.

3) These Christians became an example of the believers. The on-looking world, looking at the lives of 'anticipatory believers' in that day, was much impressed. These individuals exemplified the Lord Jesus as against being mere creatures of time.

One who anticipates the return of Christ is careful not to go anywhere, to do anything, to commit himself to any principle of which he will not be proud when Christ comes again. So it is that the doctrine of the return of Christ is a purifying hope. And every man that hath this hope in him purifieth himself even as he is pure (1 John 3:3).

4) These believers became broadcasters of the Word of the Lord (1 Thess. 1:8). Being totally confident in the return of Jesus Christ, the believers saw themselves as having a great message, a transforming hope to bring to the world. The result was a mighty and most effective program of evangelism so that, 'In every place your faith toward God is spread abroad, so that we need not to speak anything.'

In the Church of our time, the need for a strong, explosive program of evangelism and world missions is great. Still, a major proportion of the world awaits the opportunity to hear the gospel of Jesus Christ. Preoccupied with other things and overly engaged in time-serving efforts, the Church of our day could well use a new motivation for global conquest.

Broadcasting the gospel everywhere became the activity of the Thessalonians. Why? Because they believed that Christ was coming again. This doctrine produced such motivation as the world had seldom seen. No one must miss the opportunity of hearing that Jesus is coming back and that, therefore, we should trust Him. This was the motivating hope of the Thessalonians and could well be ours today.

Our Lord Jesus Christ taught that He might come back at any time, suddenly, imminently, without any notice or signs. It could happen without any warning, suddenly, catching us off guard if we're not faithfully serving our Master."[4]

So as you can see, from the Scripture, and even from the Scriptural example of the Thessalonica Church, the teaching of the Pre-Trib Rapture makes a true follower of Christ *very active*, not *lazy*. Knowing the Imminency of the Rapture will actually cause you to live for Christ more, long for Christ more, and share the Gospel of Christ as much as you can, because you want to be found faithfully serving your Master.

Yet amazingly, some will still try to deny the doctrine of Imminency and its cleansing effects by citing other verses in the Bible that they say undermine this teaching. However, a quick examination of these verses shows just how bankrupt their attempts to disprove Imminency really are, as this researcher shares:

"While the Scriptures clearly present the idea of Imminency or an any-moment coming of Christ, there are some who challenge this notion and argue that the New Testament does not teach that Jesus could come at any time. The following are three main arguments they will use to try to disprove Imminency.

First, it is alleged that since the gospel had to be preached throughout the world before Christ could return, He couldn't return at any moment (Acts 1:8).

However, in writing to the Thessalonians Paul included himself when he spoke of the Rapture. He said 'we who are alive and remain.' Evidently, he didn't see anything standing in the way of Christ coming during his lifetime or at any moment.

Second, opponents of Imminency maintain that John 21:18-19 precludes an any-moment Rapture because it says that Peter had to live to be an old man. However, Peter himself encouraged believers to look for the coming of the Lord (1 Pet1:13; 4:7). He knew that he might die suddenly (2 Pet 1:14).

Also, other believers expected Peter's early death, because when Rhoda told the believers in Acts 12 the news of his release from prison, they said, 'You are out of your mind,' and when he appeared to them 'they saw him and were amazed' (Acts 12:15-16). They apparently had no concept that he would live a long life. As they looked for the Lord's coming they certainly did not walk around every day asking, 'I wonder if Peter is dead yet?'

Moreover, the passage in John 21 was not even written and circulated to the Churches until fifteen to twenty years after Peter was already dead, so John 21:18-19 is not an impediment to Imminency.

A **third** argument against Imminency is that the Temple had to be destroyed before Christ returned (Matt 24:1-3). Yet it must be remembered that in Matthew 24 Jesus was not discussing the Rapture or the Church since the Church was still a mystery and had not yet been revealed, much less established. There is nothing in Matthew 24 which relates the destruction of the Temple to the timing of the Rapture, nor remotely suggests that it must happen first."[5]

So as you can see, try as they might, the Doctrine of Imminency is clearly established in the Bible.

Yet, the irony is, as was stated before, it's the *other* positions on the Rapture that are the ones that actually *do produce laziness*. Think about it. If I thought Jesus *couldn't* come back at *any time* to Rapture His Church like the Pre-Trib position teaches, but rather He could only come back at the midway-point of the 7-year Tribulation, or ¾ the way through with the Pre-wrath position, or all the way to the end with the Post-Trib position, then I *do know* when He's coming back, which means *I could get lazy* and goof off, right? All I would have to do is calculate the prophetic events that must take place before Jesus comes back with their version of the Rapture, like the Seal Judgments, the Trumpet Judgements, the Bowl Judgments, the Antichrist, and all that stuff, then *time my laziness* accordingly. I'll just make sure I *look busy* right before He comes back at the appointed time.

But that's just it! We don't know when He's coming back! It's *not* an appointed time, it is Imminent, it can happen at any time! The other positions on the Rapture not only *destroy* the doctrine of Imminency, but its cleansing effects as well. They actually produce the very thing they accuse the Pre-Trib position of doing, that of encouraging laziness.

Only the Pre-Trib position says there's no heads up warning whatsoever and you better get ready and be ready at *all* times! It could happen *now* and so you need to get busy sharing the Gospel *now*. It could happen *today* so you better get busy living a *holy life* for Jesus *today*! It's a "glad" teaching, not a "sad" teaching as this man shares:

"The Rapture is presented in the New Testament as an event that from man's viewpoint could occur at any moment, and believers are to be looking for it all the time. Only the Pre-Trib position allows for an imminent, any moment, signless coming of Christ for His own. Only those who believe in a Pre-Trib Rapture can honestly say, 'Jesus may come today.'

The any moment coming of Christ is one of the truths in the New Testament that is to fill us with hope, anticipation, and motivation to godly living. Believers should live with this hope every day – the hope that Jesus may come today! Only the Pre-Trib view allows for this blessed hope (Titus 2:13).

Consider the old song, *Is it the Crowning Day?* to make the point.

Jesus may come today, Glad day! Glad day!
And I would see my friend; Dangers and troubles would end
If Jesus should come today.
Glad day! Glad day! Is it the crowning day?
I'll live for today, nor anxious be,
Jesus, my Lord, I soon shall see;
Glad day! Glad day! Is it the crowning day?

However, if Mid-Tribbers or Pre-Wrathers or Post-Tribbers sang this song, wouldn't they have to sing it this way?

Jesus can't come today, Sad day! Sad day!
And I won't see my friend; Dangers and troubles won't end
Because Jesus can't come today.
Sad day! Sad day! Today is not the crowning day?
I won't live for today, and anxious I'll be,
The Beast and the False Prophet I soon shall see,
Sad day! Sad day! Today is not the crowning day?

We may get a laugh out of this parody, but it's true. The Pre-Trib view is the only view that honestly holds that Jesus could come today. The any moment coming of Christ."[6]

Again, that's why it's called the "Blessed Hope." Only the Pre-Trib teaching of the Rapture is a "glad song to the heart" of the Christian, producing joy and fruitfulness, not a "sad song of doom" instilling fear and laziness like the other positions.

Chapter Thirteen

The Spurious Objections

The **sixth accusation** against the Pre-Trib position is that **The Pre-Trib Rapture is a Recent Spurious Teaching**. Now, I don't know if it's just a last ditch effort because the other attacks against the Pre-Trib position just don't hold up under scrutiny as we've been seeing, but believe it or not, there are actually many people out there who say that they disagree with the Pretribulational Rapture because it's a "spurious" and "recent" teaching, therefore it can't be true. They basically state and accuse the Pre-Trib Rapture teaching as having been started by a man named John Darby who then is supposed to have received this "demonic" idea from a Charismatic girl named Margaret MacDonald from an utterance she made in 1830. However, when you investigate the facts of this "recent" popular accusation, the only thing you'll see that is "spurious" about it is the accusation itself. Like all the other false accusations against the Pre-Trib position, this too does not hold up under scrutiny.

The **first spurious** accusation against the Pre-Trib position is that **Recent Teachings Must Be Rejected**. First of all, this accusation that just because a teaching is "recent" or "new" therefore it cannot be true can be used both ways. If this is the basis for your rejection of the Pre-Trib position of the Rapture combined with the accusation that John Darby came up with it in 1830 via Margaret MacDonald, then surely you must likewise reject the Pre-Wrath position of the Rapture because it's even *more* recent. The Pre-Wrath Rapture of the Church was, "formally named and publicized by Marvin Rosenthal in his book *The Pre-Wrath Rapture of the Church*, published by Thomas Nelson in 1990, at the prompting of his friend Robert Van Kampen, (one of the wealthiest men in America) who went on to write *The Sign* and *The Rapture Question Answered: Plain & Simple*. In fact, had it not been for Van Kampen's wealth and determined persuasiveness, this "recent" position on the Rapture may have never even taken off, as this man shares:

"I believe that if Van Kampen were not a wealthy individual then very few, if any, of us would have ever heard of his view. Van Kampen spent a number of years searching for an advocate of his newly developed viewpoint until he was finally able to persuade Marvin Rosenthal to adopt his new theory.

I have a friend who was interviewed extensively by Van Kampen (in the 80s) for the Pastorate of the Church he attended in the Chicago area. My friend spent hours on the phone with Van Kampen, as he tried to convince him of his strange Rapture view. In the end, my friend could not agree with Van Kampen, so he did not have the opportunity to become the Pastor of that Church.

It was clear that Van Kampen was searching for someone to champion his Rapture position. Van Kampen finally convinced Marvin Rosenthal of his view. Rosenthal wrote a book called *The Pre-Wrath Rapture of the Church*, which was published by Thomas Nelson in 1990.

Van Kampen apparently subsidized the publishing of the book by buying thousands of copies and sending them to Ministers all over North America. This is how the new position was spread. Later Van Kampen came out with his own book called *The Sign* (three editions, 1992, 1999, 2000) from Crossway Books. He then had published *The Rapture Question Answered: Plain and Simple* (1997) with Revell."[1]

So let me get this straight, you reject the Pre-Trib position of the Rapture because you make the accusation that it started "recently" with John Darby via Margaret MacDonald in 1830, but here we have the Pre-Wrath position of the Rapture starting with Marvin Rosenthal via Robert Van Kampen in 1990. This is a full 160 years *more* recent. Surely you must not only "reject" this position as well, but attack it "just as vehemently" and "even more so" than the Pre-Trib position. I mean, we're talking just within a couple decades! Our own lifetime!

Now, even though I disagree with this premise, that just because something's recent it therefore cannot be true, as you can see it can work both ways on other positions of the Rapture. In fact, let's apply this same faulty premise not just to the Pre-Trib Rapture, but to other teachings in the Bible.

During the Protestant Reformation, in the 1500's, many Biblical teachings were "rediscovered" that were "covered up" for centuries by the Roman Catholic Church. For instance, such Biblical and important teachings as:

- Salvation by Faith Alone
- Salvation by Grace Alone
- Salvation by Christ Alone
- The Bible is Man's Sole Authority on Spiritual Matters
- Jesus is Our Sole Mediator between God
- The Priesthood of the Believer

Now here's my point. All these Biblical teachings, that I hope all of us as Protestants hold dear, were "rediscovered" in the 1500's. Do I therefore have to "reject" them as well since they are also a "recent" teaching like the accusation of John Darby teaching the Pre-Trib position on the Rapture in the 1800's? This is only a 300 year difference? I would surely hope you would say absolutely not!

Therefore, could it be that the teaching of the Pre-Trib Rapture was not even really a "recent" teaching at all, but rather was one that was "rediscovered" like many other teachings in the Bible, due to Ecclesiastical cover-ups? I think that will clearly present itself to be the case, as we continue in our investigation on these "spurious" accusations against the Pre-Trib Rapture. But as you can see, this is yet another "spurious" accusation. Just because a teaching is "recent," doesn't mean it cannot be true.

The **second spurious** accusation against the Pre-Trib position is that **John Darby Received it from Margaret MacDonald.** Now for the life of me, I don't even know how anyone can repeat this "spurious" accusation, let alone again and again and again as the Anti-Pre-Tribbers do, especially when you look at the facts. But that's just it. It turns out to be another case of, "If you repeat a lie loud enough, long enough, and often enough, people will believe it."

Basically this next "spurious" idea against the Pre-Trib Rapture states that, "The Pre-Trib Rapture theory was started by a Scottish girl named Margaret MacDonald who in 1830 received a demonic vision of the Last Days that included the idea of a Pre-Trib Rapture. Then this 'demonic vision' is said to have later influenced a guy named John Darby who in turn promoted and taught this idea of a Pre-Trib Rapture of the Church, making his promotion of the teaching 'demonic' because of it's supposed 'demonic' origins." As you can see, that's a pretty serious charge! However, the only thing that needs to be "cast out" of this "spurious" accusation is the "demonic lies" that it contains through and through.

First of all, this "spurious" accusation was popularized by a guy who had "spurious" motives for attacking the Pre-Trib Position in the first place. His name is Dave MacPherson and believe it or not, he blamed the Pre-Trib position for much of his pain and problems in life. Therefore, he "had" to find a way to "destroy" the Pre-Trib theory, even if it meant "promoting" this "spurious lie" that connects John Darby with Margaret MacDonald. See for yourself:

"Dave MacPherson is an individual who loves to hate Pretribulationism. In fact, he has thought up new ways to express his disdain for Pretribulationism by fabricating a false history of the Pre-Trib Rapture. For the last thirty-plus years, MacPherson has dedicated his life to full-time Rapture hating in an attempt to participate in anything that he believes will obstruct its spread.

He purports that the key elements of the doctrine of the Pretribulational Rapture originated with a young Scottish girl named Margaret Macdonald in Spring of 1830. This is the thesis put forth in a number of books and publications for over thirty years by MacPherson, a newsman turned Rapture researcher, such as *The Rapture Plot*, *The Unbelievable Pre-Trib Origin*, *The Three Rs: Rapture, Revisionism, Robbery*, *The Great Rapture Hoax*, *The Incredible Cover-Up*, *The Late Great Pre-Trib Rapture*.

MacPherson has dedicated his life to the cause of disrupting belief in the Pre-Trib Rapture, since, according to his interpretation, it has been the cause for great disruption in his own life. 'Back in 1953 I had a jolting encounter with the Rapture,' is the opening sentence in MacPherson's *Rapture Hoax* (p. 3). This is a reference to his expulsion from a Christian College in California (BIOLA) for propagating views that conflicted with Pretribulationism.

He suggests that this experience was so devastating that it accounts for a setback in his Christian life. Because of his discouragement, MacPherson and a friend went out and got drunk in Mexico and passed out. MacPherson says this was a brush with death because of the many dangers that could befall someone in such a condition in Mexico. Later, he was involved in a wreck with a car while riding his motorcycle and almost lost his left arm.

But these were not the beginning of his nor his family's troubles because of the Pre-Trib Rapture. MacPherson has a bad habit of attributing all kinds of personal tragedies to the Pre-Trib teaching: his mother's death, his sister's inability to have more children, his own failure to follow through on his calling as an evangelist, and other matters. MacPherson even states that his dog became demon possessed just about the time he was about to write his first Anti-Pretribulation book, savagely biting his writing hand several times.

So along with some other influences, MacPherson begins to project the notion that the source of the Pre-Trib Rapture is of demonic origin through a 15-year-old Scottish lassie. For MacPherson, his calling in life is a crusade to develop and sharpen his theory and to propagate it around the world."[2]

Sure looks to me like somebody has a "spurious agenda" for promoting this "spurious lie." But be that as it may, is it even true? Did John Darby get the Pre-Trib Rapture teaching from Margaret MacDonald? Not even close. Not even by a long shot!

First of all, if you read the so-called vision that Margaret MacDonald received, it's not even supporting a Pre-Trib Rapture position. Rather it's supporting a Post-Trib position with a Partial Rapture! Here, read it for yourself. It's a matter of public record. The following are relevant extracts from MacDonald's so-called utterance.

"I repeated the words, now there is distress of nations, with perplexity, the seas and the waves roaring, men's hearts failing them for fear – now look out for the sign of the Son of man. Here I was made to stop and cry out, O it is not known what the sign of the Son of man is; the people of God think they are waiting, but they know not what it is. I felt this needed to be revealed, and that there was great darkness and error about it; but suddenly what it was burst upon me with a glorious light. I saw it was just the Lord himself descending from Heaven with a shout, just the glorified man, even Jesus; but that all must, as Stephen was, be filled with the Holy Ghost, that they might look up, and see the brightness of the Father's glory....Only those who have the light of God within them will see the sign of his appearance....

Tis Christ in us that will lift us up – he is the light – tis only those that are alive in him that will be caught up to meet him in the air. I saw that we must be in the Spirit, that we might see spiritual things.... But I saw that the glory of the ministration of the Spirit had not been known. I repeated frequently, but the spiritual temple must and shall be reared, and the fullness of Christ be poured into his body, and then shall we be caught up to meet him. Oh none will be counted worthy of this calling but his body, which is the Church, and which must be a candlestick all of gold. I often said, Oh the glorious inbreaking of God which is now about to burst on this earth; Oh the glorious temple which is now about to be reared, the bride adorned for her husband; and Oh what a holy, holy bride she must be, to be prepared for such a glorious bridegroom....

I saw the people of God in an awfully dangerous situation, surrounded by nets and entanglements, about to be tried, and many about to be deceived and fall. Now will THE WICKED be revealed, with all power and signs and lying wonders, so that if it were possible the very elect will be deceived.– This is the fiery trial which is to try us.– It will be for the purging and purifying of the real members of the body of Jesus; but Oh it will be a fiery trial. Every soul will be shaken to the very centre. The enemy will try to shake in everything we have believed....

I frequently said that night, and often since, now shall the awful sight of a false Christ be seen on this earth, and nothing but the living Christ in us can detect this awful attempt of the enemy to deceive – for it is with all deceivableness of unrighteousness he will work – he will have a counterpart for every part of God's truth, and an imitation for every work of the Spirit. The Spirit must and will be poured out on the Church, that she may be purified and filled with God – and just in proportion as the Spirit of God works, so will he – when our Lord anoints men with power, so will he. This is particularly the nature of the trial, through which those are to pass who will be counted worthy to stand before the Son of man.... The trial of the Church is from Antichrist.... I frequently said, Oh be filled with the Spirit – have the light of God in you, that you may detect satan – be full of eyes within – be clay in the hands of the potter – submit to be filled, filled with God....This will fit us to enter into the marriage supper of the Lamb....

I saw that night, and often since, that there will be an outpouring of the Spirit on the body, such as has not been, a baptism of fire, that all the dross may be put away. Oh there must and will be such an indwelling of the living God as has not been – the servants of God sealed in their foreheads – great conformity to Jesus – his holy holy image seen in his people.... This is what we are at present made to pray much for, that speedily we may all be made ready to meet our Lord in the air – and it will be. Jesus wants his bride. His desire is toward us. He that shall come, will come, and will not tarry. Amen and Amen. Even so come Lord Jesus."[3]

Now, here's what's amazing if you we're paying attention to what was spoken there. The accusation is that this utterance is supposed to be the "birth place" of the Pre-Trib Rapture position that somehow influenced John Darby to influence us right on up to today. Yet even a cursory reading shows it's not even promoting a Pre-Tribulational Rapture position! Rather, based on McDonald's own statements there, it is clearly advocating a *Post-Tribulation Rapture*.

Analyze her words. The Tribulation being "the fiery trial which is to try *us*" and which will be "for the purging and purifying of *the real members* of the body of Jesus". This is the Posttribulationist position. She then describes that period as being "from Antichrist," when Satan "will try to shake in everything *we* have believed," when "the awful sight of a false Christ [will] be seen on this earth," and when "nothing but the living Christ *in us* can detect this awful attempt of the enemy to deceive," and then included herself among the faithful who would be tried *after* the Antichrist has been revealed and *during* the Tribulation period. This is completely inconsistent with the Pre-Tribulational Rapture teaching!

Therefore, how can you say this is the "birthplace" of the Pre-Trib Rapture, let alone "influenced" John Darby to "think" Pre-Trib! It's ludicrous! Sounds like somebody has a "spurious" agenda with their faulty research here. I wonder who that was?

Furthermore, Margaret MacDonald was also a historicist in that she believed that the Church was *already* in the Tribulation and had been for hundreds of years. This as well is inconsistent with the teaching of the Pre-Tribulational Rapture. All this means is that there is no way you can tie Margaret MacDonald to Pre-Trib teaching as this person admits:

"When one closely examines MacDonald's vision, it becomes clear that her vision could not have been a Pretribulational one. MacDonald looked for a "fiery trial which is to try us," and she foresaw the Church being purged by the Antichrist. Any Pretribulation Rapturist can tell you the Church will be removed before the advent of the Antichrist.

The evidence that Christians believed in the Rapture long before MacDonald does not seem to have sunk into the minds of those opposed to the Rapture. They still teach that she is the founder of Pretribulationism. When someone is presented with overwhelming proof that he or she is wrong and refuses to accept that truth, then we certainly may conclude that he or she is in spiritual darkness.

No evidence whatsoever points to MacDonald as the source of Pretribulationism. Every major prophetic author alive today claims the Word of God as the foundation for belief in the Rapture. Paul affirmed in 1 Thessalonians 4:16-18:

'For the Lord himself shall descend from heaven with a shout, with the voice of the archangel, and with the trump of God: and the dead in Christ shall rise first: Then we which are alive [and] remain shall be caught up together with them in the clouds, to meet the Lord in the air: and so shall we ever be with the Lord. Wherefore comfort one another with these words.'"[4]

Then as if that wasn't bad enough, trying to say John Darby got the Pre-Trib teaching from Margaret MacDonald when she clearly didn't even believe in it herself, another "spurious lie" propagated by Dave MacPherson is that John Darby also got the Pre-Trib teaching from a guy named Edward Irving and the Irvingites. However, they too, like Margaret MacDonald were also historicists which view the entire Church Age as the Tribulation. Also they believe that Babylon (false Christianity according to them) was about to be destroyed and then the Second Coming would occur. Irving also taught that the Second Coming was synonymous with the Rapture and even believed that Raptured saints would stay in heaven until the earth was renovated by fire and then return to the earth.[5]

This is clearly *not* Pre-Tribulational teaching, so how in the world could you say that Darby ever got influenced by Irving and the Irvingites to start "thinking" the Pre-Trib himself? It's crazy! If Darby *was* ever influenced by McDonald or Irving then he should be promoting "Post-Tribulationism" with a Partial Rapure, *not* Pre-Tribulationism! This is nuts! How could non-pretribulationists be the source of pretribulationism? It's either the worst case of research in human history or a flat out "lie" for "spurious" reasons, as this man shares:

"One of the things that facilitated the Nazi rise to power in Germany earlier this century was their propaganda approach called, 'The Big Lie.' If you told a big enough lie often enough then the people would come to believe it. This the Nazis did well. This is what Anti-Pretribulationists like John Bray and Dave MacPherson have done over the last 25 years.

Apparently 'The Big Lie' about the origins of the Pre-Trib Rapture has penetrated the thinking of the late Robert Van Kampen and Marvin Rosenthal to the extent that they have adopted such a falsehood as true. This is amazing in light of the fact that their own Pre-Wrath viewpoint is not much more than 25 years old itself."[6]

Furthermore, it is also on record that Darby even regarded the 1830 Charismatic manifestations as demonic and not of God, and thus wanted no part of it. Finally, Darby even reported that he himself *discovered* the Rapture teaching in 1827, three years before MacDonald had her vision. He admitted that the revelation of the Rapture came to him when he realized the distinction between Israel and the Church while convalescing from a riding accident during December 1826 and January 1827.[7] As one researcher points out:

"If this is true, and there is every reason to believe that it is, then all of the origin-of-the-Rapture-conspiracy-theories fall to the ground in a heap of speculative rubble. Darby would have at least a three-year jump on any who would have supposedly influenced his thought, making it impossible for all the influence theories to have any credibility."[8]

Again, it's obvious somebody is either guilty of some of the worst research in human history, or they are repeating this "Big Lie" about the Pre-Trib Rapture for "spurious" motives.

The **third spurious** accusation against the Pre-Trib position is that **John Darby Started it Himself**. Really? Did John Darby actually "start" the Pre-Trib Rapture teaching, or as with many other Biblical teachings, as we saw in the case of the examples of the Protestant Reformers, did Darby simply "rediscover" the Pre-Trib Rapture teaching, which was there the whole time in the Bible? I think the answer will be obvious once you take a historical investigation into the teachings of the Pre-Trib Rapture. In fact, this lack of honest historical research on the Pre-Trib Rapture by Anti-Pre-Tribbers, has apparently cost some of them a good chunk of change, as this man shares:

"By far the biggest mistake Post-Tribulationists have made attacking the Rapture is claiming that the Pretribulation Rapture wasn't taught before 1830. In fact, John L. Bray, a Southern Baptist evangelist, offered $500 to anyone who could prove that someone taught the Rapture doctrine prior to MacDonald's 1830 vision. Bray was first proven wrong when he wrote in a newsletter: 'Then my own research indicated that it was Emmanuel Lacunza, who in 1812 taught this theory.'

Bray stuck his neck out again when he made another $500 offer to anyone who could provide a documented statement earlier than Lacunza's 1812 writings. Apparently he had to cough up another 500 bucks. I quote him again: 'I offered $500 to anyone who would give a documented statement earlier than Lacunza's time which taught a two-stage coming of Christ separated by a stated period of time. Now I have the Photostat copies of a book published in Philadelphia,

Pennsylvania, in 1788 but written in 1742-1744 in England, which taught the Pretribulation Rapture before Lacunza.'"9

Sounds to me like it's a "losing" option to "bet against" the historical teachings of the Pre-Trib Rapture prior to John Darby! Wouldn't it be wiser just to keep your money and stop betting against the historical facts of the Pre-Trib position in exchange for faulty "spurious" motives? I think so! That's because the Pre-Trib Rapture teaching has been verified through and through in Church History. In fact, even a cursory look reveals that John Darby was NOT the first one to "promote" this teaching, that of a Pre-Trib Rapture. Rather, he was just one of many in a long line of other Biblical scholars throughout Church History that taught a Pre-Trib Rapture. See for yourself:

THE EARLY CHURCH: The Early Church fathers' such as Barnabas (100-105), Papias (60-130), Justin Martyr (110-195), Irenaeus (120-202), Tertullian (145-220), Hippolytus (185-236), Cyprian (200-250), and Lactantius (260-330) wrote on the imminent return of Jesus Christ, the central argument for the Pre-Tribulation Rapture view. Expressions of Imminency abound in the Apostolic Fathers. Clement of Rome, Ignatius of Antioch, *The Didache*, *The Epistle of Barnabas* all speak of Imminency.

- **The Didache:** As early as 70 - 180 AD, chapter 16, section 1, says, "Be vigilant over your life; let your lamps not be extinguished, or your loins ungirded, but be prepared, for you know not the hour in which our Lord will come."

- **The First Epistle of Clement:** (Written around 96 A.D. by Clement, a prominent leader of the Church at Rome who knew some of the apostles personally and probably is the Clement referred to in Phil. 4:3): "Of a truth, soon and suddenly shall His will be accomplished, as the Scripture also bears witness, saying, 'speedily will He come, and will not tarry.'"

- **Tertullian:** "But what a spectacle is that fast-approaching advent of our Lord, now owned by all, now highly exalted, now a triumphant One!"

- **Shepherd of Hermas:** It speaks of the Pretribulational concept of escaping the Tribulation. 'You have escaped from great tribulation on account of your faith, and because you did not doubt in the presence of such a beast. Go, therefore, and tell the elect of the Lord His mighty deeds, and say to them that this beast is a type of the great tribulation that is coming. If then ye prepare yourselves, and repent with all your heart, and turn to the Lord, it will be possible for you to escape it, if your heart be pure and spotless, and ye spend the rest of the days of your life in serving the Lord blamelessly.'

- **Victorinus:** (Well known by 270 and died in 303 A.D.) He wrote a commentary on the book of Revelation. In one place he made an interesting statement that reflects his idea that the Church would be removed prior to the tribulation.

- **Ephraem the Syrian:** Evidence of Pretribulationism surfaces during the early medieval period in a sermon some attribute to Ephraem the Syrian entitled *Sermon on The Last Times, The Antichrist, and The End of the World.* The sermon was written sometime between the fourth and sixth century. The Rapture statement reads as follows: 'Why therefore do we not reject every care of earthly actions and prepare ourselves for the meeting of the Lord Christ, so that he may draw us from the confusion, which overwhelms all the world? . . . For all the saints and elect of God are gathered, prior to the tribulation that is to come, and are taken to the Lord lest they see the confusion that is to overwhelm the world because of our sins.' This statement evidences a clear belief that all Christians will escape the tribulation through a gathering to the Lord. How else can this be understood other than as Pretribulational? The later second coming of Christ to the earth with the saints is mentioned at the end of the sermon. Ephraem also taught in this same sermon that the war of Gog and Magog in Ezekiel 38-39 would precede the tribulation and he taught the imminent return of Jesus. Ephraem's fascinating teachings on the Antichrist have never been published in English until now. This critically important prophecy manuscript from the fourth century of the Church era reveals a literal method of interpretation and a teaching of the pre-millennial return of Christ. Ephraem declares his belief in a personal Antichrist, who will rule the Roman Empire during the last days, a rebuilt temple, the two witnesses, and a literal Great Tribulation lasting 1,260 days. In another text by Ephraem called *The Book of the Cave of Treasure* he taught that Daniel's seventieth week will be fulfilled in the final seven years at the end of this age that will conclude with Christ's return at the Battle of Armageddon to establish His kingdom. Dr. Paul Alexander, perhaps the most authoritative scholar on the writings of the early Byzantine Church, concluded that Ephraem's text on the Antichrist taught that the Lord would supernaturally remove the saints of the Church from the earth "prior to the tribulation that is to come."

Three Clear Summary Points from the Early Church Fathers' Teachings:

- These Early Church Fathers expected Christ to physically return to earth followed by a 1000 year kingdom rule on earth.
- By many of the writings we can see they believed in the possibility of an any moment return of Christ with statements that resemble a Pre-Trib view point.
- Even though the Early Church was under heavy persecution these teachers believed there would still come a distinct time of great tribulation in the future.

THE MEDIEVAL CHURCH: By the fifth century A.D., the Amillennialism of Origen and Augustine had won the day in the established Church - East and West. It is probable that there was always some form of premillennialism throughout the Middle Ages, but it existed primarily underground.

- Dorothy deF Abrahamse notes: 'By medieval times the belief in an imminent apocalypse had officially been relegated to the role of symbolic theory by the Church; as early as the fourth century, Augustine had declared that the Revelation of John was to be interpreted symbolically rather than literally, and for most of the Middle Ages Church councils and theologians considered only abstract eschatology to be acceptable speculation.

- Since the nineteenth century, however, historians have recognized that *literal apocalypses did continue to circulate in the medieval world* and that they played a fundamental role in the creation of important strains of thought and legend. It is believed that sects like the **Albigenses**, **Lombards**, and the **Waldenses** were attracted to Premillennialism, but little is known of the details of their beliefs since the Catholics *destroyed* their works when they were found.

- Some Medieval writers such as **Abbot Ceolfrid's** Latin Codex Amiatinus (ca. 690-716) wrote statements that distinguish the Rapture from the Second Coming.

- **Brother Dolcino:** (d. 1307) He too made a distinction from the Rapture and the Second Coming. In fact, two things are fairly certain from Dolcino. First, he believed that the purpose of the Rapture was related to the escape of the saints from the end-time tribulation and persecution of the Antichrist. Second, Dolcino believed that there would be a significant gap of time between the Rapture of the saints to paradise and their subsequent descent to earth.

- It must be noted at this point that it is extremely unlikely for the Middle Ages to produce an abundance of advocates of a Pre-Trib Rapture when the more foundational belief of Premillennialism is all but absent. Thus, the Rapture question is likewise absent. This continued until the time of the Reformation, when many things within Christendom began to be revolutionized. (Or in other words "rediscovered.")

THE REFORMATION CHURCH: Premillennialism began to be revived as a result of at least three factors.

First, the Reformers went back to the sources, which for them were the Bible and Apostolic Fathers. This exposed them to an orthodox premillennialism. Specifically significant was the reappearance of the full text of Irenaeus' *Against Heresies*, which included the last five chapters that espouse a consistent futurism and cast the 70th week of Daniel into the future.

Second, they repudiated much, not all, of the allegorization that dominated mediaeval hermeneutics by adopting a more literal approach, especially in the area of the historical exegesis.

Third, many of the Protestants came into contact with Jews and learned Hebrew. This raised concerns over whether passages that speak of national Israel were to be taken historically or continued to be allegorized within the tradition of the Middle Ages. The more the Reformers took them as historical, the more they were awakened to Premillennial interpretations, in spite of the fact that they were often labeled 'Judaizers.'

- **John Calvin**, the reformer at Geneva during the 1500s and founder of the Presbyterian Church, made the following statements in some of his commentaries on books of the Bible: "Be prepared to expect Him every day, or rather every moment." "As He has promised that He will return to us, we ought to hold ourselves prepared, at every moment to receive Him." "Today we must be alert to grasp the imminent return of Christ." Commenting on 1 Thessalonians 4, the "Rapture passage," Calvin said that Paul, "means by this to arouse the Thessalonians to wait for it, nay more, to hold all believers in suspense, that they may not promise themselves some particular time…that believers might be prepared at all times."

- **Martin Luther:** In his Sermon of Consolation, declared that the hope of Christ's return is an absolute necessity for a Christian: "If thou be not filled with a desire after the Coming of this day, thou canst never pray the Lord's prayer, nor canst thou repeat from thy heart the creed of faith. For with what conscience canst thou say, 'I believe in the resurrection of the body and the life everlasting,' if thou dost not in thy heart desire the same? If thou didst believe it, thou must, of necessity, desire it from thy heart, and long for that day to come; which, if thou doest not desire, thou art not yet a Christian, nor canst thou boast of thy faith."

- By the late 1500's and the early 1600's, **Premillennialism** began to return as a factor within the mainstream Church after more than a 1,000 year reign of Amillennialism. With the flowering of Biblical interpretation during the late Reformation Period, Premillennial interpreters began to abound throughout Protestantism and so did the development of sub-issues like the Rapture.

- **The Westminster Confession**: Written by the Puritans of England during the 1600s, declared that men should "shake off all carnal security and be always watchful, because they know not at what hour the Lord will come."

- It has been claimed that some separated the Rapture from the second coming as early as **Joseph Mede** in his seminal work *Clavis Apocalyptica* (1627), who is considered the father of English Premillennialism.

- **Increase Mather:** He was a Pastor, scholar, and was the first President of Harvard College and proved, "that the saints would be *caught up into the air* beforehand, thereby escaping the final conflagration." This teaching from Mather was an early formulation of the Rapture doctrine more fully elaborated in the nineteenth century. It is clear that the application of a more literal hermeneutic was leading to a distinction between the Rapture and the second coming as separate events. Thus others began to speak of the Rapture.

- **Peter Jurieu:** in his book *Approaching Deliverance of the Church* (1687) taught that Christ would come in the air to Rapture the saints and return to heaven before the battle of Armageddon. He spoke of a Rapture prior to His coming in glory and judgment at Armageddon.

- **Philip Doddridge's** commentary on the New Testament (1738) used the term *Rapture* and spoke of it as imminent. It is clear that he believed that this coming will precede Christ's descent to the earth and the time of judgment. The purpose was to preserve believers from the time of judgment.

- **Morgan Edwards:** (Founder of Brown University) in 1742-44 saw a distinct Rapture before the start of the millennium. "I say, somewhat more because the dead saints will be raised, and the living changed at Christ's 'appearing in the air' (1 Thess 4:17) but will he and they abide in the air all that time? No: they will ascend to paradise, or to one of those many 'mansions in the father's house' (John 14:2), and so disappear during the foresaid period of time."

- **John Gill's** commentary on the New Testament (1748): Dr. Gill, a famous eighteenth-century Baptist theologian, published his commentary on the New Testament in 1748. He is considered a serious Calvinist scholar who wrote many volumes on theology. In his commentary on 1 Thessalonians 4:15-17, Dr. Gill points out that Paul is teaching a doctrine that is "something new and extraordinary." Gill calls the imminent translation of the saints "the Rapture" and calls for watchfulness because "it will be sudden, and unknown beforehand, and when least thought of and expected." "For this we say to you by the word of the Lord, that we which are alive and remain unto the coming of the Lord shall not prevent them which are asleep" (1 Thess. 4:15). In commenting on this verse Gill revealed that he understood there would be an interval of time between the Rapture and the return of saints with Christ at Armageddon. To summarize Dr. Gill's 1748 Pre-Tribulation Rapture teaching about the sequence of prophetic events it is vital to note that he declared to all:

1. The Lord will descend in the air.
2. The saints will be Raptured in the air to meet Him.
3. Here Christ will stop in the air and will be visible.
4. As yet, He will not descend on earth, because it is not fit to receive Him.
5. He'll take up the saints with Him into the third heaven, till the general conflagration and burning of the world is over.
6. He will preserve them from it.
7. And then shall all the elect of God descend from heaven to earth with Christ.

Gill then summarizes the sequence:

1) They shall be with Him wherever He is; first in the air, where they shall

meet Him.

2) Then in the third heaven, where they shall go up with Him.

3) Then on earth, where they shall descend and reign with Him a thousand years.

- **James Macknight** (1763) and **Thomas Scott** (1792) taught that the righteous will be carried to heaven, where they will be secure until the time of judgment is over.

THE MODERN CHURCH: As futurism began to replace historicism within Premillennial circles in the 1820's, the modern proponent of dispensational Pretribulationism arrives on the scene.

- **John Nelson Darby** first understood his view of the Rapture as the result of Bible study during a convalescence from December 1826 until January 1827. He is the fountainhead for the modern version of the doctrine.

- The doctrine of the Rapture spread around the world through the **Brethren movement** with which Darby and other like-minded Christians were associated. It appears that either through their writings or personal visits to North America, this version of Pre-tribulationism was spread throughout American Evangelicalism.

- Two early proponents of the view include Presbyterian **James H. Brookes** and Baptist **J. R. Graves**.

- The Rapture was further spread through annual Bible conferences such as the **Niagara Bible Conference** (1878-1909)

- Turn of the century **publications** like *The Truth* and *Our Hope*.

- **Popular books** like Brookes' *Maranatha* and William Blackstone's *Jesus Is Coming*

- Many of the greatest **Bible teachers** of the first-half of the twentieth century helped spread the doctrine such as **Arno Gaebelein, C.I Scofield** and *The Scofield Reference Bible* (1909) **A.J. Gordon, James M. Gray, R.A. Torrey, Harry Ironside**, and **Lewis S. Chafer**.

- In virtually every major metropolitan area in North America a Bible Institute, Bible College, or Seminary was founded that expounded dispensational Pretribulationism. Schools like **Moody Bible Institute**, **The Philadelphia Bible College**, **Bible Institute of Los Angeles** (BIOLA), and **Dallas Theological Seminary** taught and defended these views.

- These teachings were found primarily in independent **Churches**, Bible Churches, Baptists, and a significant number of Presbyterian Churches. Around 1925, Pretribulationism was adopted by many Pentecostal Denominations such as the Assemblies of God and The Four-Square Gospel denomination. Pretribulationism was dominate among Charismatics in the 1960s and '70s.

- **Hal Lindsey's** *Late Great Planet Earth* (1970) furthered the spread of the Pre-Trib Rapture as it exerted great influence throughout popular American culture and then around the world.

- Many **Radio** and **T. V. programs** taught Pretribulationism as well.

The Doctrine of the Rapture may not have been the most visible teaching in the history of the Church. However, it has had significant advocates throughout the last 2,000 years. It has surfaced wherever Premillennialism is taught, especially with literal interpretation, futurism, dispensationalism, and a distinction between Israel and the Church. Regardless of its history, belief in the Rapture has been supported primarily by those who attempt a faithful exposition of the Biblical text."[10]

In other words, if you stick with a literal, historical, grammatical interpretation of the Bible (which is how we're supposed to rightly interpret the Bible) then that's what you're going to come away with every single time; a Pre-Trib Premillennial view. But as you can see, based on the historical evidence, so much for it being a "recent" teaching! Who in their right mind would ever say that John Darby is the one who originated this belief in a Pre-Trib Rapture? As one man shares:

"Those who have stated that the Pre-Tribulation Rapture was never taught throughout the entire history of the Church until 1830 are simply ignorant of these important Christian texts. This constant expectation of our Lord's Second Coming is one of the characteristic features of primitive Christianity. As the

French writer Joubert once wrote, 'Nothing makes men so imprudent and conceited as ignorance of the past and a scorn for old books.'"[11]

In other words, history has vindicated time and time again the truth that the Pre-Trib Rapture is *not* a "recent" teaching, let alone a "spurious" one. Somebody clearly didn't do their homework! Which means again, these accusations against the Pre-Trib Rapture, saying that it started with Darby, are either the worst case of research in human history or a flat out "spurious" lie for some "spurious" reason, as these researchers admit:

"Christians must recognize that those who paint Pre-Tribulationists as fanatics, fringe movement Christians, or as heretics who have embraced some strange and novel idea never heard of until the 1800's, have done a disfavor to the entire body of Christ. Whatever position one holds to in this area, everyone should at the least admit good, sound, and orthodox believers have taught this view before the 1800's time period. And many today continue to see this as a valid position to hold from the Scriptures when properly interpreted in a plain, consistent, and normal manner with the words given their ordinary usage in historical context."[12]

"The Rapture of the Church is clearly *not* a new doctrine invented by a Scottish schoolgirl, or by C.I. Scofield or by John Darby. For fourteen hundred years, it was a *lost* doctrine, along with the doctrine of salvation by grace through faith.

Martin Luther didn't *discover* a new doctrine when he read Ephesians 2:8-9, he *rediscovered* what the Vatican had buried during the Dark Ages. (That's why they were *called* 'the Dark Ages' in the first place).

Luther *rediscovered* the truth that salvation comes through grace and by faith, not by paying money to a priest for absolution from purgatory.

To the degree one can credit Schofield or Darby or anybody else, it can only be for the *rediscovery* of a doctrine long buried by the Vatican for the same reason. If the Lord is to come for the *living* saints, then the Vatican dogma that requires additional purification in Purgatory collapses."[13]

In other words, somebody had a "spurious" motive to keep these truths quiet and hidden away from us. And so it is today with the teaching of the Pre-Trib Rapture. Once again, people are trying to "put a lid" on it and "keep it hidden" from the rest of us. It was there the whole time in the Bible and taught throughout Church History between bouts of Ecclesiastical stranglehold like with the Catholic Church. Yet once again, the irony is, history seems to be repeating itself. There are those in the Church today who are guilty of some "spurious" means and "spurious" motives like the Catholic Church of the past. They are trying to once again force the rest of us into another kind of stranglehold on the Blessed Hope of the Rapture, and thus put us into the Eschatalogical Dark Ages again. And all this, on the cusp of its fulfillment. The timing couldn't be more impeccable.

Yet, our loving Heavenly Father has made sure that we His Church, His beloved Bride, *rediscover* this teaching of the Pre-Trib Rapture in our lifetime when it's never been so close, closest in all of Church History. Therefore, if you're one of those in the "spurious" camp, wouldn't it be wise to just stop scoffing, stop lying, and stop promoting false "spurious" accusations against the Pre-Trib Rapture? Isn't the point to make sure you're ready yourself and then get busy saving as many as you can?

Part IV

The Problematic Positions on the Rapture

Chapter Fourteen

The Problems with Post-Trib

The **sixth thing** we're going to look to avoid being deceived is **What about the Other Positions of the Rapture**? If we are truly on a journey to not be deceived on the truth concerning the Rapture, then I think it's only fair that we not just take a look at one position, the Pre-Trib position, but all the positions. How well do they line up with the Scripture? Are they as accurate as the Pre-Trib? Do they too hold up under scrutiny? How well do they do with the accusations thrown their way? Well, I think as you'll see shortly, not only do the other positions NOT do as well as the Pre-Trib position, but they have some serious problems.

The **first position** on the Rapture that has some serious problems with it is **The Post-Trib Position**. Here's a basic explanation of their belief on the Rapture:

"Post-tribulationists believe that Christians will remain on the Earth throughout the whole 7-year Tribulation period. They will be taken up (or Raptured) to meet Christ in the air at Christs' Second Coming at the end of the 7-year Tribulation just before the battle of Armageddon and then return with Him as Christ descends to the Earth, to usher in the Millennium – the 1000-year reign of Christ on Earth. They believe the Rapture and the Return of the Lord are one event. They believe there is only one coming of the Lord - at the end of the tribulation."[1]

So as you can see, the Post-Trib position on the Rapture is radically different than the Pre-Trib position. In fact, they are at total opposite ends of the prophetic time scale spectrum. The Pre-Trib Rapture says the Church will leave the earth "prior" to the 7-year Tribulation, and the Post-Trib Rapture says the Church will remain on earth until the "end" of the 7-year Tribulation. Obviously, both cannot be true, so which one is correct? How can we not be deceived? Well, just as we put the Pre-Trib position underneath a serious microscope and dealt with the various accusations that are thrown its way, let's now do the same with the Post-Trib position. I think you will soon see, it has some serious problems.

The **first problem** with the Post-Trib teaching of the Rapture is that **It Places the Church Under God's Wrath**. Right out of the gates, based on their own definition of their own position, the Post-Tribulationists say that, "Christians will remain on the Earth throughout the whole 7-year Tribulation period." However, the problem is, you just created a contradiction in the Scripture. The Bible says that the Church is not appointed unto God's wrath, yet the 7-year Tribulation is a time when God pours out His wrath. Since God doesn't "lie" or "contradict" Himself, this premise cannot be true.

Let's take a look at that evidence again that the Church cannot be in a time frame of God's wrath, which is what the 7-year Tribulation is all about. First of all, the Scripture is clear. Jesus set His Church free from God's wrath.

Romans 5:8-11 "But God demonstrates His own love for us in this: While we were still sinners, Christ died for us. Since we have now been justified by His blood, how much more shall we be *saved from God's wrath* through Him! For if, when we were God's enemies, we were reconciled to Him through the death of His Son, how much more, having been reconciled, shall we be saved through His life! Not only is this so, but we also rejoice in God through our Lord Jesus Christ, through whom we have now received reconciliation."

1 Thessalonians 1:10 "And to wait for His Son from heaven, whom He raised from the dead – Jesus, Who *rescues us from the coming wrath*."

1 Thessalonians 5:9-11 "For *God did not appoint us to suffer wrath* but to receive salvation through our Lord Jesus Christ. He died for us so that, whether we are awake or asleep, we may live together with Him. Therefore encourage one another and build each other up, just as in fact you are doing."

So much for being a part of God's wrath! Yes, as we saw before, the Church may experience "thlipsis" or "general tribulation," here on earth today, but the Bible is clear, we will *never* experience God's "orge" or His "wrath" including the future time of "wrath" being poured out on earth during the 7-year Tribulation. Lest you think this is a foreign concept, consider this. All Christians who died in either peace or persecution throughout history have already escaped the Great Tribulation. So what's the big deal? And lest you doubt that the 7-year Tribulation is a time of God's wrath, let's take a look at these verses describing that period again.

Revelation 6:16-17 "They called to the mountains and the rocks, 'Fall on us and hide us from the face of him who sits on the throne and from *the wrath of the Lamb*! For the great day of their wrath has come, and who can stand?'"

NOTE: Even though the word "wrath" is not found in Revelation until 6:16-17, the famine, sword, pestilence, and wild beasts in the first four seal judgments are often associated with God's wrath in other places in the Bible. See (Jer 14:12; 15:2; 24:10; 29:17; Ezek 5:12, 17; 14:21). Also, the verb "has come" doesn't even mean the "wrath" started just then. It's in the Greek aorist tense which speaks of a past event. This means the "wrath" has already been going on and these people in this text are just now acknowledging it.

Revelation 11:18 "The nations were angry; and *Your wrath has come*."

Revelation 14:10 "He, too, will drink of the wine of God's fury, which has been poured full strength into *the cup of His wrath*."

Revelation 14:19 "The angel swung his sickle on the earth, gathered its grapes and threw them into the great winepress of *God's wrath*."

Revelation 15:1 "I saw in heaven another great and marvelous sign: seven angels with the seven last plagues – last, because with them *God's wrath* is completed."

Revelation 15:7 "Then one of the four living creatures gave to the seven angels seven golden bowls filled with *the wrath of God*, who lives for ever and ever."

Revelation 16:1 "Then I heard a loud voice from the temple saying to the seven angels, 'Go, pour out the seven bowls of *God's wrath* on the earth.'"

Revelation 16:19 "The great city split into three parts, and the cities of the nations collapsed. God remembered Babylon the Great and gave her the cup filled with the wine of the fury of *His wrath*."

As you can see, the Bible clearly presents the *entire* 7-year Tribulation as a time when God pours out His wrath. So how can you put the Church into this time frame, even for a second, let alone "all 7 years of it" as the Post-Trib position states, when Jesus "saved, "rescued," and has "not appointed" His Church unto God's wrath? The Pre-Tribulational Rapture position is the only position that *agrees* with the Bible on this issue. And isn't that what we're supposed to do, if we're not going to be deceived?

The **second problem** with the Post-Trib teaching of the Rapture is that **It States that the Tribulations Saints Will Be Protected**. Now we just saw that the Bible clearly teaches that God will be pouring out His wrath during the *entire* 7-year Tribulation period, therefore, the Church must be absent from it since Jesus saved us from it, otherwise you create a contradiction in the Scripture. However, rather than admit defeat, those in the Pre-Trib position try to dance around this contradiction they've created by saying that God will "protect" the Church during the 7-year Tribulation and only pour out His wrath on unbelievers." Really?

First of all, we've already seen before in great detail, the people who do get saved "during" the 7-year Tribulation are not the Church but rather a different identity altogether called the Tribulation Saints. Just like the Jewish people, during the 7-year Tribulation, God will also extend His mercy to the Gentile Nations or what's called "the inhabitants of the earth." They too will have an opportunity to be saved, but most of them will be slaughtered for it. This is the identity of the Tribulation saints. They are *not* the Church. The Church leaves at the Rapture prior to when the 7-year Tribulation begins, before God's wrath gets poured out, and these "saints" mentioned are the "Gentile Nations" who are left behind and get saved "after" the Rapture.

How do I know? Because the "context" of the word "saint" determines the meaning. The word "saint" does appear during the events mentioned in the Book of Revelation concerning the 7-year Tribulation, however, a quick look at the facts reveals it cannot be referring to the Church.

First of all the word "saint" in the Bible simply means, "holy one." And when you look at the Scripture, Old and New Testaments, you'll see that there are *many different kinds of people* being referred to as a "saint" or "holy one." There are the Old Testament saints, New Testament saints, future Tribulation saints, and even saints in the Millennial Kingdom. So just because you see the word "saint" doesn't mean it's referring to a "Church Age Saint." There are all kinds of "holy ones" throughout the Bible. Rather, what determines the "identity" of the word "saint" and to whom it's referring is the "context."

For example, take the one English word, "cool." I can use it in many different ways. Even though it's spelled the exact same way, with the exact same letter, the context determines its meaning. For instance, what if I were to state the three following sentences:

- "Wow! That outfit you have on is cool!"
- "Hey, is everything okay? Your attitude towards me is kind of cool."
- "Brrrr. The weather outside is cool."

Now notice how all three times, the word "cool" was spelled the exact same way with the exact same letters, but each time each one had a *totally different meaning*. What determined the *correct meaning* of each was the "context" in which it was used in. So it is with the word "saint." Is it referring to an Old Testament saint, a New Testament saint, a 7-year Tribulation saint, or a Millennial saint? Context determines the correct meaning.

Therefore, that's how we are to rightly interpret the word "saint" and it's usage during the horrible events of the 7-year Tribulation, including these passages:

Revelation 13:7 "He was given power to make war against the *saints* and to conquer them. And he was given authority over every tribe, people, language and nation."

Revelation 13:10 "If anyone is to go into captivity, into captivity he will go. If anyone is to be killed with the sword, with the sword he will be killed. This calls for patient endurance and faithfulness on the part of the *saints*."

Revelation 17:6 "I saw that the woman was drunk with the blood of the *saints*, the blood of those who bore testimony to Jesus."

Many people who disagree with the Pre-Tribulation Rapture position will oftentimes cite these verses and others to say, "See, the Church is in the 7-year Tribulation because it says saint." Really? Just who are these "saints" mentioned here? Remember the rule: context, context, context. Certainly these are not Old Testament saints because that time frame has already passed. Secondly, it can't be referring to the Millennial Kingdom saints because that's still in the future.

Likewise neither can it be referring to the New Testament Church Age saints because as we've already seen, these saints are under God's wrath and the Church Age saint is not appointed unto God's wrath. This does not even take into account all the other strong evidences we saw earlier detailing how the New Testament Church leaves at the Rapture of the Church prior to the events of the 7-year Tribulation. Therefore, that only leaves one other final option. These passages must be referring to the Tribulation saints who get saved "after" the Rapture and "during" the 7-year Tribulation.

First of all, we know that people can and will get saved during the 7-year Tribulation due to the powerful evangelism campaign going on in the world through the 144,000 male Jewish evangelists, the two witnesses, and the angel that flies through the sky declaring the eternal gospel.

Revelation 7:4,9 "Then I heard the number of those who were sealed: 144,000 from all the tribes of Israel. After this I looked and there before me was a great multitude that no one could count, from every nation, tribe, people and language, standing before the throne and in front of the Lamb. They were wearing white robes and were holding palm branches in their hands."

Revelation 11:3 "And I will give power to my two witnesses, and they will prophesy for 1,260 days, clothed in sackcloth."

Revelation 14:6 "Then I saw another angel flying in midair, and he had the eternal gospel to proclaim to those who live on the earth – to every nation, tribe, language and people."

Therefore, the Tribulation saints, those who get saved "during" the 7-year Tribulation, are the "saints" mentioned in the Book of Revelation. They cannot be the Church. The lesson is they should've gotten saved at the present time, "before" the Rapture occurred prior to the 7-year Tribulation. Yes, they finally got saved, praise God for that, but now they're in a heap of trouble. Why? Because unlike what the Post-Trib position would have you and I believe, there is *no protection* going on here. Rather most of them will be horribly murdered and martyred and have their heads chopped off.

Revelation 6:9-11 "When he opened the fifth seal, I saw under the altar the souls of those who had been slain because of the word of God and the testimony they had maintained. They called out in a loud voice, 'How long, Sovereign Lord, holy and true, until You judge the inhabitants of the earth and avenge our blood?'

Then each of them was given a white robe, and they were told to wait a little longer, until the number of their fellow servants and brothers who were to be killed as they had been was completed."

Revelation 7:9,13-15 "After this I looked and there before me was a great multitude that no one could count, from every nation, tribe, people and language, standing before the throne and in front of the Lamb. They were wearing white robes and were holding palm branches in their hands. Then one of the elders asked me, 'These in white robes – who are they, and where did they come from?' I answered, 'Sir, you know.' And he said, 'These are they who have come out of the great tribulation; they have washed their robes and made them white in the blood of the Lamb.'"

Revelation 20:4 "And I saw the souls of those who had been beheaded because of their testimony for Jesus and because of the word of God. They had not worshiped the beast or his image and had not received his mark on their foreheads or their hands."

So much for being "protected" during this time frame of God's wrath being poured out as the Post-Trib position would have you and I believe! These people are *not* being preserved. They're being killed. That's why, to avoid this contradiction, the Pre-Tributionalist would simply state that these "martyred people" are *not* referring to the Church but rather the Tribulation Saints who get saved "after" the Rapture. No contradiction with these saints. And isn't that what we're supposed to do if we're not going to be deceived?

The **third problem** with the Post-Trib teaching of the Rapture is that **It Replaces Israel with the Church**. Not only does the Post-Trib position get the identity of the "saints" wrong in the 7-year Tribulation and create another contradiction, but they also confuse Israel with the Church messing things up even more. Just one example would be their citation of Matthew 24:22:

Matthew 24:22 "If those days had not been cut short, no one would survive, but for the sake of the elect those days will be shortened."

Here the Post-Tribber would state that the identity of the "elect" mentioned here is "irrefutable evidence" that the Church will go through the 7-year Tribulation. Really? Now, you got it right that the time frame spoken of here is during the 7-year Tribulation, but once again you got the identity wrong. The elect is *not* the Church. In fact, it cannot be the Church because as we saw before in great detail, Matthew 24 is *not* dealing with the Church *at all*, but rather Israel.

First of all, just as the word "Church" is absent in Revelation 4-18, so the word "Church" is absent in Matthew 24. Why? Because the context in Matthew 24 clearly reveals it has nothing to do with the Church. The Church does not even come into existence until Acts Chapter 2. Rather, Matthew 24 is dealing with the Jewish people who are one of the reasons why there is a 7-year Tribulation in the first place.

Furthermore, we know Matthew 24 cannot be referring to the Church because Jesus starts the Chapter off by saying that the Jewish Temple will be torn down to the ground and destroyed, which did happen in 70 AD. But then a few verses later He says a rebuilt Jewish Temple comes back into existence with Jewish people apparently worshipping at it again. We see this with His reference to the Abomination of Desolation in the Book of Daniel where as we saw, the Antichrist goes up into that Temple and declares himself to be god halfway into the 7-year Tribulation. The point is this. The Jewish Temple being destroyed or rebuilt has no significance for the Church. Jesus says the Church doesn't need a manmade Temple because we have become the Temple of God by the indwelling Holy Spirit.

1 Corinthians 3:16 "Don't you know that you yourselves are God's temple and that God's Spirit lives in you?"

So the Church is only concerned about "being" God's temple, not a "destroyed" or "rebuilt" Jewish Temple. However, a manmade Jewish Temple being destroyed and rebuilt is a *very* significant issue for the Jewish people to whom this Chapter is addressed.

Furthermore, Jesus also tells the people during that time frame to "flee to the mountains."

Matthew 24:16 "Then let those who are in Judea flee to the mountains."

Notice He says, "those in Judea." Where's that? Israel! This is not the Church nor can it be the Church. Think about it. Only a small minute fraction of the Church, i.e. Christians live in Israel. If this were referring to the Church it would make this command to flee absolutely meaningless.

Secondly, the command to flee is, "to the mountains." Most scholars believe the place referred to here is the ancient rock city of Petra. Question: "Can the whole Church fit into Petra?" I think not. However, the remnant of the Jewish People can.

Next we see Jesus mentioning that those people of that time are apparently "keeping the Sabbath Day."

Matthew 24:20 "Pray that your flight will not take place in winter or on the Sabbath."

Question: "Does the Church observe a traditional Jewish Saturday Sabbath?" No. But the Jewish people do, even to this day! We Christians not only worship on Sunday in honor of the Resurrection of Jesus Christ, but we are never given the command to worship on the Jewish Sabbath day. Why? Because we have the Lord of the Sabbath Himself, Jesus Christ. We have the "reality" not the "shadow." That's why the Bible says this when referring to the Church and the Jewish Sabbath:

Colossians 2:16-17 "Therefore do not let anyone judge you by what you eat or drink, or with regard to a religious festival, a New Moon celebration or a Sabbath day. These are a shadow of the things that were to come; the reality, however, is found in Christ."

Technically, we are free to worship Jesus any day we want as New Testament Christians. However, traditionally we usually come together "the first day of the week" (Sunday) in honor of the Resurrection of Jesus.

Acts 20:7 "On the first day of the week we came together to break bread."

Therefore, the point is this. How could Jesus be talking about the Church in Matthew 24 when He says these people need to "pray that their flight doesn't take place on the Sabbath" if the Church doesn't worship on the Sabbath? Could it be He's referring to the Jewish people who still *do* to this day worship on the Sabbath? I think so.

So why would the events of Matthew 24 be speaking of the Church when the whole Chapter is referring to Israel, not the Church? So much for "irrefutable evidence" that the Church will go through the 7-year Tribulation by citing Matthew 24:22 let alone any passage from that chapter! Looks like someone is guilty of ignoring the "context" again, as these researchers state:

"The reason why some are teaching that the Church will be present during this terrible time (the 7-year Tribulation) is the failure to distinguish between God's plan for Israel and His plan for the Church, especially in the prophecy revealed by Christ in Matthew 24.

In the passage in Matthew 24, Christ is on the Temple Mount explaining to His Jewish disciples the events that will occur in Israel and in other nations that will lead to the return of Christ as their Jewish Messiah. The disciples' question that Jesus was answering concerned the coming of Israel's long-promised Kingdom, not the coming of Christ for His Church (which they did not even know about).

It is easy to forget that, at this point, before the crucifixion of our Lord and the coming of the Holy Spirit at Pentecost, there was no such thing as a Christian Church. If you had told one of the disciples during the week before Christ's crucifixion that someday there would be an organization based on Christ's teachings, called the Church, and that 99 percent of its members would be uncircumcised Gentiles who would follow neither Jewish law nor offer Temple sacrifices, he would probably have fallen off his chair in shock and disbelief.

One of the classic mistakes in interpretation is to take this conversation between Christ and His Jewish disciples concerning the messianic kingdom and read back into it the reality of the Christian Church which did not come into existence until the Jews rejected Christ and God breathed life into His Body of believers.

Since Christ does not mention the Church to His disciples in this conversation, the plain interpretation is that Israel is the primary focus of the Prophecy of Matthew 24. Because Revelation places a strong emphasis on Israel during the Tribulation, and not on the Church, most Post-Tribulationists have adopted a replacement theology view in order to maintain the focus on them.

Replacementism is the view that Israel, having failed God, has been replaced by the Church. The Church is now seen as spiritual Israel and spiritual Jerusalem. This teaching claims that all the promises and blessings, in fact Israel's entire inheritance, now belongs to the Church. However, God has separate strategies for dealing with the Church and the Jews. When you consider the change in focus, during the tribulation, from the Church to Israel, the Pre-Trib Rapture provides a good explanation for this transfer of attention.

To say that Israel is no longer God's chosen people is really playing with fire because the Antichrist will likely be saying the same thing when he tries to destroy the Jews during the Tribulation. I look for people that hold to replacementism to be in the cheering section when the Beast goes on his Jew-killing campaign."[2]

In other words, that is a camp you don't want to be a part of. Why? Because God doesn't take kindly to those who mess with Israel or His Church. Both have special plans for special purposes. But as you can see, just as it was with the word "saint" so it is with the word "elect." Just because these words appear in a particular passage in the Bible does *not* mean that they refer to the Church. Context determines the meaning, that is, if you're going to avoid a contradiction. And isn't that what we're supposed to observe if we're not going to be deceived?

The **fourth problem** with the Post-Trib teaching of the Rapture is that **It Confuses the Rapture with God's Judgment**. Not only do Post-Tribbers misquote Matthew 24:22 and falsely state that the "elect" mentioned there is referring to the Church when it clearly is not as we just saw, but they also misquote another passage in Matthew 24 and likewise falsely state that it is dealing with the Rapture of the Church when it is not. Here's that passage:

Matthew 24:29-31,40-41 "Immediately after the distress of those days, the sun will be darkened, and the moon will not give its light; the stars will fall from the sky, and the heavenly bodies will be shaken. At that time the sign of the Son of Man will appear in the sky, and all the nations of the earth will mourn. They will see the Son of Man coming on the clouds of the sky, with power and great glory. And He will send his angels with a loud trumpet call, and they will gather his elect from the four winds, from one end of the heavens to the other. Two men will be in the field; one will be taken and the other left. Two women will be grinding with a hand mill; one will be taken and the other left."

Now what the Post-Tribber would state is that this "gathering of the elect" mentioned here in Matthew 24 at the end of the 7-year Tribulation is referring to the Rapture of the Church at the end of the 7-year Tribulation. However, as we just saw by the context, the word "elect" here in this Chapter is *not* referring to the Church but Israel.

Furthermore, this "gathering" is not even speaking about the "Rapture" but rather the "Angel Harvest" of both the wicked and righteous at the end of the 7-year Tribulation. The one person being "gathered" while another is left is talking about the "elect" or Israel being "gathered" to enter the Millennial Kingdom while the "others" are the unbelieving unredeemed who are "taken" and cast into hell. Obviously, they don't get to be a part of the Millennial Kingdom. We see this "Angel Harvest" at the end of the 7-year Tribulation in Revelation 14, or the "pulling" of the Wheat and Tares of Matthew 13, and the "separation" of the "Sheep and Goats" in Matthew 25.

Revelation 14:14-16 "I looked, and there before me was a white cloud, and seated on the cloud was one 'like a son of man' with a crown of gold on His head and a sharp sickle in His hand. Then another angel came out of the temple and called in a loud voice to him who was sitting on the cloud, 'Take your sickle and reap, because the time to reap has come, for the harvest of the earth is ripe.' So he who was seated on the cloud swung his sickle over the earth, and the earth was harvested."

Matthew 13:36-43 "Then He left the crowd and went into the house. His disciples came to Him and said, 'Explain to us the parable of the weeds in the field.' He answered, 'The one who sowed the good seed is the Son of Man. The field is the world, and the good seed stands for the sons of the kingdom. The weeds are the sons of the evil one, and the enemy who sows them is the devil. The harvest is the end of the age, and the harvesters are angels. As the weeds are pulled up and burned in the fire, so it will be at the end of the age. The Son of Man will send out his angels, and they will weed out of his kingdom everything that causes sin and all who do evil. They will throw them into the fiery furnace, where there will be weeping and gnashing of teeth. Then the righteous will shine like the sun in the kingdom of their Father. He who has ears, let him hear.'"

Matthew 25:31-34,41,46 "When the Son of Man comes in His glory, and all the angels with Him, He will sit on His throne in heavenly glory. All the nations will be gathered before Him, and He will separate the people one from another as a shepherd separates the sheep from the goats. He will put the sheep on his right and the goats on his left. Then the King will say to those on his right, 'Come, you who are blessed by my Father; take your inheritance, the kingdom prepared for you since the creation of the world.' Then he will say to those on His left, 'Depart from me, you who are cursed, into the eternal fire prepared for the devil and his angels.' Then they will go away to eternal punishment, but the righteous to eternal life."

Again, as we saw, the Church is not mentioned in Matthew 24 at all, therefore this Angel Harvest cannot be referring to the Church. Also, it has nothing to do with the Rapture but rather the End Time "gathering" of the "elect" of Israel in order to return them to the land for the Millennium, while the "others" who are "taken" are the unbelieving "weeds" or "goats" who are cast into hell. This has *nothing* to do with the Church, let alone the Rapture in the first place!

Furthermore, we know this cannot be referring to the Rapture because one, if we are resurrected at this time, (which happens at the Rapture) why would we need angels to gather us? In the resurrection, we will be like the angels, able to travel in the air at will.

Matthew 22:30 "At the resurrection people will neither marry nor be given in marriage; they will be like the angels in heaven."

Two, this premise that that Angel Harvest is really speaking of the Rapture creates another contradiction in that we would have the wicked being "Raptured" at this same time as well. As we saw, Matthew 13 says the angels will not only gather the "elect," but also the "wicked." Therefore, if you're going to say this "gathering" is speaking of the Rapture then you would have to say that *both* the "wicked" and the "righteous" are getting Raptured and that would be ludicrous.

Third, both the wicked and the righteous cannot be taken *first*. In 1 Thessalonians 4, the passage that really *does* speak about the Rapture of the Church, we see that only the "righteous" (the dead in Christ and live Church Age saints) are taken and the wicked are "left behind."

1 Thessalonians 4:16-17 "For the Lord himself will come down from heaven, with a loud command, with the voice of the archangel and with the trumpet call of God, and the dead in Christ will rise *first*. After that, we who are still alive and are left will be caught up together with them in the clouds to meet the Lord in the air. And so we will be with the Lord forever."

So as you can see, in the real Rapture, the "dead in Christ" or "righteous" go first with the live Church Age saints being "caught up" together with them. However, in Matthew 13 it says the "wicked" are taken first.

Matthew 13:30,49 "Let both grow together until the harvest. At that time I will tell the harvesters: *First* collect the weeds and tie them in bundles to be burned;

then gather the wheat and bring it into my barn. This is how it will be at the end of the age. The angels will come and separate the wicked from the righteous."

So who goes first if the Rapture and Angel Harvest are the same event as the Post-Trib position would have you and I believe? The "righteous" or the "wicked?" The only way to reconcile these two passages is to admit that they *cannot* be speaking of the same event. Both can't be gathered *first* and God doesn't contradict Himself. Therefore, it has to be speaking of two separate events, the Rapture of the Church prior to the 7-year Tribulation being taken "first" and the Angel harvest of the "elect Israel" and the "unbelieving wicked" later at the end of the 7-year Tribulation where the "unbelieving wicked" will be taken "first" before Israel *at that time*. Any other interpretation creates a serious contradiction. And isn't that what we're supposed to avoid if we're not going to be deceived?

The **fifth problem** with the Post-Trib teaching of the Rapture is that **It Confuses the Rapture with the Day of the Lord**. Another huge mistake the Post-Tribbers make is in stating that the event known in the Bible as the "Day of the Lord" is the same as and/or is linked with the Rapture of the Church. However, we know this *cannot* be true because once again it would create another contradiction in the Scripture which God does not do.

First of all, the Bible clearly states that the Rapture comes "before" the Day of the Lord. We see this in 1 Thessalonians 4-5. As one researcher states:

"The order of events is striking. First Thessalonians 4:13-18 deals with the Rapture of the Church to meet the Lord in the air. Then, in 1 Thessalonians 5:1, a new subject is introduced by Paul with the words, "Now as to" (peri de in Greek). This Greek phrase is one of Paul's favorite ways in his letters to change subjects. So, it's clear that he is finished focusing on the Rapture. But what is the next subject in 5:1-9? The Day of the Lord or the coming time of Tribulation.

'Now as to the times and the epochs, brethren, you have no need of anything to be written to you. For you yourselves know full well that the Day of the Lord will come just like a thief in the night' (1 Thess 5:1-2).

Why is this significant? Because of the order of the events. Which event is mentioned first, the Rapture or the Tribulation? It's the Rapture first, then the Tribulation or Day of the Lord. The Tribulation is pictured as a separate and subsequent event from the Rapture.

The order is clear.

| 1 Thessalonians 4:13-18 | The Rapture |
| 1 Thessalonians 5:1-9 | The Day of the Lord (Tribulation)"[3] |

Therefore, how can these be the "same" event, let alone somehow "linked?" Answer: They can't! The Post-Trib argument falls to pieces based on the context of Scripture. They are "separated" events not the "same" event or "linked" events.

Secondly, we've already seen in great detail, the Church is not appointed unto God's Wrath and if you study the Day of the Lord, it is clearly speaking of the 7-year Tribulation where God pours out His Wrath. Therefore the Church *cannot* be "linked" with this time frame.

In both the Old and New Testaments, The Day of the Lord speaks of a horrible time frame when God pours out His wrath and judgment on this wicked world. It's not a literal twenty-four hour day, or a single event, but a period of time which starts "after" the Rapture of the Church and incorporates the entirety of the 7-year Tribulation period. Therefore, the Day of the Lord does not mention and has no application whatsoever to the Church. Again, it's concerning Israel and the godless Gentile Nations of the earth.

Which is precisely why the Thessalonians were freaking out and why the Apostle Paul had to respond a *second time* to the Thessalonica Church about the Rapture and tell them you're not going to be a part of this horrible day.

2 Thessalonians 2:1-5 "Concerning the coming of our Lord Jesus Christ and our being gathered to him, we ask you, brothers, not to become easily unsettled or alarmed by some prophecy, report or letter supposed to have come from us, saying that the Day of the Lord has already come. Don't let anyone deceive you in any way, for that day will not come until the rebellion occurs and the man of lawlessness is revealed, the man doomed to destruction. He will oppose and will exalt himself over everything that is called God or is worshiped, so that he sets himself up in God's temple, proclaiming himself to be God. Don't you remember that when I was with you I used to tell you these things?"

So here we see the Apostle Paul *comforting* and *reassuring* the Thessalonians from a misconception going around at that time by some false teachers saying these Christians missed the Rapture because the Day of the Lord had already come! But Paul says, "No! No! No! No!" Christians are *not* going to be around during that time and he's emphatic about it! Why? Because the Bible says the Day of the Lord is all about God's judgment and bringing people low. It's a time when He pours out His wrath, and anger, and desolation, and vengeance, and destruction, and it's terrible. It's a time of gloominess and darkness and distress and trouble, and refers to the cataclysmic final judgment of God on the wicked, not the Church! The Church is *not* appointed unto His wrath! That's why Paul says "Don't be deceived" *and* you should know better! "Don't you remember I already told you this?" In essence, "Why are you falling for this? You know you can't be there! I already went over this with you guys. Christians are nowhere around in the 7-year Tribulation! We left at the Rapture, prior to the 7-year Tribulation!" So in essence he says, "Don't freak out and listen to these false teachers!"

Besides, if the Thessalonians *thought* that the Rapture came after the 7-year Tribulation started, and you received a letter from Paul saying that the Day of the Lord had already started which occurs during the 7-year Tribulation, then would they not be excited beyond words? Of course! They would be hopeful that the Rapture was at the door because the 7-year Tribulation had already begun! They wouldn't have been troubled or fearful. They would have been excited!

Yet that's precisely the point. The Apostle Paul is writing to alleviate their *fears* and *troubled hearts* concerning the fake letter that said the Day of the Lord had already begun and thus they were in the Tribulation. This *lie* is what freaked them out because they *knew* the Rapture occurred *before* this horrible time frame. This is why Paul says *comfort* or *encourage* one another with these words. You're not going to be here. Calm down. The Rapture occurs before all that!

But as you can see, there is no way you can "link" the "Day of the Lord" with the "Rapture of the Church" as the Post-Trib position does. Not only is the Rapture pictured in the Bible as occurring "first" *before* the Day of the Lord, but there is no way you can "involve" the Church *in* the Day of the Lord when that Day clearly deals with God's wrath being poured out in which Jesus has "saved" "rescued" and "not appointed" His Church unto. Any other interpretation creates a contradiction. And isn't that what we're supposed to avoid if we're not going to be deceived?

The **sixth problem** with the Post-Trib teaching of the Rapture is that **It Confuses the Rapture with the Second Coming**. Believe it or not, not only do Post-Tribbers falsely "link" the "Day of the Lord" with the "Rapture of the Church," but they likewise error by "blending" the "Second Coming of Jesus" with the "Rapture of the Church." However, as we saw previously in our study, it is actually an *easy* thing to demonstrate that the Rapture of the Church *cannot* be the same thing as the Second Coming of Jesus. They are clearly two distinct events. Here are just 20 of the differences we shared before.

The Rapture	The Second Coming
Christ comes in the air	Christ comes to the earth
Christ comes for His saints	Christ come with His saints
Believers are taken away	Unbelievers are taken away
Christ claims His bride	Christ comes with His bride
Christ gathers His own	Angels gather the elect
Christ comes to reward	Christ comes to judge
There are no signs. It is imminent	Many signs precede it
Revealed only in New Testament	Revealed in both Old and New Testaments
Mystery	Foretold
The Mount of Olives is unchanged	Mount of Olives is divided
It is a time of blessing and comfort	It is a time of destruction and judgment
Involves believers only	Involves Israel and the Gentile nations
Will occur in a moment the blink of an eye	Will be visible to the entire world
Tribulation begins	Millennium begins
The Lord takes believers to heaven	Believers return from heaven
Living believers obtain glorified bodies	Elect remain in same bodies
Believers go to the Father's House	The Elect stay on earth
Satan remains free	Satan is bound
False Prophet & Antichrist at large	False Prophet & Antichrist thrown into Lake of Fire
Unbelievers remain on earth	Unbelievers go to hell[4]

As you can see, the Rapture and the Second Coming are two distinct separate events. Therefore, how in the world can you "link" or "blend" these two events into "one" as the Post-Trib position would have you and I believe? Talk about a serious contradiction!

Furthermore, if the Rapture and the Second Coming were one and the same event, then why do we see no mention of the Rapture *at all* in the passages that *do* describe the Second Coming? Here are just two of them. One from the New Testament, one from the Old Testament.

Revelation 19:11-21 "I saw heaven standing open and there before me was a white horse, whose rider is called Faithful and True. With justice He judges and makes war. His eyes are like blazing fire, and on His head are many crowns. He has a name written on Him that no one knows but He himself. He is dressed in a robe dipped in blood, and His name is the Word of God. The armies of heaven were following Him, riding on white horses and dressed in fine linen, white and clean. Out of His mouth comes a sharp sword with which to strike down the nations. 'He will rule them with an iron scepter.' He treads the winepress of the fury of the wrath of God Almighty. On His robe and on His thigh he has this name written: KING OF KINGS AND LORD OF LORDS. And I saw an angel standing in the sun, who cried in a loud voice to all the birds flying in midair, 'Come, gather together for the great supper of God, so that you may eat the flesh of kings, generals, and mighty men, of horses and their riders, and the flesh of all people, free and slave, small and great.' Then I saw the beast and the kings of the earth and their armies gathered together to make war against the rider on the horse and His army. But the beast was captured, and with him the false prophet who had performed the miraculous signs on his behalf. With these signs he had deluded those who had received the mark of the beast and worshiped his image. The two of them were thrown alive into the fiery lake of burning sulfur. The rest of them were killed with the sword that came out of the mouth of the rider on the horse, and all the birds gorged themselves on their flesh."

Now, do you see any Rapture in here? I don't! I do though see the Church "coming down" or "back" (the armies of heaven) as the Pre-Trib position teaches. However, I do *not* see a "going up" of the Church as the Post-Trib position teaches. Now let's take a look at an Old Testament passage referring to the Second Coming:

Zechariah 14:1-9 "A Day of the Lord is coming when your plunder will be divided among you. I will gather all the nations to Jerusalem to fight against it; the city will be captured, the houses ransacked, and the women raped. Half of the city will go into exile, but the rest of the people will not be taken from the city. Then the LORD will go out and fight against those nations, as He fights in the day of battle. On that day His feet will stand on the Mount of Olives, east of Jerusalem, and the Mount of Olives will be split in two from east to west, forming a great valley, with half of the mountain moving north and half moving south. You will flee by My mountain valley, for it will extend to Azel. You will flee as you fled from the earthquake in the days of Uzziah king of Judah. Then the LORD my God will come, and all the holy ones with Him. On that day there will be no light, no cold or frost. It will be a unique day, without daytime or nighttime-a day known to the LORD. When evening comes, there will be light. On that day living water will flow out from Jerusalem, half to the eastern sea and half to the western sea, in summer and in winter. The LORD will be king over the whole earth. On that day there will be one LORD, and His name the only name."

Do you see a Rapture there? Not me! I do see Him "coming back" with holy ones, but I don't see the Church mentioned here at all let alone "going up." Why? Because the Rapture of the Church and the Second Coming of Jesus are not the same event! In fact, logically, you'd think that *if* the Rapture and the Second Coming *were* the same event, then the Rapture would at least be mentioned in these passages somewhere, anywhere. However, it's nowhere! As one man states:

"Some may call this an argument from silence, yet this silence speaks quite loudly. This is the biggest event in the history of the Church, where hundreds of millions of people are resurrected – and it's not mentioned in Revelation 19 or Zechariah 14. Why?"[5]

I'll tell you why. Because the Rapture and the Second Coming are *not* the same event and *do not* happen at the same time. One happens "before" the 7-year Tribulation (Rapture) and the other happens at the "end" of the 7-year Tribulation (Second Coming). Any other interpretation creates a major contradiction. And isn't that what we're supposed to avoid if we're not going to be deceived?

The **seventh problem** with the Post-Trib teaching of the Rapture is that **It Creates a Problem with the Millennium Population**. Not only does the Post-Trib position create all kinds of contradictions, contextual errors, and timing issues in the Bible, which again, is something we should avoid because God doesn't' lie, but they also produce yet another serious destructive outcome with their belief system, that is concerning the people who enter the Millennial Kingdom. If the Post-Trib position is true, where they say the Rapture happens at the end of the 7-year Tribulation, and the Church then makes an immediate U-turn with Jesus at His Second Coming, then who is left to populate the Millennial Kingdom? Other researchers put it this way:

"The Bible teaches that when Christ returns to earth He will establish His kingdom on earth that will last for 1,000 years (Rev 20:1-6). Old Testament saints, Church Age saints, and the Tribulation saints *who died* during the 7-year Tribulation, will all enter the Millennial Kingdom in *new glorified bodies*.

However, believers who come to faith in Christ during the tribulation (Tribulation saints) *and live* until the Second Coming will enter the millennial kingdom of Christ in their *natural, human bodies*. They will carry on ordinary occupations such as farming and building houses, and they will bear children, populating the Messianic kingdom (Isa 65:20-25).

Here is the problem. It would be impossible for people to enter the 1,000 year reign of Christ in *natural bodies* if all saints were caught up at the Second Coming, as Post-Tribulationists teach. Why? Because everyone would already have a *glorified body* and therefore there would not be anyone left in natural bodies to populate the kingdom.

All Raptured Christians before the 7-year Tribulation receive their glorified bodies (Romans 8:22,23; 1Corinthians 15:50-54) and there are no children born to glorified bodies (Matthew 22:23-30). Also, all unsaved are cast into Hell before the 1,000 Year Kingdom Reign of Christ (Revelation 19:11-21 and Matthew 25:41).

Therefore, if the Rapture is Post-Tribulation, at the end of the 7-year Tribulation, then several problems arise with impossible solutions. Where do the natural mortal bodies come from of those that are *born* during the Millennium and *rebel* at the conclusion of the Millennium (Revelation 20:7-10)? There would be no lost people alive to have children, so they cannot come from them. All of the saved have their glorified bodies. No children can be born to them as a result of a Post-Tribulation Rapture.

At the end of Christ's 1,000 Year Reign there are unbelievers who will give their allegiance to satan in an attempt to defeat Christ. (Revelation 20:7-10). Glorified people with glorified bodies can't do this. They no longer have a sin nature to rebel. So how do these people get their human sinful bodies? Placing the Rapture at the end of the Tribulation and the start of the Millennium makes an impossible situation.

However, because the Pre-Tribulationists have at least a seven-year interval between the removal of the Church at the Rapture and the Return of Christ to the earth, this is not a problem because millions of people will be saved during the interval and thus be available to populate the millennium in their natural bodies that still have a sin nature in order to fulfill Scripture. Only the Pre-Trib viewpoint can account for this Post-Trib problem.

The Post-Tribulationists have no satisfactory answer to this dilemma. Therefore, the philosophy of a Post-Tribulation Rapture is impossible."[6]

Why? Because like all the other examples already given, the Post-Trib position creates serious contradictions with the rest of the Bible concerning the Millennial Kingdom and other prophetic events. And since God doesn't lie, isn't that what we're supposed to avoid if we're not going to be deceived?

The **eighth problem** with the Post-Trib teaching of the Rapture is that **It Creates a Problem with the Millennium Separation**. Just when you thought it couldn't get any worse for the Post-Trib position on the Rapture, yet another problem they have created by their contextual errors is with God's judgment and separation of the people at the end of the 7-year Tribulation. Just prior to the establishment of the Millennial Kingdom, the Bible clearly reveals that God will "separate" as we saw with the Angel Harvest, the "sheep" from the "goats" in preparation of establishing the Millennial Kingdom. Let's take a look at that teaching:

Matthew 25:31-34,41,46 "When the Son of Man comes in His glory, and all the angels with Him, He will sit on His throne in heavenly glory. All the nations will be gathered before Him, and He will separate the people one from another as a shepherd separates the sheep from the goats. He will put the sheep on His right and the goats on His left. Then the King will say to those on His right, 'Come, you who are blessed by My Father; take your inheritance, the kingdom prepared for you since the creation of the world.' Then He will say to those on His left, 'Depart from Me, you who are cursed, into the eternal fire prepared for the devil and his angels.' Then they will go away to eternal punishment, but the righteous to eternal life."

As we saw earlier, this passage, along with others, is dealing with the Angel Harvest where God separates those who are still alive, albeit few, who managed somehow to survive the horrible events of the 7-year Tribulation. This is at the end of the 7-year Tribulation, after the Second Coming of Jesus, just prior to the establishment of the Millennial Kingdom. Therefore, God "separates" the remaining people in preparation to the 1,000 year reign of Christ. He takes the "believers" who are left, the "sheep," and allows them to enter this

"Kingdom" specially prepared for them, and then He takes the "unbelievers" the "goats" and casts them into "eternal punishment" or "hell." Again, the Angels are the instruments of this "separation" and it has nothing to do with the Rapture.

Now here's the problem. The Post-Trib position destroys this ability for there to be a "separation of the sheep from the goats" prior to the Millennial Kingdom as these other researchers point out:

"If the Rapture happens in conjunction with the Second Coming, as Post-Tribulationists say, and all living believers are caught up to heaven to meet Jesus and escort Him back to earth, then who are the sheep on earth when Jesus arrives? Everyone left on earth would be goats. There would not be any sheep. All the sheep would have just been Raptured. To state it another way: How would both saved and unsaved, still in their natural bodies, be separated in judgment right after the Second Coming, if all living believers are caught up at the Second Coming?

Also, there would not be any need for Jesus to separate the sheep from the goats when He gets to earth because the Rapture would have already accomplished the separation. Separation will have taken place in the very act of translation.

But if the Rapture occurs before the 7-year Tribulation as the Pre-Trib position states, there would be time for many people to come to know the Lord during the 7-year Tribulation. These Tribulation believers would be the 'sheep' of Matthew 25:31-46 when Jesus returns. Once again, the issue is solved by taking a Pre-Trib position with its gap of at least seven years.

Furthermore, it is important to recognize that when Jesus returns to set up His Kingdom there is NO Rapture, i.e., no one is 'caught up' into the air to be with the Lord. People who become believers during the Tribulation Period will 'enter into' the Millennium with their earthly bodies, not be 'Raptured.'

Thus, it can be concluded that a Post-Tribulational time of the Rapture makes no logical sense, is incongruous with the sheep-goat nation judgment, and, in fact, eliminates two critical end-time events. However, a Pre-Tribulational Rapture avoids all of these insurmountable difficulties."[7]

In other words, it avoids all these horrible contradictions. And isn't that what we're supposed to do if we're not going to be deceived?

The **ninth problem** with the Post-Trib teaching of the Rapture is that **It Creates a Problem with the Christian Rewards**. Not only does the Post-Trib position of the Rapture create all kinds of timing issues and contextual errors with the Rapture of the Church, but not so surprisingly, it also messes up the Rewarding of the Church. This "rewarding time" is also known as the Bema Judgment of the Church. This is what Paul is referring to in this passage:

2 Corinthians 5:10 "For we must all appear before the judgment seat of Christ, that each one may receive what is due him for the things done while in the body, whether good or bad."

The word "judgment seat" is the Greek word "bema" which simply means, "a tribunal, a raised platform mounted by steps where a ruler viewed and judged people at the games." It's kind of like in the Olympics where people, who after competing in a race, would appear before the "judge" on their "raised platform" to receive their respective "crowns" or rewards. This is the Bema Seat and is what is pictured as the Bema Judgment of Christ for His Church. It is not a time of "punishing" for our "punishment" has already been taken by Jesus by His work on the Cross. Rather, this is a time for Him to reward His Church. Just like in the Olympics, after the Rapture occurs before the 7-year Tribulation, our race here on earth is over, and now it is time to see what "rewards" or "crowns" we will receive. The Bible actually mentions five of them:

- **1st Crown – Incorruptible Crown** (the victor's crown)

  1 Corinthians 9:25 "Everyone who competes in the games goes into strict training. They do it to get a **crown** that will not last; but we do it to get a crown that will last forever."

- **2nd Crown – Crown of Life** (the martyr's crown)

  Revelation 2:10 "Be faithful until death, and I will give you the **crown** of life."

- **3rd Crown – Crown of Glory** (the shepherd's or elder's crown)

  1 Peter 5:1,4 "To the elders among you, I appeal as a fellow elder, a witness of Christ's sufferings and one who also will share in the glory to be revealed: And when the Chief Shepherd appears, you will receive the **crown** of glory that will never fade away.”

- **4th Crown – Crown of Righteousness** (the longing for Jesus crown)

  2 Timothy 4:8 “Now there is in store for me the **crown** of righteousness, which the Lord, the righteous Judge, will award to me on that day – and not only to me, but also to all who have longed for His appearing.”

- **5th Crown – Crown of Rejoicing** (the soul winner's crown)

  1 Thessalonians 2:19 “For what is our hope, our joy, or the **crown** in which we will glory in the presence of our Lord Jesus when He comes? Is it not you? Indeed, you are our glory and joy.”

The crowns mentioned here in the Bible are an incentive for faithfulness in the Christian life and fruitfulness in Christian service. Now, does this mean that some Christians are better than other Christians because they end up with more crowns than others? No! Revelation 4 shows us that we will *all* lay our crowns before the Lord.

Revelation 4:10-11 “The twenty-four elders fall down before Him who sits on the throne, and worship him who lives for ever and ever. They lay their crowns before the throne and say: You are worthy, our Lord and God, to receive glory and honor and power, for you created all things, and by your will they were created and have their being.”

Now as we saw before in great detail, the 24 Elders mentioned here is clearly speaking of the Church. So the question is, “Why do we the Church toss our crowns before the Lord?” Because He is the One Who gave us the ability to receive the crowns in the first place that was awarded to us at the Bema Judgment! He gets the glory for it all. This is not a time to boast that, “My crown is bigger than your crown,” or “I've got more crowns than you.” Rather it is a time when we *all* acknowledge Christ is to be honored and worshipped through and through because He gave us all the privilege and ability to even earn a crown in the first place, however many of them, in order to have the privilege to lay them at His feet.

But I said all that to get to this. This “rewarding” of the Church takes place after the Rapture prior to the 7-year Tribulation. In fact, it has to. Why?

Because if the Rapture occurs simultaneously with the Second Coming of Jesus Christ as the Post-Trib position states at the end of the 7-year Tribulation, there is not enough time for the Bema Judgment. Remember, they would picture you and I being Raptured up and then taking an "immediate" U-turn down with Jesus at the Second Coming. Therefore, just like the "timing" of the separation of the "sheep and the goats" gets messed up by having the Rapture at the end of the 7-year period as the Post-Trib position states, so it is with the "timing" of the "Rewarding of the Church." Everything gets ruined. There just isn't enough time with their postion, as this man shares:

"The Bema seat is a literal event, not a symbolical fancy. It cannot and will not be fulfilled all in one fleeting moment. The lives of the saints must be reviewed, their works must be tested, the rewards will be administered."[8]

In other words, you can't "squeeze" the rewarding of the Church in a short U-turn. It's illogical and makes no sense. Also, the Post-Trib position not only does not allow enough time for the Bema Judgment, the "crowning" of the Church, but neither does it fit the "sequence" or the "timing" of the 24 Elders "wearing" their crowns who are the Church. Question: "How can the Church, the 24 Elders in heaven, already have their crowns as is mentioned in Revelation 4:4-10 before the events of the 7-year Tribulation are mentioned in Revelation Chapters 6-18, if the Rapture hasn't taken place yet?" Answer: "The Rapture must have already taken place." This clearly fits the Pre-Trib position. All other positions including the Post-Trib position create yet another contradiction. And isn't that what we're supposed to avoid if we're not going to be deceived?

The **tenth problem** with the Post-Trib teaching of the Rapture is that **It Creates a Problem with the Resurrection**. Now, believe it or not, at this point a Post-Tribber might step in and actually cite the following verse to try to salvage their faulty view.

Revelation 20:4-6 "I saw thrones on which were seated those who had been given authority to judge. And I saw the souls of those who had been beheaded because of their testimony for Jesus and because of the word of God. They had not worshiped the beast or his image and had not received his mark on their foreheads or their hands. They came to life and reigned with Christ a thousand years. (The rest of the dead did not come to life until the thousand years were ended.) This is the first resurrection. Blessed and holy are those who have part in the first resurrection. The second death has no power over them, but they will be priests of God and of Christ and will reign with Him for a thousand years."

Now here is what the Post-Tribber would have you and I believe about this text to try to convince us to accept their crumbling position. And I quote:

"The Apostle Paul describes the First Resurrection occurring just before the Church is Raptured at Christ's appearing. And Revelation 20 states that the First Resurrection will take place after the rise of the Antichrist and the Mark of the Beast is instituted, which will happen only after the Tribulation is under way at Christ's Coming. The Resurrection of the dead in Christ at His Coming is obviously the First Resurrection as well. They are one and the same. This clearly proves that a Pre-Tribulation Rapture contradicts the Scriptures."[9]

Really? How about we take a look again at the context of these passages dealing with the First Resurrection and the Rapture, and see who is really contradicting God's Word. You see, the first problem with this premise, by the Post-Trib position, is that they equate the "first resurrection" mentioned in Revelation 20 as being the "same" resurrection mentioned in 1 Thessalonians 4. Yet, the Bible clearly teaches that there is more than one resurrection, as this man points out:

"The New Testament teaches multiple resurrections, not just a single event at the end of time. There are multiple resurrections of believers that do not occur at the same time but are sequential as follows:

1) The resurrection of Jesus Christ as the first fruit of many to be raised. (Rom. 6:9; 1 Cor. 15:23; Col. 1:18; Rev. 1:18).

2) The resurrection of the redeemed at Christ's coming. (Dan. 12:2; Luke 14:14; John 5:29; 1 Thess. 4:16; Rev. 20:4, 6)

    a) Resurrection of the Church at the Rapture, prior to the 7-year Tribulation.
    b) Resurrection of Old Testament believers at the Second Coming (Jews and Gentiles) at the end of the 7-year Tribulation, seven years after the Resurrection at the Rapture of the Church.
    c) Resurrection of all martyred tribulation saints at the Second Coming (Jews and Gentiles) at the end of the 7-year Tribulation, seven years after the Resurrection at the Rapture of the Church.
    d) Resurrection of all millennial believers, after the millennium (implied).

3) The resurrection of the unredeemed from throughout history (Rev. 20:11-14)."[10]

So as you can see, the Resurrection mentioned in Rev. 20:4-6 is actually one of many Resurrections mentioned in the Bible. And notice that particular Resurrection actually occurs "after" the Second Coming of Christ and therefore contradicts the idea of a Post-Trib Rapture that would happen "at the same time" as the coming of Christ. Also, even a Post-Tribulationist would have to recognize that in his order of events, the resurrection of Rev. 20:4-6 is not the "first" resurrection to occur.

Second, the reason why this particular Resurrection is referred to as the "first" resurrection is not because it's the "first" that ever took place, but rather, based on the context, it's being juxtaposed with the "second" death.

Revelation 20:14-15 "Then death and Hades were thrown into the lake of fire. The lake of fire is the second death. If anyone's name was not found written in the book of life, he was thrown into the lake of fire."

According to the Bible, the second death is referring to the act of being chucked into the Lake of Fire at the end of the Millennial Kingdom after the Great White Throne judgment. All the unrighteous dead are raised up from hell and thrown into the Lake of Fire; a "second" ultimate nightmare! You thought hell was bad, you haven't seen anything yet! You go from hell, to the Great White Throne Judgment, to the Lake of Fire! That's the second death! It just got worse for you forever!

This is why the Resurrection mentioned "prior" to the "second" death in this passage's context is called the "first" resurrection. It's not the "first" resurrection to ever occur, but rather it's drawing a distinction between those who are "blessed" to be a part of this "first" event in the context of this passage at the beginning of the Millennial Kingdom, and those who are "not blessed" and are thus thrust into the nightmarish "second" event and the end of the Millennial Kingdom. This "first" event is being juxtaposed with the "second" event. That's it!

Third, the Resurrection in Revelation 20 is not even dealing with the Resurrection of the Church, but as you saw, it's actually speaking of the Resurrection of the Old Testament believers and the martyred Tribulation saints. The Resurrection of the Church Age saints had already occurred seven years prior!

Fourth, you're also falsely assuming that the Rapture of the Church and the Resurrection are one and the same event when they're not, as this researcher states:

"The Resurrection and the Rapture are not the same event. Resurrection is for the dead while the Rapture will be for the living (we who are alive and remain 1 Thess. 4:17). It is a common ploy by non-Pre-Tribulationists to just assume that Resurrection and Rapture are the same, since that is what they believe. Then they want to conclude that there must be a single resurrection event, which, if true, would militate against Pre-Tribulationism.

Second, it is true that a Resurrection takes place in conjunction with the Rapture in 1 Thessalonians 4. However, Paul treats them as separate phases of the overall event described in 1 Thessalonians 4:13–18. Verse 14 speaks of the Resurrection of *deceased* Church Age believers, followed by verses 15–17 that describe the Rapture of *living* Church Age believers. Paul says, 'Then we who are alive and remain shall be caught up together with them in the clouds to meet the Lord in the air' (verse 17). Thus, it is clear that the Resurrection and 'the catching up' (i.e., Rapture) are not the same exact event, even though they occur in close sequence with one another."[11]

Looks to me like someone's guilty of taking things out of context again. And I guess this is why this researcher has this remark:

"One should never use one statement in Scripture to argue against the clear meaning of another passage, as if they are pitted against one another. However, since there are no contradictions in the Bible, all passages should be interpreted in their contexts in such a way that Scripture is harmonized with itself. This is the approach that should be taken in dealing with these passages in relation to the Rapture. When this approach is followed, it does not result in Anti-Pre-Trib conclusions."[12]

In other words, keep things in context and you're going to come out Pre-Trib every single time, not one of the other faulty positions on the Rapture like Post-Trib. And isn't that what we're supposed to do if we're not going to be deceived?

The **eleventh problem** with the Post-Trib teaching of the Rapture is that **It Creates a Problem with the Antichrist**. Yet another "timing" issue that gets messed up with the Post-Trib position is in reference to the "disappearance" of the Church and the "appearance" of the Antichrist. The Bible puts the timing of these two events as such:

2 Thessalonians 2:7-8 "For the secret power of lawlessness is already at work; but the one who now holds it back will continue to do so till he is taken out of the way. And then the lawless one will be revealed, whom the Lord Jesus will overthrow with the breath of his mouth and destroy by the splendor of his coming."

So here we clearly see an order of events that must take place in the Bible concerning the Antichrist. In essence Paul says he, the Antichrist, the lawless one, will *not* be revealed *until* "the one who now holds it back" is taken "out" of the way. So the big question is, "Who is this identity that has to be taken out before the Antichrist can appear on the scene?" As we saw before, it is none other than the Church.

First of all, the phrase there, "holds it back" is "katecho" in the Greek and it simply means, "to restrain, to hold back, or to hinder the course or progress of." Secondly, it is preceded by the word "now" as in "now holds it back" which is the Greek word "arti" and it means, "right now, at this very time, at this very moment." Third, the word "one" as in "the one who now holds it back" is referred to in both the neuter and masculine. And fourth, the phrase there "taken out of the way" are the Greek words "ginomai meso" which means, "to arise from the midst" or "be made or finished from among."

So you put all this together in the context and I think you can begin to narrow it down. Whoever this "one" is must be "removable," and must be also at the same time "powerful enough to hold back" or "restrain evil" and the "appearance of the Antichrist" right now. To me, that would leave you with only one option and that is the Holy Spirit's presence in the Church today.

Think about it. Are we not to be the "salt and light" of the earth, maintaining God's righteous decrees which "restrains" evil from marching forward without total restraint? Also, is not our presence here on earth "preventing" the appearance of the Antichrist? I mean, wouldn't we be the very first ones pointing him out to the world, blowing the whistle, ruining his plans and warning everyone not to fall for his lies and deceptions? Of course! Therefore, once we the Church "arise from the midst" and are "taken out of the way" before this time period begins, the 7-year Tribulation, then there's nothing "holding back" the Antichrist from "appearing" and his "evil plans" and "evil in general" from spreading "unrestrained."

Furthermore, the Holy Spirit's presence in the Church is the only explanation that also answers the identity of the "one" as being "both" neuter and masculine at the same time. In the Bible the word for Spirit is "pneuma" which is neuter, and yet at the same time the Bible consistently refers to the Holy Spirit in the masculine. Case closed. The "one" who is both neuter and masculine at the same time is the Holy Spirit's presence in the Church today.

Now, notice I didn't say this identity was "just" the Holy Spirit Himself but the Holy Spirit's "presence" in the Church today. That's because the Holy Spirit is God Who is omnipresent and thus cannot be removed from the earth completely. Secondly, we also know, as has already been mentioned, that millions of people will be saved during the 7-year Tribulation which requires the Holy Spirit to still be functioning on earth convicting them of the need for salvation. Therefore it has to be Holy Spirit's "restraining influence" in the Church today.

Now here's the problem that's created if you hold to the Post-Trib position. Paul says that the Antichrist *cannot* appear *until* the "one who holds it back" is "taken out of the way," that is, the Church. So how can you say the Church is Raptured or "taken out of the way" at the *end* of the 7-year Tribulation, when the Antichrist has *already* made his "appearance" at the *beginning* of the 7-year Tribulation? (Revelation 6; Daniel 9:27) You just created another serious contradiction in the Scripture. Yet, God doesn't contradict Himself so you can't be right in your position.

The only way to harmonize this "appearing" of the Antichrist with the "timing" of the Church being "taken out of the way" is to hold to the Pre-Trib position which states that the Church is "removed" or Raptured *prior* to the 7-year Tribulation *prior* to the appearance of the Antichrist at the beginning of the 7-year Tribulation. No contradiction, perfect harmony, as these researchers state:

"The Church will be removed from the earth BEFORE the appearing of the Antichrist (2 Thessalonians 2:7,8). If the Antichrist came to power with the Church still here, I do not see how he could operate. When Hitler was fighting to take over England, a number of Christians were praying for victory. Hitler made mistake after mistake, and England outperformed its enemy at every stage of the conflict. It is difficult to measure the impact of intercessory prayer in physical warfare. Little is known of how great a role praying saints played in the defeat of Nazi Germany.

If the Church were to reside on earth during the tribulation, I am sure she would give the Antichrist fits. In Revelation 11:3, the two witnesses alone give the

Antichrist enough headaches. Millions of Christians who know their Bibles well would recognize the man of sin and pray fire down on his head. The Post-Trib view would have to plan on the Church just rolling over and playing dead the whole seven years.

Furthermore, 2 Thessalonians 2:3-10 establishes that the removal of the Church will be before the manifestation of the Man of Sin, a fact which places the Rapture before Revelation 13 and as far back in the chronology of that book as 6:1, before the opening of the first seal and the rider upon the white horse.

Such a review should convince any candid mind that the place of the Rapture in the chronology of the Revelation and in the order of prophetic events is clearly Pre-Tribulational. On the other hand, since intervening events required a marked interval between the Rapture and the revelation, the whole Post-Tribulational idea that these two phases of our Lord's return are only moments apart, if not simultaneous, is demonstrated to be utterly untenable."[13]

In other words, it cannot be true. The Bible clearly states that the Church *cannot* be on earth the *same time* as the Antichrist. The Post-Trib position, once again, makes mish mash out of the Scripture and creates even more serious contradictions. And isn't that what we're supposed to avoid if we're not going to be deceived?

The **twelfth problem** with the Post-Trib teaching of the Rapture is that **It Destroys the Meaning of Jesus' Wedding**. Just when you thought the "timing issues" of the Post-Trib position couldn't get any worse, we have yet another one. Believe it or not, their position totally messes up the Wedding of Jesus. The Bible says that we the Church are His Bride and that He's coming back to receive us to Heaven, where we will celebrate our wedding, and then return to earth with Him. The Post-Trib Position destroys all this timing. Let me demonstrate:

1st – The Church is the Bride of Christ

Ephesians 5:28-32 "In this same way, husbands ought to love their wives as their own bodies. He who loves his wife loves himself. After all, no one ever hated his own body, but he feeds and cares for it, just as Christ does the Church – for we are members of His Body. 'For this reason a man will leave his father and mother and be united to his wife, and the two will become one flesh.' This is a profound mystery – but I am talking about Christ and the Church."

Now, I would assume that the Post-Tribber would agree that the Church is the Bride of Christ, as presented in the Scripture, so no problem there. However, it is from here forward that their timing gets messed up.

2nd – The Church is Received by Christ

John 14:2-3 "In My Father's house are many rooms; if it were not so, I would have told you. I am going there to prepare a place for you. And if I go and prepare a place for you, I will come back and take you to be with Me that you also may be where I am."

So here we see another classic passage on the Rapture where Jesus clearly states that He is coming back to get His Bride (at the Rapture) to be with Him in heaven. Question: Why would Jesus prepare a place for us in heaven and then not take us there as the Post-Trib position would have you and I believe? Remember, they have us going up at the end of the 7-year Tribulation in a Rapture and then making an immediate U-turn back to earth. However, this leaves no time for the Church to be taken into heaven, the Father's House, as Jesus promised! The Post-Trib position totally contradicts Jesus, which I don't recommend doing by the way.

Now let's take a look at the next problem created by the Post-Trib position concerning the Wedding of Jesus.

3rd – The Church Celebrates with Christ

Luke 12:36 "Like men waiting for their master to return from a wedding banquet, so that when he comes and knocks they can immediately open the door for him."

So here we see the Bible clearly tells us that when Jesus comes at His Second Coming, He will be returning from a Wedding banquet. Question: How can Jesus return from a Wedding Banquet if the Wedding hasn't even taken place yet, as the Post-Trib position would have you and I believe? The only way for the Marriage to have already occurred including the time for the Wedding Banquet, is to have the Church leave "prior" to the 7-year Tribulation as the Pre-Trib position teaches, not at the end as the Post-Trib Position states. The Post-Trib position leaves no time for this event to take place either.

Also, it just so happens, as we saw before in the study of the Jewish Marriage Ceremony, that according to Jewish tradition, once the couple returned to the father's house, they would consummate the marriage and celebrate their wedding feast or banquet *for the next seven days* (during which the bride remained closeted in her bridal chamber).

So it is that we too, the Bible says, are whisked away and closeted in our Bridal Chamber, during the 7 year Tribulation. We're up there enjoying our Wedding Day while the unbelieving world is unfortunately undergoing God's Wrath. This is clearly the same teaching as the Pre-Trib position.

Now let's take a look at yet another thing the Post-Trib position messes up with Jesus' Wedding.

4th – The Church Returns with Christ

After the Marriage Supper, Jewish tradition records that this is when the bride and groom are presented to the world as "man and wife." And this just also happens to correspond to the time when Jesus returns to earth at the end of the 7-year Tribulation *accompanied* by His Bride "dressed in fine linen, white and clean."

Revelation 19:11-14 "I saw heaven standing open and there before me was a white horse, whose rider is called Faithful and True. With justice he judges and makes war. His eyes are like blazing fire, and on His head are many crowns. He has a Name written on Him that no one knows but He Himself. He is dressed in a robe dipped in blood, and His Name is the Word of God. The armies of heaven were following Him, riding on white horses and dressed in fine linen, white and clean."

As we saw before, the identity of the "armies of heaven" is clearly speaking of the Church, the Bride of Christ. The clothing mentioned here "dressed in fine linen, white and clean," is the clothing of the Church. Therefore, this passage is telling us that the Bride of Christ, the Church, *returns with Jesus* at His Second Coming.

Question: How can this happen with a Post-Trib scenario? The Post-Trib position teaches that the Church goes *up* to *meet* Jesus at His Second Coming, but the *Bible* says that the Church *comes back* with Jesus at His Second Coming. Major, major contradiction here. Only the Pre-Trib position remedies this Post-Trib timing problem, as these researchers also admit:

"When Jesus returns to earth at the Second Coming, He will return from a wedding (Luke 12:36). At the Rapture, Jesus is married to His Bride, the Church.

After the wedding, He will return to earth. The Bride of Christ, the Church, is made ready to accompany Christ to earth (Revelation 19:7-8,14) before the Second Coming, but how could this reasonably happen if the Church is still on the earth awaiting the Second Coming? If the Rapture of the Church takes place at the Second Coming, then how does the Bride (the Church) also come with Christ at His Return?"

"The Marriage of the Lamb must occur in heaven after the Rapture but before the return to earth. This event has long been anticipated; it has been looked for with much rejoicing (Rev. 19:7) and will not be hurried. The Bride has time to make herself ready (19:7). There is worship and praise involving all of the hosts of heaven (19:6). The Hallelujah Chorus of the redeemed must be sung, and with all eternity ahead it will not be limited to "the first and the last stanza"!

Before the marriage and the supper will be the presentation of the bride. This is the most glorious, crowning experience in all the long history of the Church, and will be a time of greatest joy for the Christ who redeemed her. When all the saints go marching in, "He shall see the travail of his soul, and shall be satisfied" (Isa. 53:11).

The presentation of the Bride and the marriage supper cannot be fulfilled in one fleeting moment. The Bride will prepare herself and be presented to Christ, the marriage must be performed and the marriage feast celebrated and enjoyed.

Yet for the sake of a theory, some would have us believe that all these blessed experiences occur in an instant, in the twinkling of an eye, as part of the downward sweep of the Lord to earth, with no preview of heaven, and with no glimpse of the "many mansions" prepared by a loving Savior for the Bride whom He will receive unto Himself when He comes again (John 14:2,3).

The Post-Tribulational paradigm of the Church being Raptured and then immediately brought back to earth leaves no time."[14]

In other words, it messes things up and creates even more contradictions. And isn't that what we're supposed to avoid if we're not going to be deceived?

The **thirteenth problem** with the Post-Trib teaching of the Rapture is that **It Destroys the Purpose of the Rapture**. As we saw before, one of the major purposes of the teaching of the Rapture in the first place was to offer a "blessed hope" or an "encouraging truth" to the Church that although we may have had it rough here on earth for a little while, defending and living for Jesus, He will nonetheless "keep us" from "the hour of trial that is going to come upon the whole world to test those who live on the earth", that is, the time period where God pours out His wrath on this wicked and rebellious world, the horrible 7-year Tribulation.

However, if you think about it, the Post-Trib position actually destroys this encouraging word, this Blessed Hope. In fact, it would make it utterly meaningless, as this man shares:

"Post-Tribulationists maintain that the Rapture happens in conjunction with the Second Coming. Believers will be caught up to meet the Lord Jesus in the air as He is coming from heaven to judge the world, then will come right back to earth with Him. But this raises a very important question that often gets overlooked in this discussion. If God has miraculously preserved the Church throughout the entire tribulation as they falsely state, why even have a Rapture? Why bother? It's inconsequential. The Lord will not be delivering His Bride from anything. There's really no purpose in it. But if Christ comes before the Tribulation, His coming is filled with purpose. He will rescue us from the wrath to come."[15]

In other words, only the Pre-Trib position maintains the purpose of the Blessed Hope. It is the only one that maintains the encouraging word of the Rapture. However, the Post-Trib position makes the Rapture inconsequential and meaningless. You might as well change it to the "Blessed Nothing" or the "No Big Deal Promise" and I think our Lord Jesus gives much better promises than that!

Furthermore, as we saw before, one of the benefits of the Rapture is the affect that its Imminency has upon the Church in the meantime. In other words, we don't know when the Rapture occurs, it can happen at any time, it is Imminent, thus we always need to be ready for His return. We need to get busy living a holy life for Him, being a positive example to those around us for Him, as we share His Gospel and get rid of any and all procrastination since today could be our last day here on earth as a Christian. All of this is maintained *if* the Rapture is Imminent!

However, the Post-Trib position destroys the "cleansing effects" of the Imminency of the Rapture that only the Pre-trib position maintains. In a Post-Trib scenario, there is no urgency and we're not even looking for an Imminent Rapture. Rather we're looking for "signs" to calculate the Return of Jesus' and thus we now have 7 years of "excuses" to get lazy and procrastinate. The exact opposite of the Pre-Trib position.

This is because the Second Coming is preceded by many signs and can be calculated. Only the Pre-trib position allows for the Rapture to remain an unknown hour. If I find myself IN the 7-year Tribulation then the "unknown" event becomes a "known" event, because I can "calculate" it, based on the signs given during that 7-year period. All I have to do is pay attention to all the "signs" that take place during the 7-year Tribulation that's mentioned in the Book of Revelation and Matthew 24 and elsewhere, like the Seal Judgments, the Trumpet Judgements, the Bowl Judgments, the Antichrist, all that stuff, and calculate accordingly.

The Pre-Trib position is the only position that says there is no heads up warning, and thus you better *get ready* and *be ready* at *all times*! It makes sure your life as a Christian *stays cleaned up* because how do you want the Lord to find you? Goofing off or sharing the Gospel? Living for Him, or sinning again? This is the power of Imminency that only the Pre-Trib position maintains. The Post-Trib Position destroys all this cleansing benefit of Imminency, as these researchers share:

"Post-Tribulationists have not adequately dealt with Titus 2:13 where believers are exhorted to look for 'the glorious appearing' of Christ to His own. If the Rapture follows the Tribulation, believers would then look for signs instead of His coming. It denies the New Testament teaching of Imminency – that Christ could come at any moment – since there are intervening events required in that view. We believe there are no signs that must precede the Rapture.

Furthermore, the biggest problem with Post-Tribulationism is that it makes Jesus appear to be misleading. Jesus said of the time of His return, 'No man knows the day nor the hour.' Yet if the Post-Tribulationalist is correct and Christ's return is at the end of the Tribulation, then from the very moment that the anti-Christ comes on the scene at the outset of the Tribulation, you can know that exactly seven years later Jesus will come. Hence, you would know exactly the time and the hour of the Lord's coming.

Consequently, in the Post-Trib position, it makes Jesus appear to be a liar."[16]

And that, my friend, is something you don't want to do! Furthermore, concerning the Rapture, Paul mentions not once but twice in 1 Thessalonians 4 and 5, "encourage one another" with these words, that is, the truth about the Rapture.

1 Thessalonians 4:18 "Therefore *encourage* each other with these words."

1 Thessalonians 5:11 "Therefore *encourage* one another and build each other up, just as in fact you are doing."

So here's the logical common sense question. How in the world am I going to encourage someone, let alone myself, if I know that I'm not only going to be *in* the horrible 7-year Tribulation, the worst time in the history of mankind when God unleashes His wrath upon the planet in utter fury, but be *in it* for *the whole 7-years* as the Post-Trib position would have you and I believe! That's not encouraging, that's *discouraging*! And that's precisely what the Post-Trib position does! It destroys the purpose and the encouraging hope of the Rapture, as this man shares:

"Pre-Trib belief antagonists are on the rise. Christ's call to believers, they say, just isn't going to happen before Christians suffer at least part of the terrors of that beastly era. Those of us who believe there is coming a supernatural Rapture-escape from these judgments on sinful mankind are just living in fantasy land is the collective message I infer from emails and articles that increasingly assault my senses.

That I, and all of you, should begin prepping with food, water, gold, silver, and finding a good bunker in which to hunker down during these upcoming days seem to me to be the things these Rapture naysayers are presenting.

Seldom do I hear coming from our opponents on the question of the Rapture the admonition to be trying to witness with all our might the gospel of Jesus Christ. While the Pre-Trib proponent holds at the heart of his effort winning as many souls to Christ as possible so those saved won't go through that time of horrors, many of the anti-Rapture antagonists want to do things to make sure they are more comfortable while trying to survive that hellish time.

Coincidentally–or perhaps not–these just happen to, in some cases of TV and other ministries who openly disdain the thought of a Rapture, offer for sale all of these things for survival. The packaged food items invariably are proclaimed to have shelf lives of three decades or longer. So, we can, if we survive, have these supplies to partake of well into the Millennium, I suppose. This, based upon the general theme that they believe the seven-year Tribulation, not the Rapture, is imminent.

I wish to mention only one Rapture factor here: Where's the Comfort? By that we ask: What comfort is there in the argument that Christians will go through the Tribulation?

Paul the apostle first assures us of this fact: "For God hath not appointed us to wrath, but to obtain salvation by our Lord Jesus Christ" (1 Thessalonians 5:9). But, it is the next thought from the mind of God that should cause warm reassurance in the spiritual heart of every believer: "Wherefore comfort yourselves together, and edify one another, even as also ye do." (1 Thessalonians 5:11).

Get it? We are to "comfort" ourselves, not wring our hands looking for these things to destroy us or to look for Antichrist. We are to be looking for our "blessed hope" (Titus 2:13).

There is no comfort –nor is there directive in God's Word–to be had in anticipating going through the time of God's wrath and almost certain martyrdom (probably by beheading). There is no comfort in looking for the worst dictator in the planet's history to hunt us down and lop off our heads.

Here is what God's Word promises instead of the dreaded scenario proposed by the Rapture antagonists:

'For this we say unto you by the word of the Lord, that we which are alive and remain unto the coming of the Lord shall not prevent them which are asleep. For the Lord himself shall descend from heaven with a shout, with the voice of the archangel, and with the trump of God: and the dead in Christ shall rise first: Then we which are alive and remain shall be caught up together with them in the clouds, to meet the Lord in the air: and so shall we ever be with the Lord. Wherefore comfort one another with these words.' (1 Thessalonians 4:15-18)"[17]

Sounds to me like the Pre-Trib position is the only position that agrees with the comforting purpose of the Rapture, which means all the other positions are not only not true, but they cannot be true. Why? Because once again they create yet another contradiction in Scripture. And isn't that what we're supposed to avoid if we're not going to be deceived?

Chapter Fifteen

The Problems with Pre-Wrath

The **second position** on the Rapture that has some serious problems with it is **The Pre-Wrath Position**. Or should I say more accurately, the Three-Quarters Rapture Position. The title is a little deceptive because it doesn't tell you the timing of when they think the Rapture will take place. But let us take a look at where and when this theory on the Rapture started:

"The person who conceived the "Pre-Wrath" view of the Rapture was a man named Robert Van Kampen (1938-1999). Van Kampen became one of America's richest men through his involvement in investment banking. During his lifetime he accumulated one of the largest private collections of rare and antique Bibles in North America.

In the 1970's Van Kampen began developing the "Pre-Wrath" concept of the timing of the Rapture. Once he had completed his work on the concept, he started trying to find a well-known person in the field of Bible prophecy to endorse his new view. That person finally turned out to be Marvin Rosenthal, who at the time was serving as the director of a very influential ministry called Friends of Israel.

Rosenthal tried to convince the board of the ministry to abandon its commitment to the Pre-Trib view and accept the new viewpoint. They refused, and Rosenthal was forced to depart. He went to Florida where he built the Holy Land Experience – a Christian theme park which has since been taken over by the

Trinity Broadcasting Network. Today, Rosenthal serves as the director of Zion's Hope, a ministry located in Winter Garden, Florida.

Rosenthal's book was financed by Van Kampen's fortune, and he mailed out thousands of copies to pastors all over America. Later, Van Kampen wrote his own books about the "Pre-Wrath" view, the most important being *The Sign* (1992)."[1]

Now that you know where it started, let's take a look at a basic explanation of their belief on the Rapture:

"Van Kampen's three-quarters Rapture view is a blend of Mid-Tribulational and Post-Tribulational rationale. He has the Church continuing through the first three-quarters of the 7-year Tribulation until the Rapture occurs. Thus, the three-quarters Rapture theory.

Instead of seeing the terms describing the seventieth week of Daniel as denoting various characteristics of a single period, Van Kampen chops them into compartmental segments that contain either the wrath of man and satan, or the wrath of God.

Through redefinition, Van Kampen limits the wrath of God to the final year and three-quarters of the seven-year period, and deduces that the Rapture occurs right before that time period.

First, he chops the seventieth week of Daniel into three parts: 1) the beginning of birth pangs (first three and a half years), 2) the great tribulation (first half of the second half of the seven years), 3) the Day of the Lord (last half of the second half of the seven years, plus a thirty day period after the Second Coming).

By arbitrarily compartmentalizing the seventieth week of Daniel in this way, Van Kampen prepares the way for his view by saying that the first two periods (first three-quarters of the seven-year period) is the wrath of man and satan, but not God's wrath.

By speculating that God's wrath only occurs during what he labels as 'The Day of the Lord' (the last quarter of the seventieth week of Daniel), therefore, he says the Rapture occurs at that point and keeps the Church out of the wrath of God, as promised in the New Testament Epistles."[2]

So as you can see, the Pre-Wrath position on the Rapture is not only frankly confusing, but it's totally different than the Pre-Trib position. In fact, I'm not the only one who admits to its self-imposed confusion. So does this researcher:

"The Pre-Wrath view is not a Pre-Tribulational view because it insists that the Church will be *present on earth* during most of the seven years of Daniel's 70th week (all except for the last phase which this view calls the Day of the Lord).

The Pre-Wrath view is not a Mid-Tribulational view because it insists that the Rapture will occur *after* the midpoint of the final seven years, somewhere around the middle of the last 3½ years.

The Pre-Wrath view is a Post-Tribulational view in the sense that it teaches that the Rapture will occur after the Great Tribulation. However, this view *redefines* the Great Tribulation period in a way that is unusual. Instead of saying that the Great Tribulation ends at the same time Daniel's 70th week ends (at the end of this 7-year period), this view says that the Great Tribulation ends just prior to the Day of the Lord which they say takes place a significant time prior to the end of Daniel's 70th week. Thus this view is Post-Tribulational but not post-"Daniel's 70th week." This view teaches that the Rapture will take place toward the end of Daniel's 70th week but not at the end."[3]

Now, you got that? Kind of confusing, isn't it? I think the confusion arises over several deviations of the Scripture as we will see in a moment. But since God is not a God of confusion, this is a good indicator that that "hand of man" is messing things up concerning the Rapture and is what's "creating" this confusion. I say that because God wrote His Word for us, the Bible, so that we might clearly understand what He is trying to say to us. He does not play "cat and mouse" with us and neither does He speak with a "forked-tongue." He *wants us to know clearly* what He is saying to us. He doesn't play games and He certainly doesn't purposely confuse things so that only the rich and famous or spiritually elite can come away with the "correct" meaning and disseminate it to the rest of us ignorant folk. Rather, He wants *all people* to clearly know what He is saying in the Bible and therefore He wrote it in a manner that anyone can come away with the correct meaning using common sense principles.

Therefore, if some teaching is supposed to be "derived from the Bible" and yet comes out "totally confusing" like the Pre-Wrath Rapture theory, then again, this is a good indicator that "the hand of man" is in there twisting the

Scripture to make it say what "man" wants it to say. That's not only *not* how we're supposed to interpret the Bible, but it's one of the fastest ways to being deceived.

But the basic core difference concerning the Pre-Wrath Rapture is this. The Pre-Wrath Rapture says the Church will remain on earth until "3/4ths" of the 7-year Tribulation, while the Pre-Trib Rapture says that the Church will leave the earth "prior" to the 7-year Tribulation and escape it altogether. Obviously, both cannot be true, so which one is correct? How can we know? How can we not be deceived? Well once again, just as we put the Pre-Trib position underneath a serious microscope and dealt with the various accusations that are thrown its way, let's now do the same with the Pre-Wrath position. And I think you will see in a moment, just like the Post-Trib position, this position, the Pre-Wrath position, also has some serious problems.

The **first problem** with the Pre-Wrath teaching of the Rapture is that **It Confuses the Timing of God's Wrath**. Now even though the Pre-Trib position would agree with the Pre-Wrath position on the premise that, "The Church will not be appointed unto God's wrath," as you saw, their version of when God's wrath takes place is all jumbled up. In fact, it's not just jumbled up, it's flat out wrong! The Pre-Wrath position would have you and I believe that God's wrath is "limited" to only the final quarter of the 7-year Tribulation. But as we saw again in great detail in the previous section dealing with the problems of the Post-Trib position, *all* of the 7-year Tribulation is a time when God pours out His wrath. *All* 19 judgments mentioned in Revelation Chapters 6-18 are God's wrath, not just some of them.

Also, the seal judgments, which are opened at the very *beginning* of the 7-year Tribulation, are brought forth not by man or satan, but by the Lamb Himself, the Lord Jesus Christ. The Lamb, Jesus (God) is opening the seals from *His throne* and the order is given for judgment to begin. This is not coming from man or satan, but God Himself, and that at the very beginning of the 7-year Tribulation. To say this is man or satan is an abomination. God is the One giving the order for His wrath to begin and it continues all the way to the end of the 7-year period.

Therefore, the whole premise for the Pre-Wrath theory limiting God's wrath to the final quarter of the 7-year Tribulation is not only wrong, it is really blasphemous. Think about it. How can you give man or even satan credit for what God Himself will be doing! Who in their right mind would do this?

Well, I think the answer arises when you see how the "confusion" over the timing of God's wrath in the 7-year Tribulation was created in the first place by a "confused" motive from Van Kampen. When he came up with his theory on

the Rapture, instead of sticking with what the Bible says and allowing the Bible
to speak out to him what it says, which is how we're supposed to interpret the
Bible, he tried to "reconcile" two positions into one, as this researcher points out:

"Van Kampen claims that he was torn between the Pre-Tribulation and Post-
Tribulation views of the Rapture. He agreed with his Pre-Tribulation friends that
the Church will not see the wrath of God. But he agreed with his Post-Tribulation
friends that the elect will someday become targets of Antichrist's persecution. He
felt that there must be a common denominator to balance these teachings. That's
when he came up with the idea that the persecution by Antichrist during the great
tribulation will be the wrath of satan not the wrath of God.

Using Revelation 12:12, Van Kampen says that satan's wrath is the persecution
of God's elect. This verse states:

Revelation 12:12 "Therefore rejoice, you heavens and you who dwell in them!
But woe to the earth and the sea, because the devil has gone down to you! He is
filled with fury, because he knows that his time is short."

When one studies this passage, it is clear that satan's wrath is a reaction to God's
wrath. God punishes satan by casting him down to earth. This makes him angry.
The proper way of seeing the Tribulation is that it is the time of both God's wrath
and satan's wrath as he struggles against the sovereignty of God."[4]

Wow! Talk about twisting the Scripture! We just saw that the *entire* 7-
year Tribulation is a time when God pours out His wrath; it's not satan instituting
it. How can you attribute *any of it* to satan when it's *all* from God? Besides,
satan's wrath isn't even the same as God's wrath. It's just a *reaction* to God's
wrath *and* it's not even occurring at the same time! How can you come up with
this?

Oh, I get it. You committed the fatal error. You didn't allow the Bible to
speak out to you what it says, but you entered into it with a preconceived idea of
what you "wanted it to say," and tried to reconcile your preconceived idea with
the Bible and therefore had to twist things accordingly. No wonder it's
confusing! In fact, as I mentioned at the beginning, the very name itself is
confusing, as this man also shares:

"The Pre-Wrath Rapture name is both confusing and vague. It is confusing
because both the Pre-Trib and Mid-Trib views are 'Pre-Wrath.' The Pre-Trib

view argues that the entire 7 years of the Tribulation (Daniel's 70th Week of Years) constitutes a pouring out of the wrath of God. The Mid-Trib view takes the position that only the second half of the Tribulation is the period of God's wrath. So, Rosenthal's name for his viewpoint does not distinguish it from the Pre-Trib and Mid-Trib views. All three are 'Pre-Wrath' views.

The 'Pre-Wrath' name is also vague because it does not give a clue as to *when* the Rapture occurs in relation to the Tribulation. The name of the Pre-Trib view signifies a belief that the Rapture will occur before (pre) the Tribulation begins. The name of the Mid-Trib view clearly indicates a belief that the Rapture will occur in the middle of the Tribulation. The name of the Post-Trib view puts the Rapture after (post) the Tribulation. But the name, 'Pre-Wrath' gives no indication of when the Rapture will occur with relation to the Tribulation."[5]

Sounds to me like somebody came up with a "confusing" title for a "confusing" belief on the Rapture. Again, this should not be too surprising. God is not the author of confusion, man is. Once you veer off the Scripture and enter into it with your mind clouded with preconceived ideas, deception and confusion are sure to follow.

However, if we stick with the Bible and allow it to speak out to us what it wants us to know (which is how we're supposed to interpret it) you will see clearly that the whole of the 7-year Tribulation is a time of God's wrath and therefore the Church is exempt from all 7 years as the Pre-Trib position states. One man puts it this way:

"God's wrath involves the whole 7-Year Tribulation. The Pre-Wrath Rapture view has the Church Raptured just before the bowl judgments (Revelation 16) that occur during the last quarter of the Tribulation. The bowl judgments are the only judgments this view considers to be the wrath of God, leaving the Seal and Trumpet judgments as wrath from man and Satan.

But, isn't it Jesus Himself who breaks the seals that launch each of the Revelation 6 seal judgments which occur at the beginning of the Tribulation?

Also, the seven angels who blow the trumpets that initiate each of the trumpet judgments are given their trumpets at the throne of God (Revelation 8:2).

And, Revelation 15:1 states that the bowl judgments at the end of the Tribulation finish the wrath of God, not begin His wrath.

Because these judgments are initiated by Jesus Himself at the beginning of the Tribulation, the whole Tribulation must be God's wrath, which the Church is exempt from."[6]

In other words, the timing of God's wrath in the 7-year Tribulation will make perfect sense if you just leave the Bible alone. If you don't want to be confused, then don't mess with God's timing for His wrath by trying to "squeeze into it" what you "want it" to say. Let the Bible speak for itself. And isn't that what we're supposed to do if we're not going to be deceived?

The **second problem** with the Pre-Wrath teaching of the Rapture is that **It Confuses the Timing of the Day of the Lord**. As you just saw, the Pre-Wrath Rapture theory not only has a "confusing" name and a "confused" timing of God's wrath in the 7-year Tribulation, but it also "confuses" the timing of the "Day of the Lord." Why? Because just like with a house of cards, once you start tweaking with the foundation, the Bible and Biblical truth, what comes next is a crumbled mess.

As we already saw in great detail, including the previous section dealing with all the Post-Trib problems, the Day of the Lord is a time period that encompasses the *entirety* of the 7-year Tribulation. It is a time when God pours out His wrath, and anger, and desolation, and vengeance, and destruction, and it's terrible. It's a time of gloominess and darkness and distress and trouble, and refers to the cataclysmic final judgment of God upon the wicked, not the Church! Again, the Church is *not* appointed unto His wrath.

Now here's the problem, even though the Pre-Wrath position would agree with the Pre-Trib position concerning the Biblical teaching that the Church is not appointed unto God's wrath, the Pre-Wrath position has to "forcibly tweak" the timing of the Day of the Lord to "fit into" their preconceived belief system concerning the Rapture. Rather than concede and/or admit that the Bible clearly presents the Day of the Lord as a time when God pours out His wrath during the *entire* 7-year period, they "redefine" it to say no, the Day of the Lord occurs only in the "final quarter" of the 7-year Tribulation and thus the Church is Raptured out just prior to this period and thereby "saved" from God's wrath.

Say what? Talk about twisting the Scripture again. No wonder it's a confusing mess. The Day of the Lord clearly encompasses *all* of the 7-year Tribulation. You can't just chop it up conveniently to fit your preconceived idea and timing of the Rapture as these researchers state:

"The Great Day is a title borrowed from the OT (Joel 2:11, 31; Zeph. 1:14; Mal. 4:5) The primary passages from which John draws his images in the description of the sixth seal prove the reference of this phrase to be to the Day of the Lord (Joel 2:11, 30-31; cf. Isa. 2:10-11, 19-21; 13:9-34;13; 34:4, 8; Ezek. 32:7-8; Hos. 10:8). This passage links all the seal judgments to God's wrath, in contrast to Van Kampen, and even associates it with the Day of the Lord.

Such Biblical facts contradict the recent Rapture view of Van Kampen. This would also support the Pre-Trib understanding that the Day of the Lord includes the entire seventieth week of Daniel and thus a time of God's wrath from which the Church is promised deliverance.

Rosenthal invests much in his belief that the Day of the Lord is limited to the final quarter of the seventieth week of Daniel. 'If expositors get the starting point of the Day of the Lord right,' insists Rosenthal, 'the timing of the Rapture becomes clear' (Rosenthal, Pre-Wrath, p. 117). This is true! But Rosenthal is not able to answer points relating to the Day of the Lord and the timing of the Rapture.

In order to make their view work in the abstract, Van Kampen must redefine the nature and scope of terms like the Day of the Lord. However, their work does not fit when all of Scripture is considered. Further, their wrong understanding of the key Biblical terminology sets the stage for their erroneous conclusion that the Rapture will occur three-quarters of the way through the seventieth week of Daniel, instead of before."

"Van Kampen defines only the final quarter of Daniel's seventieth week, as the Day of the Lord, which according to him is the only time of God's wrath. He sees the first three quarters as the wrath of man and satan. But does the Bible make such distinctions? I do not believe it does.

Wrath in Zephaniah

Zephaniah 1:14-18 heaps together a cluster of terms that characterize the future Day of the Lord. Verse 14 labels this time as "the great Day of the Lord" and "the Day of the Lord." Then verses 15-18 describe this time with the following descriptions: "that day is a day of wrath," "a day of trouble and distress," "a day of wasteness and desolation," "a day of darkness and gloominess," "a day of clouds and thick darkness," "a day of the trumpet and alarm," "I will bring distress upon men," and "the Day of the Lord's wrath." The context supports the notion that all these descriptives apply to the Day of the Lord. Such Biblical usage does not allow an interpreter to chop the Day of the Lord into compartmental segments as Van Kampen insists.

The text plainly says that the Day of the Lord is a time of both tribulation and God's wrath. All of the many descriptives in this passage provide a characterization of the Day of the Lord that applies to the entire seven-year period. The Zephaniah passage clearly contradicts the basis upon which Van Kampen attempts to build his recently developed theory. Zephaniah is not alone in providing an obstacle to the Van Kampen speculation.

Wrath in Revelation

Revelation 6:1-17 records the six seal judgments, which are the first reported judgments of the tribulation. Revelation 6 and the seal judgments also contradict the Van Kampen formulation since the Bible describes all six judgments as 'the wrath of the Lamb: For the great day of his wrath is come' (Rev. 6:16c-17a). Even though Van Kampen cannot recognize God's wrath, the unbelievers at the beginning of the seven-year tribulation will be able to.

Revelation 5 reveals that only the Lamb (Christ) was qualified to open the seals that would begin the first judgments of the tribulation. As we connect the dots of Revelation 5 and 6, there is no basis for saying that the events of the seal judgments are somehow disconnected from Scripture's characterization as God's wrath. The following observations about the seal judgments support such a connection:

The Lamb is the Individual Who breaks, and thus initiates, all six of the seals (Revelation 6:1,3,5,7,9,12) clearly indicating that He (God) is the source of the events or wrath. These are explicit references to the wrath of God, not the wrath of man or satan as taught by Van Kampen.

One quarter of the earth's population is killed (Rev. 6:8).

The fifth seal reveals that multitudes of Tribulation saints are slain as a result of seal activity, which has to be considered the wrath of the Lamb. God allows this to occur when the Lamb breaks the seal in this part of the seal judgments.

At the end of the six seal judgments an assessment is given as follows: 'Fall on us, and hide us from the face of him that sitteth on the throne, and from the wrath of the Lamb: For the great day of his wrath is come; and who shall be able to stand?' (Rev. 6:16-17).

'Him that sitteth on the throne' is God the Father as indicated in chapter 4, thus it is clearly God's wrath. It is also the Lamb's wrath (Christ). The passage clearly says 'the Great Day of His wrath is come,' meaning that all six of the seal judgments are classified as God's wrath.

The above information provides ample Biblical proof that all six seal judgments are the wrath of God (Lamb). Therefore, this passage does not support the Van Kampen interpretation. Since the Church is promised deliverance from the wrath of God (Rom. 5:9, 1 Thess. 1:10, 5:9, and Rev. 3:10), it is clear in light of Revelation 6 that the Church will be Raptured before the seventieth week of Daniel."

"Also, if the Day of the Lord commences with the judgments at the end of the Tribulation as the Pre-Wrath proponents would say, then how can it begin with a time of peace and safety (1 Thessalonians 5:2,3)? Even a superficial knowledge of the Tribulation does not give the impression that there will be any time of peace and safety, except perhaps at the very beginning; certainly not at the end.

In the first 3½ years of tribulation, Revelation 6 says the earth is in *chaos*, the worldwide *economy collapses* and *inflation* is so rampant it takes a day's wage just to buy food. Not to mention all this causes *1/4 of the earth to die* from *war* and *wild beasts*!" (So much for peace and safety!)

"It should be clear that Van Kampen must resort to strained characterizations of things like the Day of the Lord, the tribulation, and the scope of God's wrath in order to first avoid Pre-Tribulationism, and second, to support his new three-quarters Rapture view.

Bible believing Christians, though, should continue to draw strength and hope from the fact that our Lord could Rapture His Church at any moment. We will not be left standing when our Lord moves history to the point of the commencement of the seventieth week of Daniel. This is our true Blessed Hope. Maranatha!"[7]

In other words, if you don't want to be confused, then don't go into the Bible with preconceived ideas and mess up God's timing of the Day of the Lord.

Let the Bible speak for itself. Don't try to "squeeze into it" what you "want it" to say. And isn't that what we're supposed to avoid doing if we're not going to be deceived?

The **third problem** with the Pre-Wrath teaching of the Rapture is that **It Confuses the Timing of the Judgements of the Lord**. Once again, if you tweak with the Scripture, everything begins to fall apart. And this is precisely what has happened with the Pre-Wrath position on the judgments of God. All because you want the Bible to "fit in" with your preconceived ideas on the Rapture, you totally messed up the "real timing" of the judgments of God mentioned in the 7-year Tribulation. Everything falls apart. For instance, here's the typical timing of the judgments in the 7-year Tribulation with the Pre-Trib view:

The Seven Year Tribulation - Daniel's 70th Week
(Daniel 9:24-27)

Rapture   Second Coming

                                    7 years

Begin   3 ½ years   3 ½ years   End
|_____|
Seals   Trumpets   Bowls
Rev. 6:17-8:60   Rev. 8:7-9:21   Rev. 16:1-21
                               Rev. 11:15-19[8]

As you can see, it's pretty straightforward. God's wrath is clearly being poured out through the entirety of the 7-year Tribulation and thus the Church is absent from all of it as well just like the Bible teaches. Here's a summary of the Pre-Trib view via the chart:

"The Biblical view of the Pre-Tribulationalists is that the whole of the seven years, called the Tribulation, Daniel's 70th Week, or the Time of Jacob's trouble, is a period of God pouring out His wrath. God will do this in a series of three judgments upon the earth which will end with His Second Coming.

The Book of Revelation teaches the judgments or wrath of God on earth begin at the start of the seven years of Tribulation with the Seal Judgments (Rev. 6:17, 8:1-60) , followed by the Trumpet Judgments (Rev. 8:7-9:21, 11:15-19) and subsequent and final Bowl (Vial) Judgments (Rev. 16:1-21).

As each judgment is released upon the earth they grow in intensity and are increasingly more devastating. The last 3 ½ years of the seven years of the Tribulation will be the worse period and is referred to as the Great Tribulation (Matt. 24:21)."[9]

Now let's take a look at the timing of the judgments of the 7-year Tribulation according to the Pre-Wrath view as contrasted in this following chart:

THREE-QUARTERS RAPTURE THEORY

	1	2	3	4
70th Week	Reclamation	Restoration	Millennium	
3 ¦ Years 3 ¦ Years	30 DAYS	45 DAYS	1000 YEARS	

BEGINNING OF BIRTH PANGS — GREAT TRIBULATION — THE DAY OF THE LORD

WRATH OF MAN AND SATAN   WRATH OF GOD

Antichrist Paralyzed   Armageddon

10

Okay, can you say, "Jumbled mess of confusion?" Wow! Where do you even begin with this? As you can see, there is a huge massive difference between these charts in the timing of God's judgments. The Pre-Trib position is pretty straightforward, while the Pre-Wrath position is all mixed up. The differences in the charts really brings home the truth again that once you tweak with the Scripture with your preconceived ideas, as the Pre-Wrath position does, everything begins to fall apart. Because you approached the Bible with a wrong motive and wanted it to "fit your pre-conceived idea" of the Rapture, you totally messed up the "real timing" of the judgments in the 7-year Tribulation. But don't take my word for it. Let's look at the proof:

The Seals/Trumpets/Bowls Chronology:

The 3/4 Trib Rapture violates the chronology of the book of Revelation. The Seal Judgments are continued over into the second half of the 7 year period, the Trumpet Judgments are moved to the end of the second half, and the Bowl Judgments are appended to a 30 day period after the close of Daniel's 70th Week!

The Pre-Wrath view makes a CONFUSING distinction and discontinuity between the seals, the trumpets and the bowls. This view says that the seals involve only the wrath of man, not the wrath of God and will take place during the first 3½ years of Daniel's 70th week and also during the Great Tribulation.

The trumpets involve the wrath of God and will take place during the Day of the Lord. The bowls involve the wrath of God also, but they will be poured out after Daniel's 70th week has been completed (during the 30 days following).

Thus, according to this view the seals are totally different in nature and character than the trumpets and bowls. However the Bible presents the seals/trumpets/bowls as being UNIFIED. They all come from the hand of God (Rev. 5:1). They are all part of ONE UNIFIED SCROLL (Rev. 5:2).

The Pre-Wrath view is forced to say that the seals contain only the wrath of man. They cannot contain the wrath of God. Why not? Because according to this view the Church is on earth during the seal judgments. Yet, according to the Bible, Church Age believers are not appointed unto WRATH (1 Thess. 5:9). Thus, the only way to keep Church saints on earth during the seal judgments is to say that these judgments do not involve the wrath of God.

This then forces the Pre-Wrath advocates to make the unbiblical distinction between the seals and the trumpets and bowls. Does the Bible really warrant such a distinction? To say that a judgment which reduces the world's population by a fourth has nothing to do with the wrath of God is incredulous (see Revelation 6:7-8, the 4th seal judgment).

The Great Tribulation Chronology:

The Pre-Wrath view holds to the CONFUSING position that the Great Tribulation was shortened by God from a period of 3½ years to an unknown period of time less than 3½ years. This is based upon Matthew 24:22, 'And except those days should be shortened, there should no flesh be saved: but for the elect's sake those days shall be shortened.' Rosenthal's understanding of this verse is essential to the Pre-Wrath position.

All agree that the Great Tribulation begins at the time of the abomination of desolation, at the midway point of Daniel's 70th week (after the first 3½ years). The key question is not when the Great Tribulation begins but when it ends.

The Pre-Tribulational position says that the Great Tribulation is the second half of Daniel's 70th week (the 7-year Tribulation) and therefore it lasts 3½ years. The Pre-Wrath view says it lasts *less than* 3½ years. How does that add up to 7 years, hence the 70th week or 7-year Tribulation?

Yet Rosenthal makes it clear that Daniel's 70th week is not shortened. Hence we have this confusing series of events."[11]

On top of that the Pre-Wrath view totally separates the Great Tribulation (the second half of the 7-year Tribulation) from the Day of the Lord (the entirety of the 7-year Tribulation). How can you separate the two when they're totally interlocked and meshed together? Where did you get that from? Well, one research may have the answer:

"I came across an article published by the Worldwide Church of God, the cult founded by H. Armstrong. I was amazed to find that these people hold to the identical view of Rosenthal when it comes to the Great Tribulation as being totally distinct from the Day of the Lord. Hence, some of Rosenthal's ideas are not new. The Worldwide Church of God cult has been teaching these things since 1986 and probably long before that."[12]

Hmmm. I wonder who's copying who? Furthermore, this tweaking of the Day of the Lord and the Great Tribulation makes mish mash out of the "birth pains" analogy that Jesus used to describe the 7-year Tribulation. One man puts it this way:

"Rosenthal's view is confusing. If the first 3½ years are the beginning of birth pangs and if the period prior to the Day of the Lord (p. 174) is the time of hard labor (the Great Tribulation), then what kind of pains are there during the Day of the Lord? If the time of man's wrath is likened to beginning labor and hard labor, what shall the time of God's wrath be likened to?

Rosenthal's view confuses the childbirth analogy. In childbirth, the beginning labor and the severe labor are followed by the birth! The difficult time is followed by a wonderful and joyous time! Daniel's 70th week (with its beginning and hard labor) is followed by a glorious time (the Lord's return to earth and millennial bliss). However, in Rosenthal's view we do not have this.

In the Pre-Wrath view the beginning labor and the severe labor are followed by the Day of the Lord, the most intense time of God's wrath the world has ever known! Thus, this mother who thought she would be relieved by giving birth, discovers to her horror that SHE HAS GIVEN BIRTH TO A MONSTER! How confusing!! Imagine telling a woman who has just completed hard labor: "Your worst time is still ahead!"

Rosenthal's view does not make sense. The Great Tribulation is the greatest time of trouble the world will ever know (Matt. 24:21), but Rosenthal says that the Day of the Lord follows it! The Great Tribulation is a time of hard and severe birth pangs, but Rosenthal teaches that the Day of the Lord follows it! When we should be expecting birth and a time of rejoicing, Rosenthal plunges us into the horrors of the Day of the Lord. Confusing!"[13]

The Second Coming Chronology:

The Pre-Wrath view of the Second Coming is CONFUSING in that it teaches that 'there is only one Second Coming' which includes, 'the Rapture of the Church, the outpouring of God's wrath during the Day of the Lord, and Christ's physical return in glory.' It also means, 'a coming and continuing presence.'

From this view one gets the impression that Christ meets the Church in the air at the Rapture and then Christ and the Church continue to gradually descend to the earth during the Day of the Lord.

However the Bible teaches that when Christ comes to Rapture the believers He will receive His believers unto Himself 'that where I am, there ye may be also' (John 14:3). The context is referring to the Father's house in heaven (John 14:1-3). According to our Lord, the Rapture involves Christ receiving His Bride (the Church) and taking her with Him to heaven.

The Pre-Wrath view does not allow for this because it insists upon the Lord's 'continued presence' with respect to the earth (once He comes He must remain present and not return to heaven). Thus it is very significant that in a 300-page book dealing with the Rapture, Rosenthal does not once even mention John 14:3 which is one of the key passages on the Rapture. The reason is clear: John 14:3 does not fit in with the Pre-Wrath theory and thus it is best to ignore contradictory data.

Furthermore, one of the strangest parts of Rosenthal's book is chapter 16 (pages 215-230). In this chapter he attacks the Pre-Trib Rapture view as espousing two separate comings of the Lord. He then proclaims: 'There is not even a hint – anywhere – of two separate comings' (page 222).

In response to this attack, I would like to point out that the Pre-Trib view does not present two comings of the Lord. Instead, it advocates an appearing of the Lord (the Rapture) followed at least 7 years later by the coming of the Lord (the Second Coming). Jesus does not return to the earth at the Rapture. He appears in the heavens for His Church, receives them, and then returns to Heaven with them.

But what is so weird about Rosenthal's attack is that his end time viewpoint presents multiple comings of the Lord – so many, in fact, that it is hard to chart them.

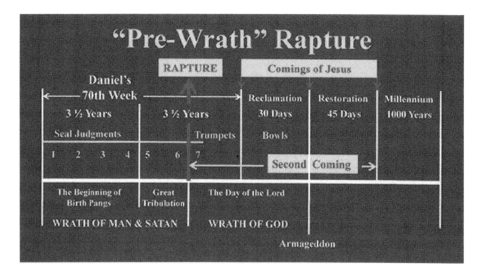

According to his view, at the end of Daniel's 70th Week, Jesus returns to earth to save Israel from annihilation, after which He returns to Heaven. Then, at the end of the '30 days of Reclamation' Jesus returns again to defeat satan at the Battle of Armageddon. Following the '45 days of Restoration,' Jesus returns to Heaven, gathers His Church, and returns to begin His thousand year reign.

So, Rosenthal has a total of four 'comings' of Jesus, yet he has the audacity to assert there is only one 'coming' of the Lord and he condemns the Pre-Trib view for having two! This amounts to mass confusion."

The Destruction of the Heavens & Earth Chronology

"The Pre-Wrath view CONFUSES the purging of the heavens and the earth by fire (2 Peter 3:10-12) with judgments which take place near the end of Daniel's 70th week. This view says that the dissolving of the universe will be *before* the millennium rather than *after* the millennium and this view also teaches that the new heavens and the new earth will be realized *during* the Millennium (see pages 127-134).

The passing away of the heavens and the melting of the elements are included as part of the Day of the Lord in 2 Peter 3:10: "But the Day of the Lord will come as a thief in the night; in the which the heavens shall pass away with a great noise, and the elements shall melt with fervent heat, the earth also and the works that are therein shall be burned up."

Since Rosenthal limits the Day of the Lord to a very short period of time (less than 3½ years) and since he teaches that the end of the Day of the Lord coincides with the end of Daniel's 70th week, then a post-millennial event cannot be included in the Day of the Lord. Indeed, Rosenthal cannot include any of the Millennium as being part of the Day of the Lord either because the Day of the Lord 'is exclusively a time of devastating judgment' and 'no blessing is associated with it' (p. 127).

An objective reading of 2 Peter 3:10-12 reveals that Peter is describing the total dissolving and melting of the present universe by means of fire: 'But the Day of the Lord will come as a thief in the night; in the which the heavens shall pass away with a great noise, and the elements shall melt with fervent heat, the earth also and the works that are therein shall be burned up. Seeing then that all these things shall be dissolved, what manner of persons ought ye to be in all holy conversation and godliness, Looking for and hasting unto the coming of the day of God, wherein the heavens being on fire shall be dissolved, and the elements shall melt with fervent heat?'

If we interpret these verses LITERALLY, then how could this possibly be a description of what shall take place *during* Daniel's 70th week? If such were to take place during Daniel's 70th week, how could there be any survivors? When the world was judged by water there were only eight survivors! If God were to judge the earth by fire during Daniel's 70th week in such a way that the very elements dissolve, how could anyone survive? Rosenthal fails to interpret 2 Peter Chapter 3 literally.

The Book of Revelation places the new heavens and the new earth *after* the Millennium. The Millennium is described in Chapter 20 and the new heavens and the new earth is introduced after the Millennium in chapter 21 (see verse 1). The Lord Jesus predicted that there would come a time when heaven and earth would pass away (Matt. 24:35). When would this event take place?

In 2 Peter 3 we are given a very important chronological clue as to exactly when the heavens and the earth will be judged by fire: 'But the heavens and the earth, which are now, by the same word are kept in store, reserved unto fire against the day of judgment and perdition of ungodly men' (2 Peter 3:7). God is reserving the present universe for a great final judgment (a fire judgment). When will this take place?

At the 'day of judgment and perdition of ungodly men' (2 Pet. 3:7). On what day will ungodly men be judged and sent into perdition [into the lake of fire]? This will take place at the time of the GREAT WHITE THRONE JUDGMENT (Rev. 20:11-15). This is confirmed in Revelation 20:11, 'And I saw a great white throne, and him that sat on it, from whose face the earth and the heaven fled away [compare 2 Pet. 3:7,10-12]; and there was found no place for them.'

Notice carefully that the Great White Throne judgment is post-millennial (after the Millennium) and therefore the dissolving of the universe by fire, spoken of in 2 Peter 3, must take place *after* the Millennium. This also perfectly harmonizes with Revelation 21:1, 'And I saw a new heaven and a new earth: for the first heaven and the first earth were passed away; and there was no more sea.'

In 2 Peter 3:13 we learn that righteousness will find its home in this new heaven and new earth: 'Nevertheless we, according to his promise, look for new heavens and a new earth wherein dwelleth righteousness.' This is because 'there shall in no wise enter into it any thing that defileth, neither whatsoever worketh abomination, or maketh a lie: but they which are written in the Lamb's book of life' (Rev. 21:27). During the Millennium the Lord Jesus will exercise a righteous rule and will swiftly punish unrighteousness, but sin will still be present in the hearts of men and righteousness will not find its true home on earth at that time.

Moving the elemental destruction of the heavens and the earth to a time *before* the Millennium creates more problems than it solves, and does not respect the chronology given to us in 2 Peter 3:7 and the Book of Revelation."

The Last Trumpet Chronology:

Because Paul, in 1 Cor. 15:52 and 1 Thes 4:16, said believers would be Raptured at the sounding of a trump, many folks have tried to make it appear that the Rapture trumps are the same trumpets found in Revelation 11:15-18, Joel 2:1, and Matt. 24:31 which all occur during the tribulation.

The problem with the reference to the trumpets in Joel 2:1 is that the context of that passage is the Day of the Lord, not the Rapture. Also, Matt. 24:31 is in reference to the angel harvest at the end of the 7-year Tribulation, also not the Rapture.

And Pre-wrath proponents say that the seventh trumpet blown in Rev 11:15-18 is the same last trump Paul spoke of in 1 Cor 15:52. However, they fail to take into account the fact that John wrote Revelation 40 years after Paul wrote his first epistle to the Corinthians. So how could Paul refer to something that was not yet revealed? It just doesn't make sense, but that does not deter the critics from trying to twist the scriptures to fit their pre-conceived views of a Pre-Wrath Rapture.

To further add to the Pre-Wrathers' error and confusion, we must note that there are several 'last trumpets' in the Bible and Jewish tradition. When you have trumpets commonly used throughout the Bible, I think it's foolish to just assume any two of the 62 trumps or trumpets are prophetically related.

In the movies Ben-Hur and The Wizard of Oz, I recall hearing the sounding of trumpets. Are both these trumpets somehow prophetically related?

If your friend John said he went to his favorite restaurant last night, and another friend Larry said he also went to his favorite restaurant last night, is it logical for you to assume they both went to the same restaurant? Obviously not, because even though John and Larry went to their favorite restaurants, they may have had two different eating establishments in mind.

The same logic should apply with the word trumpet. With such a blind devotion to this one similarity, I have to wonder if these last tumpeters are able to distinguish the difference between Tylenol and Exlax. They're both over-the-counter drugs, they come in pill form, and they can also be found in a medicine cabinet. Of course, one will make your headache disappear and the other will make your toilet paper disappear."[14]

In other words, if you don't want to make a "mess" out of things and get seriously confused, then don't go into the Bible with your preconceived ideas about the timing of God's judgements in the 7-year Tribulation. Let the Bible speak for itself and define the terms itself and everything will turn out just fine. And isn't that what we're supposed to do if we're not going to be deceived?

The **fourth problem** with the Pre-Wrath teaching of the Rapture is that **It Confuses the Identity of the Church**. Just like the Post-Trib position, the Pre-Wrath Position also makes the same fatal error in their citations of Scripture to support their timing of the Rapture. They too confuse the identity of the Church and Israel, and the Church Age believers with the Tribulation saints. Why? Because they have a "preconceived idea" that the Church "must be" IN the 7-year Tribulation, therefore they have to "squeeze" the identity of the Church into that time period somewhere.

However, as we saw before, the whole purpose of the 7-year Tribulation has to do with the Jewish people and the Gentile nations, not the Church. It is the classic passage of Daniel 9:20-27 that gives us the purpose and reason for the 7-year Tribulation in the first place. And as we saw, the verbiage is all about Israel, not the Church.

- Verse 20 – "my sin and the sin of my people Israel" (Daniel & the people of Israel)
- Verse 20 - "making my request to the LORD my God for his holy hill" (Daniel & Jerusalem)

- Verse 22 – "Daniel, I have now come to give you" (Daniel a Jewish Person)
- Verse 24 – "Seventy 'sevens' are decreed for your people and your holy city" (The Jewish people & Jerusalem)
- Verse 25 – "From the issuing of the decree to restore and rebuild Jerusalem" (Jerusalem)
- Verse 26 – "The people of the ruler who will come will destroy the city and the sanctuary" (Jerusalem)
- Verse 27 – "And on a wing of the temple he will set up an abomination that causes desolation" (Rebuilt Temple in Jerusalem)

Question, "Where is the Church in any of this?" Answer: *Nowhere*! Why? Because the verbiage clearly reveals that it's all about the Jewish people and Jerusalem and their rebuilt Jewish Temple, *not* the Church. Also, we saw there just happens to be a "gap" between the 69th week and the 70th week (the 7-year Tribulation) of Daniel's 70th week prophecy. Why? Because this is where the "mystery of the Church" fits in. During this 2000 year gap God has been:

- Building His Church (Acts 2:47; 1 Cor. 3:6-9; 12:18; Eph. 2:21-22; 1 Pet. 2:5).
- Taking out of the nations a people for His Name (Acts 15:14).
- Bringing in the fullness of the Gentiles (Rom. 11:25).
- Placing believers into a living organism (1 Cor. 12:13).
- Saving a "showcase" that will eternally display His matchless grace (Eph. 2:7).
- Manifesting Himself through His Body which is upon the earth (1 Tim. 3:15-16).[15]

Once the timing of the "mystery of the Church" is fulfilled or what's called the "fullness of the Gentiles," the Church is Raptured out and the 70th week begins. The Church is nowhere around during this final 70th week, at least, if you stick with the Bible. And that's what we're supposed to do, by the way. The 7-year Tribulation, is clearly dealing with Daniel a Jewish person, all the Jewish people, Jerusalem, and the Jewish Temple, and not the Church; the audience is Jewish through and through. It's for the "House of Israel", not the "Body of Christ." It is a "time of trouble for Jacob," not a "time of trouble for the Church." It's not "Paul's Doom" or "Peter's Demise" or even "Ananias' Agony." No! It's Jacob's trouble, a Jewish name, for a Jewish people, for a Jewish time, not the Church.

So how in the world can you "confuse" the identity and history of the Church with Israel? It makes no sense. Unless of course, you're entering the Scripture with a "preconceived idea" and you "want" the Church to be *in* the 7-year Tribulation. But that's not how we're supposed to interpret the Bible as this man points out:

"The Pre-Wrath view CONFUSES the mysterious and parenthetical nature of the Church Age. It confuses CHURCH HISTORY with ISRAELITE HISTORY. God has a program for the Church and God has a distinct program for His people Israel. The two must not be confused.

The clearest and most complete chronological prophecy that God has given to us is the 70-week prophecy in Daniel 9:24-27. These 70 weeks involve 490 years of Jewish history: 'Seventy weeks are determined UPON THY PEOPLE AND UPON THY HOLY CITY.' These 490 years pertain to the Jews and to Jerusalem, not to the Church.

Of the 490 years, the last seven years are yet unfulfilled. After the first 69 weeks the Messiah was cut off and we know that the Church Age began less than two months after the Messiah was cut off. Daniel's 70th week has remained unfulfilled for nearly 2000 years. The prophetic time clock has stopped ticking for all these years. The clock stopped ticking after the 69th week and has not yet resumed ticking. How can we explain this large 2000 year gap between the 69th week and the 70th week? The answer is revealed on the pages of the New Testament. This 2000 year gap, God is involved with the Church.

Just as the Church had an abrupt beginning on the day of Pentecost shortly after the conclusion of the 69th week, so it should be expected that the Church will have an abrupt removal shortly before the beginning of the 70th week. The Pretribulational model harmonizes perfectly with Daniel's 70th week prophecy while at the same time recognizing the parenthetical and mysterious nature of the Church Age.

It is 'mysterious' in the sense that Church truth was unrevealed on the pages of the Old Testament and the Church Age was not foreseen by the prophets. The Old Testament prophets did not tell us about the gap simply because they did not see the gap. It was unrevealed to them. They saw only the two mountain peaks which represent the first and second comings of Christ but they did not see the large valley in between.

The Pre-Wrath view sees the Church as being on earth during a large part of Daniel's 70th week (the Church will be on earth, according to Rosenthal's charts, for approximately 3/4 of the last seven years). This mixes up and confuses God's purpose for Israel and God's purpose for the Church. THE CHURCH HAS NEVER AND WILL NEVER BE PRESENT ON EARTH DURING ANY OF ISRAEL'S 70 WEEKS."[16]

  Oh, but that's not all. The Pre-wrath view not only "confuses" the identity of the Church with Israel, but it also confuses the identity of the Tribulation saints. Why? Because once again, you are approaching the Bible with your "preconceived idea" that the Church "must be" *in* the 7-year Tribulation, therefore you have to "squeeze" their identity into there somewhere. But as we saw before, the Tribulation saints are not the same as the Church Age saints.

  The Tribulation saints are those who get saved "after" the Rapture "during" the 7-year Tribulation, but they are not the Church. Just like the Jewish people, God will extend His mercy during this time to the Gentile Nations or what's called "the inhabitants of the earth." They too will have an opportunity to be saved, but most of them will be slaughtered for it. Again, this is the identity of the Tribulation saints. They are *not* the Church.

  The lesson is they should've gotten saved at the present time, "before" the Rapture occurred prior to the 7-year Tribulation. Yes, they finally got saved, praise God for that, but now they're in a heap of trouble. Most of them will be horribly murdered and martyred and have their heads chopped off. This is why the promise of the Rapture is a "Blessed Hope" for us *now* in the "Church age." If you get saved *now* you avoid the whole thing, praise the Lord! But once again, the Pre-Wrath view has to "mess things up" with their "preconceived idea" as these researchers state:

"The Pre-Wrath Rapture view is CONFUSING in its identification of those who are saved during the 70th week of Daniel. Keep in mind that according to the Pre-Wrath view, Daniel's 70th week belongs primarily to CHURCH HISTORY. Approximately 3/4 of these last seven years (5+ years) will belong to the Church Age. Only the very last phase of Daniel's 70th week will be a time when the Church will be absent from earth. Thus everyone who is saved during the first 5+ years will be a member of the Church of Jesus Christ and will be a part of the Rapture, according to this view.

This carries with it several implications. What about the 144,000 Jewish witnesses described in Revelation 7 and 14? If these are saved during the first 5+

years, then they would be members of the Church and they would be taken up in the Rapture (unless we are to teach a partial Rapture). Why are these saved persons not included in the Rapture?

What about the great multitude from every nation described in Revelation 7:9? They are identified as those who have come out of great tribulation (Rev. 7:14). Rosenthal says that this multitude is the Raptured Church. However, the great host of Church Age saints never came out of great tribulation because they lived on earth prior to Daniel's 70th week. Hence, if the Raptured Church consists only of those who have come out of great tribulation, then we must have a partial Rapture.

Absolutely, nothing in this passage can even remotely be understood as referring to believers in the current Church Age who will be Raptured before the Tribulation begins. Revelation 6:9-11 is referring to saints who have believed after the Tribulation has begun. These saints are not part of the current dispensation of the Church Age. These are Jews and Gentiles who believed on Jesus Christ after the Rapture and every one in this group were killed for their testimony for Christ.

All believers in this present dispensation have not been killed for their testimony of Jesus Christ. Clearly, this is a different group of believers and not those of the present Church Age. First, if these are all the Raptured saints of God, of this age, it would require that all those who are Raptured must be slain and martyred. Of course this is not the case. Second, it does not explain what happens to believers who have died in Christ Jesus. Once again the Pre-Wrath heresy is refuted by the word of God.

Another point revealed in this passage and overlooked or ignored by the Pre-Wrath position is that all these saints, both in heaven and on the earth are seen as one group. However, a part of the group is shown as having been slain and are in heaven. The other part of the group is still on earth and waiting to join the slain saints in heaven, by experiencing their eventual deaths as well at the hands of the Antichrist.

Thus is revealed another flaw in the Pre-Wrath view. It has part of believers Raptured and part awaiting the Rapture! These cannot be Church Age saints. 1 Thessalonians 4:17 has all believers, both dead and alive Raptured and taken to meet the Lord in the air at the same time. Nothing in the New Testament suggests a partial Rapture of some believers and others are left behind.

This plainly is not a reference to the Rapture of believers of the Church Age, but rather to those who believed and were saved in the seven year Tribulation.

The Pre-Wrath view says that during most of Daniel's 70th week God is placing believers into the body of Christ and dealing with the Church. When it comes to salvation and who the people of God are, it is the Church that is prominent during the greater part of these final seven years. This is very confusing in light of the fact that the 70 weeks of Daniel's prophecy pertain to the Jews and Jerusalem, not to God's called out assembly, the Church. When clear-cut dispensational distinctions are ignored much confusion results."[17]

Oh, but it gets even worse. Again, like a house of cards, once you begin tweaking with the foundation, what the Bible really says and what it speaks out to us, what comes out next is surely to be a toppled mess. Not so surprisingly, that's exactly what has happened with Matthew 24 and the "preconceived idea" of Pre-Wrath "having to have" the Church be *in* there somewhere. However, again, as we saw in the section dealing with the problems with the Post-Trib position, Matthew 24, the whole chapter, has nothing to do with the Church, but rather it's all about Israel.

First of all, just as the word "Church" is absent in Revelation 4-18, so the word "Church" is absent in Matthew 24. Why? Because the context in Matthew 24 clearly reveals it has nothing to do with the Church. The Church does not even come into existence until Acts Chapter 2. Rather, Matthew 24 is dealing with the Jewish people who, as we saw, are one of the reasons why there is a 7-year Tribulation in the first place.

Also, we know Matthew 24 cannot be referring to the Church because Jesus starts the Chapter off by saying that the Jewish Temple will be torn down to the ground and destroyed, which did happen in 70 AD. But then a few verses later He says a rebuilt Jewish Temple comes back into existence with Jewish people apparently worshipping at it again. The point is this. The Jewish Temple being destroyed or rebuilt has no significance for the Church. Jesus says the Church doesn't need a manmade Temple because we have become the Temple of God by the indwelling Holy Spirit.

Furthermore, Jesus also tells the people during that time frame to "flee to the mountains." Can the whole Church fit into the "mountains" or what many believe to be Petra?" I think not. However, the remnant of the Jewish People can.

Next we see Jesus mentioning that those people of that time are apparently "keeping the Sabbath Day." Question: "Does the Church observe a traditional Jewish Saturday Sabbath?" No. But the Jewish people do, even to this day! So why would the events of Matthew 24 be speaking of the Church when the whole Chapter is referring to Israel, not the Church? Answer: It's *not* speaking about the Church!

And as we saw before, neither is the "gathering of the elect" referring to the Church. In fact, it's not even a Rapture passage at all! Rather it's speaking of the "Angel Harvest" of both the wicked and righteous at the end of the 7-year Tribulation. The one person being taken while another is left is talking about the "elect" or Israel being "gathered" to enter the Millennial Kingdom while the "others" are the unbelieving unredeemed who are "taken" and cast into hell. Obviously, they don't go into the Millennial Kingdom. It has nothing to do with the Church as these men point out:

"The Pre-Wrath view CONFUSES the re-gathering of the nation Israel with the Rapture of the Church. This view teaches that Matthew 24:31 is a description of the Rapture of the Church: 'And he shall send his angels with a great sound of a trumpet, and they shall gather together his elect from the four winds, from one end of heaven to the other.' It is far better to understand Matthew 24:31 as the final re-gathering of the nation Israel, an event repeatedly mentioned in the Old Testament Scriptures.

The fact is, when Jesus gave His explanation of future events, known as the Olivet Discourse (Matthew 24), the Church and its destiny, including the Rapture, was still a mystery. This information would later be revealed to the Apostle Paul. If Christ had discussed the course of the Church Age and the Rapture, it would have been very confusing to the disciples at that time. The Church came into existence on the Day of Pentecost (Acts 2), and little by little, the organization took shape.

Van Kampen complains that when the Pre-Tribulation teachers relegate the events of the Olivet Discourse to Israel, they fail to teach the entire Gospel message. (*Rapture*, p. 103) We agree that students of the Word should accept that all Scripture is profitable (2 Timothy 3:16), and that all of it should be taught. However, not all sections apply to all people. Everything in the Gospels is important and *instructive* to the Church, but some portions are *about* the history of Israel, beyond the age of the Church. To fail to make that distinction is to do a great disservice to the Bible student."[18]

In fact, not only does this "gathering of the elect" in Matthew 24 have nothing to do with the Church, but rather those who are being "gathered" to enter into the Millennium, but again, once you mess with the timing of these events in the Bible, everything else starts to fall apart. As was the case with the Post-Trib timing of the Rapture, so it is with the Pre-Wrath timing of the Rapture. Both mess up the "gathering of the elect" to enter the Millennium, as this researcher shares:

"As it was in the Post-Trib position, so it is with the Pre-Wrath position. Who is left to populate the Millennial Kingdom? If the Rapture were to take place just before the battle of Armageddon, and all the believers were taken just before the final events of the Tribulation, what people would become believers at the very last moments so that there would be godly people to populate the Millennial Kingdom?

Van Kampen's thought is that this is where the 144,000 come in. (*Rapture*, pp. 53-54). We agree that there will be many Jewish people who believe at the end when they see the Lord whom they have pierced and mourn for Him. (Zechariah 12:10). However, according to Revelation 7, the 144,000 are sealed *before* any destruction occurs: 'Do not harm the land or the sea or the trees until we put a seal on the foreheads of the servants of our God. Then I heard the number of those who were sealed: 144,000 from all the tribes of Israel.'

According to Matthew 25:31-46, there will be a judgment of "sheep" and "goats" based on how people treated Israel. In the Pre-Tribulation view, surviving believers of the Tribulation period will qualify as the 'sheep.' In the Pre-Wrath view, all believers would have been taken at the Rapture and only a remnant from Israel itself would become believers at the very end. It is difficult to imagine that these new converts could be the 'sheep' who acted kindly toward Israel.

Van Kampen offers a very unorthodox explanation of this dilemma. Since it is obvious that these Gentile survivors have not yet accepted Christ (or they would have gone up at the Rapture shortly before this time), he says that they will have trusted Christ when they saw Him face to face 'when the Son of Man comes in His glory.' (Matthew 23:31) (*Sign*, pp. 403-405)

I didn't notice any mention of this theory in his later book, probably because of difficulties in supporting this view."[19]

In other words, it's a bunch of bologna! But that's still not all. The "coming of Jesus" in Matthew 24 is likewise not dealing at all with the Rapture, but rather the Second Coming of Jesus. So not only is this *whole chapter not dealing with the Church*, but it has *nothing* to do with the Rapture period. The Rapture has already taken place. Yet, because of the Pre-Wrath's "preconceived idea" that the Church "must be" *in* the 7-year Tribulation, they mess up this whole Chapter, as this researcher admits:

"The key passage for the Pre-Wrath view is the Olivet Discourse (Matthew 24). Matthew 24:30 states that, 'They will see the Son of Man coming on the clouds of the sky, with power and great glory.' Van Kampen says this is the Rapture. However, there are many differences between the Rapture and the Glorious Return of Christ. Here are some of these differences:

The Rapture	**The Glorious Return**
Christ Comes for His Own 1 Thessalonians 4:13-18	Christ Returns with His own Revelation 19:4
Believers taken to the Father's House John 14:3	Believers come to Earth Matthew 24:30
Seen only by Believers 1 Corinthians 15:52	Every Eye will See Him Revelation 1:7;19:11-16;Matthew 24:30
No Reference to satan	satan Bound Revelation 20:1-3
Earth not Judged	Earth Judged Revelation 20:4-5
A Mystery 1 Corinthians 15:51	Foretold in Old Testament Daniel 12:1-3;Zech 12:10;14:4

If we are to read Matthew 24:29-30 literally and understand it in a normal and natural way, we can only conclude that immediately after the Great Tribulation the Son of Man will come in power and great glory. This is normally and naturally understood to be a reference to our Lord's glorious coming to the earth to judge His enemies and establish His kingdom.

The Second Coming of the Lord to the earth will be very visible indeed, but not the Rapture. The Rapture will take place "in a moment [in a split second of time], in the twinkling of an eye" (1 Cor. 15:52). If something takes place that quickly how can it be seen? It reminds us of Enoch who "walked with God, and he was not; for God took him" (Gen. 5:24). The people did not see God take him because it took place too quickly. All they could see was that "he was not" (he had disappeared). So it will be with the translation of the Church at the Rapture.

The Pre-Wrath view confuses the Rapture with the second coming in glory to the earth. It also confuses the blackout which occurs during the 6th seal with the blackout which occurs immediately prior to the Lord's return to the earth. May God help us to distinguish those things which differ, rightly dividing His Word of truth."[20]

And isn't that what we're supposed to do if we're going to avoid being deceived? I'll let this researcher close us out on this problem of the Pre-Wrath Rapture theory confusing the identity of the Church:

"A carefully and scholarly study of the Book of Revelation shows that between Revelation 3:22 and 19:1 there is no mention of Church Age saints. The events between these two references reveal the progression of the seven year Tribulation until it ends with the Second Coming of the Lord Jesus Christ. Saints of God are mentioned within these Chapters, but each time it is referring to those who believed within the seven years of the Tribulation and were saved by God.

Christians who have been saved since Pentecost are not in view in this final seven years of the Old Testament dispensation. The Lord Jesus will take His Bride, which are believers in this present age to be with Him at the Rapture. Jesus Christ will once again be presented to Israel as the Messiah as the 144,000 saved Jews preach the Gospel around the world.

The Church Age will end before the seven year Tribulation and the last seven years of the Old Testament period will start. God will complete His purposes and promises for the nation of Israel, His chosen people. The current dispensation of the Church Age will end with the Rapture of all believers, both dead and alive, before God begins to renew His covenant with Israel. (1 Thess. 4:13-18) There is nothing in Matthew 24 that refers to Church Age saints. Those saved in the Tribulation are a different group of believers."[21]

The **fifth problem** with the Pre-Wrath teaching of the Rapture is that **It Confuses the Placement of the Church**. As we saw in great detail in the section dealing with the problems with the Post-Trib position, once you place the Church in the 7-year Tribulation, like the Pre-Wrath theory does as well, you put them up against the Antichrist and this just simply cannot be. Why? Because as we saw before, the Bible does not put the Church "with" the Antichrist:

2 Thessalonians 2:7-8 "For the secret power of lawlessness is already at work; but the one who now holds it back will continue to do so till he is taken out of the way. And then the lawless one will be revealed, whom the Lord Jesus will overthrow with the breath of his mouth and destroy by the splendor of his coming."

Again, here we see the order of events that must take place in the Bible concerning the Antichrist. Paul says the Antichrist, the lawless one, will *not* be revealed *until* "the one who now holds it back" is taken "out" of the way. We clearly saw "repeatedly" that the "one" who is "taken out of the way" is the Church! The Church is the "restrainer."

Therefore, according to the Bible, how can you have the Church and the Antichrist in the same time frame? Answer: You can't! I know you have a "preconceived idea" that you "want" the Church to be *in* that time frame under the Antichrist's persecution, but that is simply not what the Bible states. And because of this "preconceived idea" the Pre-Wrath theory must get "inventive" with the identity of the "restrainer" or the "one who holds" the Antichrist back. Here's who they replace the Church with:

"The Pre-Wrath position makes the CONFUSING claim that the angel Michael is the Restrainer referred to in 2 Thessalonians chapter 2 (p. 260, 271). This view cannot identify the Restrainer with God the Holy Spirit in the Church because the presence of the Restrainer will prevent the man of sin from being revealed (2 Thess. 2:6-8).

According to the Pre-Wrath view *the Church* (Indwelt by God the Holy Spirit) *will still be on earth at the time when the Man of Sin is revealed.* They believe the Church will be on earth to suffer the severe persecutions of Antichrist during the Great Tribulation!

Hence, Rosenthal must find someone else to play the role of the Restrainer. His confusing and unwarranted identification of the Restrainer with the archangel Michael is ably refuted."[22]

And we did that repeatedly in our study earlier where we saw clearly that the Church *is* the "restrainer" not the Archangel Michael or some other wacky theory. We the Church fulfill this role of the "restrainer" today by maintaining God's righteous decrees which "restrains" evil from marching forward without total restraint. Also, it is our presence here on earth today that is "preventing" the appearance of the Antichrist. Why? Because think about it. We would be the very first ones pointing him out to the world, blowing the whistle, ruining his plans and warning everyone not to fall for his lies and deceptions if we're in the same time frame!

Therefore, once we the Church "arise from the midst" and are "taken out of the way" before this time period begins, the 7-year Tribulation, then there's nothing "holding back" the Antichrist from "appearing" and his "evil plans" and "evil in general" from spreading "unrestrained." Total harmony *if* you stick with the Scripture. Unfortunately, that's *not* what the Pre-Wrath Theory does. Yet, is that not what we're supposed to do if we're not going to be deceived?

The **sixth problem** with the Pre-Wrath teaching of the Rapture is that **It Confuses the Promises to the Church**. As we saw before, one of the great promises to the Church was in fact the very teaching of the Rapture. It is our "Blessed Hope" that becomes an "encouraging truth" to the Church that although we may have had it rough here on earth for a little while, defending and living for Jesus, He will nonetheless "keep us" from "the hour of trial that is going to come upon the whole world to test those who live on the earth" that is, the time period where God pours out His wrath on this wicked and rebellious world during the horrible 7-year Tribulation.

However, if you think about it, all other positions on the Rapture, save the Pre-Trib position, destroy this encouraging word, this Blessed Hope. And so once again, the Pre-Wrath opponents with their "preconceived idea" have to "dance around" this promise and therefore mess it up as well. Here's what they try to do:

"Rosenthal's Pre-Wrath handling of Revelation 3:10 (kept from the hour) is total CONFUSION. Rosenthal wants this verse to support the Pre-Wrath position. How does he understand it? The time of testing spoken of in this verse refers to the Great Tribulation, according to Rosenthal. The Rapture and the Day of the Lord will follow this time of testing (p. 241).

His understanding is as follows: 'Because you (the Church of Philadelphia) have kept the word of My patience (during the 'beginning of sorrows' or the first 3½ years), I will keep you from the hour of testing (the Great Tribulation)' (p. 241). Do you see the confusion in this position?

Rosenthal claims that Revelation 3:10 promises that God will keep the Church from the Great tribulation, and yet the Pre-Wrath view insists that the Church will be on earth during the entire time of the Great Tribulation.

Moreover, the Pre-Wrath view teaches that believers will be severely persecuted during the Great Tribulation: 'Some will be sent into captivity. Others will be slain' (p. 236).

Thus, the Pre-Wrath view presents two confusing, contradictory statements: (1) Believers will be on earth to be persecuted, to suffer and the die during the Antichrist's reign of terror known as the Great Tribulation *and* (2) Believers will be kept from the Great Tribulation (according to the promise of Rev. 3:10).

Do these two statements harmonize and make sense or are they very confusing and contradictory?

Rosenthal also makes the confusing statement that Revelation 3:10 'has nothing whatever to do with the Rapture.' He teaches that the Rapture will take place after the Great Tribulation. God's promise to keep His people (Rev. 3:10) will be fulfilled during the Great Tribulation and has nothing to do with the Rapture. He teaches that the Rapture will keep the Church from the Day of the Lord, but it will not keep the Church from the time of Great Tribulation. The Church will be on earth during this tribulation time, tested severely by the Antichrist.

Rosenthal's view on Revelation 3:10 is startling! To paraphrase it: 'Because you have kept the word of My patience during the 'beginning of sorrows' (the first 3½ years), I am going to send you into a far more severe test, even into the Great Tribulation!'

Thus, their reward for passing the test of the first 3½ years is to be exposed to a far greater time of testing and trouble, the greatest time of trouble the world has ever known! If the Church is involved in this time of testing and suffering under the persecution of Antichrist, then how is the Church kept from it?

Finally Rosenthal makes this confusing statement: 'It is only the Church of Philadelphia which is promised exemption from the hour of temptation....To apply the promise given to the Church of Philadelphia to all of Christendom is to interpret the Scriptures non-literally' (p. 237).

If this is so then the promise of Revelation 3:10 has absolutely nothing to do with believers living in the 20th century. There is no Church of Philadelphia in Asia Minor today. And yet Rosenthal on page 239 does apply this verse to a future generation of believers, even to those believers who are steadfast under the stress and pressure of the first 3½ years and who will thus be protected from the Great Tribulation.

In what sense are these believers part of the Church of Philadelphia? Confusing!"[23]

But that's just it. The promise of the Rapture and being kept from the 7-year Tribulation is not meant to be confusing but a blessing! And that's precisely why the Apostle Paul mentions not once but twice in 1 Thessalonians 4 and 5, "encourage one another" with these words, that is, the truth about the Rapture.

1 Thessalonians 4:18 "Therefore *encourage* each other with these words."

1 Thessalonians 5:11 "Therefore *encourage* one another and build each other up, just as in fact you are doing."

So again, as we saw before, here's the logical common sense question. How in the world am I going to encourage someone let alone myself if I know that I'm not only going to be *in* the horrible 7-year Tribulation, the worst time in the history of mankind when God unleashes His wrath upon the planet in utter fury, but be *in it* for three-quarters of the duration as the Pre-Wrath position would have you and I believe! That's not encouraging, that's *discouraging*! Like all other positions on the Rapture, save the Pre-Trib position, the Pre-Wrath position destroys the purpose and the encouraging hope of the promise of the Rapture. You tell me if their belief is a wonderful promise to look forward to:

"According to the Pre-Wrath theory, the Church will be on earth when the Antichrist makes a treaty with Israel which marks the beginning of the 70th week. The Church must enter the 70th week (p. 19, 137). The Church must pass through all of the first 3½ years. Indeed, the Church must be on earth during a significant part of the second half of the 70th week (p. 138). The Church must be on earth during the entire period called the Great Tribulation and will not be Raptured until after the Great Tribulation is over, but immediately prior to the Day of the Lord.

Thus Church saints must be on earth to decide if they will accept the mark of Antichrist (p. 36) and they must be willing to suffer and die for Christ, if necessary, under the persecution of the Antichrist (p. 34). The true Church will be on earth when the Antichrist is personally present, empowered by satan (Rev. 13:4), demanding that the world bow down and worship him (p. 137). Thus the Church will be present on earth 'during a significant part of the 70th week of Daniel' (p. 138)."[24]

So much for an "encouraging promise." Wow! And as if that wasn't bad enough, the Pre-Wrath theory also destroys the Imminency of the Rapture. Is this, the following scenario, what you're looking forward to? Is this what motivates you to share the Gospel as fast as you can and get busy living for Jesus because He could come back at any moment as the Pre-Trib position declares? Let's take a look at Pre-Wrath's version of Imminency:

"The Rapture of the Church is not an imminent event (p. 292). It cannot take place today. It is impossible for the Lord Jesus to come for His Church today. The Rapture cannot take place next week, next month or next year. Indeed the Rapture cannot take place for several years at the very earliest. The Pre-Wrath view CONFUSES, yea, TOTALLY REJECTS the doctrine of the imminent return of Christ (the doctrine that Jesus Christ *may* come for His Church at any time).

- Instead of looking for the Savior from heaven (Phil. 3:20), we should be looking for the signing of the treaty (Daniel 9:27).
- Instead of looking for that blessed hope, even the glorious appearing of our great God (Titus 2:13), we should be looking for the coming of Antichrist.
- Instead of looking for the Bridegroom (John 14:3), we should be looking for the man of sin.
- Instead of rejoicing in the fact that 'we shall not all sleep' (1 Cor. 15:51) we should be bracing ourselves to face the persecutions of Antichrist resulting in physical death for believers.
- Instead of the Lord being at hand (Phil. 4:5), He is at least several years away.

- Instead of rejoicing in the fact that His coming is drawing nigh (James 5:8), we should be sobered at the thought that the 70th week of Daniel is drawing nigh.
- Instead of looking for the mercy of our Lord Jesus Christ (Jude 21), we should be looking for the greatest time of tribulation that this world has ever known (Matt. 24:21).
- Instead of waiting expectantly for His Son from heaven (1 Thess. 1:10) we should be waiting for the abomination of desolation.

How can the Pre-Wrath Rapture be a COMFORTING HOPE (see 1 Thess. 4:18) if we are told that we will be on earth to face the wrath of satan (Rev. 12:12), the fury of the Antichrist (Rev. 13) and the greatest time of trouble the world has ever known (Matt. 24:21)?

Where in all of the Church epistles are believers told to be looking for the tribulation? Where are we told to be looking for the Antichrist or the Abomination of Desolation? Repeatedly in the epistles believers are told to be looking expectantly for the Savior who is OUR LIFE: 'For ye are dead, and your life is hid with Christ in God. When Christ, who is our life, shall appear, then shall ye also appear with him in glory' (Col. 3:3-4).

Indeed, God will keep us from (keep us out of) the hour of temptation which shall come upon all the world, to try them that dwell upon the earth (Rev. 3:10). "Even so, come, Lord Jesus!"

To the one holding the Pre-Wrath Rapture view this question can be asked, '*Do you believe that the Lord Jesus Christ could come for you today?*' He would have to deny this with an emphatic 'NO!'"[25]

So much for a "blessed hope" if you hold to the Pre-Wrath Rapture theory! If I have to say an emphatic "no" to that question, then what "hope" is there? What kind of a position is that? Where's the encouragement? Rather, if I stick with what the Bible says and allow it to speak out to me what it says, not try to "squeeze" into it what my "preconceived ideas" want it to say, then I *do* get to answer that question in the affirmative. *YES!* Jesus could come back for me today because the Blessed Hope of the Rapture is just that; a blessed hope! It declares that God will "keep me from that hour", the horrible 7-year Tribulation, all of it, and rescue me His Church before it all begins. No wonder Paul said "encourage one another with these words." But all that is stripped away and destroyed in the Pre-Wrath theory, as this man points out:

"Pre-Wrathers believe they should plan for the worst-case scenario because if they're wrong, they conclude it won't matter. But if they're right, they'll be prepared. This is a horrible way to live. Instead of living boldly for the Lord, knowing He is coming to take us home, the Pre-Wrathers worry about the Antichrist coming! But, in fact, if you live to see the Antichrist you've missed the Rapture!

'And you know what restrains him now, so that in his time he will be revealed. For the mystery of lawlessness is already at work; only He who now restrains will do so until he is taken out of the way (via the Rapture). Then that lawless one will be revealed...' 2Th. 2:6-8

One of the cornerstones of Bible prophecy doctrine is that we're to keep our eyes looking up to heaven, to our future home, not down on this earth. One of the biggest downsides to the 'Pre-wrath' theory is that it robs believers of the joy and expectation of the coming Rapture. The end of the Church Age is something to look forward to, not fear. We are to look for Jesus Christ, not the Antichrist!

The Pre-Wrath Rapture view says that we, the Bride of Christ, will go through the first 3 1/2 years of tribulation, meaning, we'll be severely persecuted before our wedding day with the Lord. Really?

Do you actually believe the Lord will unload on the Church, the Bride of Christ, death and destruction, tearing us apart limb from limb, just before He marries us? Oh good grief! Not much to look forward to there!

No, we, the "Bride of Christ," are to look forward to our marriage to the God of Love.

'Let us rejoice and be glad and give the glory to Him, for the marriage of the Lamb has come and His bride has made herself ready.' Rev. 19:7

These are just a few of the problems with the Pre-Wrath theory. There are many more – too many to write about."[26]

Why? Because you violated the Biblical rule. You're supposed to let the Bible speak out to us what it has to say, not enter into it with your "preconceived ideas." By so doing, you turned the "Blessed Hope" into a "Beating of the Bride." And I don't think that's what God had in mind when He gave the Blessed

Promise of the Rapture to His Beloved Church. Let the Scriptures speak for themselves. Don't "twist" them in to what you "want" them to say. And isn't that what we're supposed to do if we're not going to be deceived?

The **seventh problem** with the Pre-Wrath teaching of the Rapture is that **It Confuses the Atonement of the Church**. Just when you thought it couldn't get even more messed up with the Pre-Wrath Rapture theory, it gets even worse. In fact, dare I say totally blasphemous. I say that because another one of the major false tenants of the Pre-Wrath theory is not only a "confusion" of the identity of the Church and the promises made to the Church by the Lord Jesus, but also a horrible "confusion" as to the "cleansing" of the Church. Believe it or not, the Pre-Wrath Rapture theory says it's *not* Jesus Who cleanses us! The following researcher points out this fatal flaw:

"The Pre-Wrath view states that the *reason* for believers going through part of the Tribulation is that 'the Church' needs to go through a period of *cleansing* before the Rapture. The period of persecution, according to the Pre-Wrath view, is necessary to return 'the Church' to serving the Lord and *purging* it of sin."[27]

Excuse me? What did you just say? The Bible says that it is Jesus Christ and Him *alone* Who cleanses us and purges us from our sins!

Titus 2:11-14 "For the grace of God that brings salvation has appeared to all men. It teaches us to say 'No' to ungodliness and worldly passions, and to live self-controlled, upright and godly lives in this present age, while we wait for the blessed hope – the glorious appearing of our great God and Savior, Jesus Christ, Who gave Himself for us to redeem us from all wickedness and to *purify* for Himself a people that are His very own, eager to do what is good."

Hebrews 1:3 "The Son is the radiance of God's glory and the exact representation of His being, sustaining all things by His powerful Word. After He had provided *purification* for sins, He sat down at the right hand of the Majesty in heaven."

Hebrews 10:14 "Because by one sacrifice He has made *perfect forever* those who are being made holy."

1 John 1:7 "But if we walk in the light, as He is in the light, we have fellowship with one another, and the blood of Jesus, his Son, *purifies* us from *all sin*."

1 John 1:9 "If we confess our sins, He is faithful and just and will forgive us our sins and *purify us* from *all unrighteousness*."

Not only is the Rapture our "blessed hope" but so is the Cross of Christ. What makes us "worthy" to be with Christ in heaven, including our departure to heaven via the Rapture, is His atoning sacrifice on the Cross and that *alone*. Anything else is not trusting *soley* upon the work of Jesus Christ and therefore is not only dangerous but blasphemous! How far can you push this and no longer be trusting in the Good News of the Gospel anymore? Think about it. If we somehow "purify" ourselves during the 7-year Tribulation to make ourselves "acceptable" to God, then why in the world did Jesus go to the Cross in the first place!

Furthermore, how is this blasphemous idea that the Church is "cleansed" and "purged" of sin during the 7-year Tribulation any different than the false blasphemous teaching of the Roman Catholic Church called "purgatory?" That is the false belief that a person "purges" (hence purg-atory; a place to purge) themselves of sin through their own suffering to be made acceptable to God? Answer: The Pre-Wrath false cleansing teaching is the *same false teaching* of Purgatory only applied to the Rapture! It's blasphemous through and through as these researchers also admit:

"The problem with this idea (that the Church needs to go through a period of *cleansing* before the Rapture in the 7-year Tribulation) is brought into the light by the question, 'What about all the Christians saved in the past 2000 years who have died and are with the Lord?' Why should a handful, in comparison to all the believers who have lived since Pentecost, have to endure this supposed cleansing?

Where in the New Testament does God state that He will purge 'the Church' of sin in the 7-year Tribulation before believers are Raptured? God says in Christ are all sins forgiven. Where then is the supposed need of a cleansing before the Rapture can occur?

The Pre-Wrath people may counter by saying 'the Church' has gone into apostasy and in the first 3 ½ years of the Tribulation it will be purged and cleansed through persecution. The problem with that conclusion is that false doctrine has always, through the past two thousand years plagued Churches, and false religion will continue to flourish in the first half of the Tribulation with the Antichrist and the false prophet joining all the religions of the world in to a one world religion. The false 'Christian' Churches will certainly go into the Tribulation as will the cults.

Nothing in God's word says there will be a purifying of 'the Church' before the Rapture can occur. The Bible says that the blood of Jesus is sufficient to cleanse us of all sin (1 John 1:7). The idea that the Church needs to be purified creates a Christian Purgatory, which is a blasphemy of the blood of Jesus."[28]

And that, my friend, is something you desperately *do not* want to do. But that's what you get when you twist things around like the Pre-Wrath Rapture theory does to "make" their "preconceived ideas" supposedly work.

However, if you allow the Bible to speak to you, (which is what we're supposed to do) you come away with a "blessed assurance" and a "blessed hope" and Jesus *alone* and His work on the Cross is what purifies us from *all* our sins, and therefore we are *already* worthy to leave with Him at the Rapture prior to the 7-year Tribulation. That is what you get *if* you stick with the Bible. And isn't that what we're supposed to do if we're not going to be deceived?

Chapter Sixteen

The Problems with Mid-Trib

The **third position** on the Rapture that has some serious problems with it is **The Mid-Trib Position**. Now, even though this position is also relatively new and more in the minority position, I still nonetheless feel we need to cover at least the highlights of it. Here is a basic explanation of their belief on the Rapture:

"The Mid-Tribulation Rapture seems to be a compromise between the Pre-Tribulation and the Post-Tribulation views. According to this view the seven-year tribulation is divided into two halves; the first half described as the wrath of man, and the last half as the wrath of God. (Hence some people call this position the 'original' pre-wrath position.) The Rapture of the Church will take place at the middle of the tribulation period three-and-one-half years prior to the Second Coming of Jesus Christ."[1]

So as you can see, the Mid-Trib position on the Rapture is also radically different than the Pre-Trib position. The Pre-Trib Rapture says the Church will leave the earth "prior" to the 7-year Tribulation, and the Mid-Trib Rapture says the Church will remain on earth until the "middle" of the 7-year Tribulation. Obviously, both cannot be true, so which one is correct? How can we not be deceived? Well, just as we put the Pre-Trib position underneath a serious microscope and dealt with the various accusations that are thrown its way, let's now do the same with the Mid-Trib position. I think you will soon see, it has some serious problems.

The key word there in the description is "compromise." Another fatal error. This is something you definitely *do not* want to do when you approach the Bible in order to discover its truth. Just like with the "preconceived ideas" of the Pre-Wrath Rapture theory, so it is with the Mid-Tribulation Rapture theory. Once you approach the Bible with "preconceived ideas" or in this case, an "attitude of compromise," what comes next is a jumbled mess of "confusion" and "errors." This is part of the reason why the Mid-Trib position of the Rapture is in a minority view, as this man states:

"In a real sense, Mid-Tribulationalism is a compromise view between the other two alternate positions and lacks the strength of either, meanwhile being involved in additional problems peculiar to its own prophetic system. The slender number of its advocates and the dearth of convincing Mid-Tribulational literature both put a large question mark over the validity of the viewpoint."[2]

In other words, it's so full of problems not many hold to it. But nonetheless, let's now take a look at some of these problems and "errors" created by this "attitude of compromise" concerning the Rapture.

The **first problem** with the Mid-Trib teaching of the Rapture is that **It Places the Church in the 7-year Tribulation**. Now, as we go through these various problems with the Mid-Trib position, you will notice that several of them have already been covered in great detail in the previous two sections dealing with the problems with the Post-Trib and Pre-Wrath positions, not to mention the rest of the study prior. We've already covered such problems with the other positions such as:

- They Place the Church Under God's Wrath.
- They State that the Tribulation Saints Will Be Protected.
- They Replace Israel with the Church.
- They Confuse the Rapture with God's Judgment.
- They Confuse the Rapture with the Day of the Lord.
- They Confuse the Rapture with the Second Coming.
- They Create a Problem with the Millennium Population.
- They Create a Problem with the Millennium Separation.
- They Create a Problem with the Christian Rewards.
- They Create a Problem with the Resurrection.
- They Create a Problem with the Antichrist.
- They Destroy the Meaning of Jesus' Wedding.
- They Destroy the Purpose of the Rapture.

- They Confuse the Timing of God's Wrath.
- They Confuse the Timing of the Day of the Lord.
- They Confuse the Timing of the Judgments of the Lord.
- They Confuse the Identity of the Church.
- They Confuse the Placement of the Church.
- They Confuse the Promises to the Church.
- They Confuse the Atonement of the Church.

Therefore, to avoid a total redundancy for those who may have skipped straight through to this section on the Mid-Tribulation position of the Rapture *before* familiarizing yourself with the previous material, I encourage you to review those other sections. But as you saw, right out of the gates, just like the Post-Trib and Pre-Wrath theories on the Rapture, the Mid-Trib position also places the Church in the 7-year Tribulation. Yet, as we saw before, in great detail, this cannot be. Why? Because the purpose of the 7-year Tribulation as mentioned in the Book of Daniel has nothing to do with the Church.

One, the Church was a "mystery" and nowhere around when Daniel was writing concerning the 70th week or 7-year Tribulation. Its purpose is all about God restoring and redeeming a remnant of Israel preparing them for the Millennial Kingdom, as well as pouring out His wrath on the Gentile nations or "inhabitants of the earth", not the Church. (See sections on the problems of Post-Trib and Pre-Wrath)

Two, the 7-year Tribulation is a time when God pours out His wrath during the *entire* 7 years, not 3½ years as the Mid-Trib position would have you and I believe. (See sections on the problems of Post-Trib and Pre-Wrath.) Therefore, since the Church is not "appointed unto God's wrath" the Church cannot be in this time frame. One researcher puts it this way:

"One problem with the Mid-Tribulation Rapture timing view is that it believes that the Church will go through the Tribulation period for three and a half years but be removed before the great tribulation starts. This would assume that the Church will undergo some of God's wrath but not the worst of it. This is completely contradictory to the rest of the Bible.

The Scriptures (1 Thessalonians 5:9) tell us that the Church is not destined to wrath. And to say that we would experience wrath is to contradict God's ways and character. So, this is another reason why the Mid-Tribulation Rapture timing view fails the test of sound and logical analysis."[3]

Why? Because you went into the Bible with an "attitude of compromise" and you came out with a "tangled mess." Yet, the Scripture is clear. The Church is not "appointed unto" God's wrath. Therefore they cannot be in the 7-year Tribulation. Let the Bible speak for itself and define the terms itself and everything will turn out just fine. And isn't that what we're supposed to do if we're not going to be deceived?

The **second problem** with the Mid-Trib teaching of the Rapture is that **It Removes God's Wrath in the 7-year Tribulation**. Instead of admitting that the Church has no basis for being in the 7-year Tribulation at all, as the Bible declares, the Mid-Trib position, just like the Post-Trib and Pre-Wrath positions on the Rapture, begin to "dance around" this issue and tweak the Scripture in order to "make" their "compromise" work. That's why the Mid-Trib position would have you and I believe that God's wrath does *not* include the full 7 years, but rather only the final 3 ½ years, so as to "fit" their version of the Rapture which they say takes place in the middle. Therefore, they say the Church is not around to experience God's wrath, so problem solved. Nice try, but as we saw before in great detail, this is simply not true.

First of all, as was stated earlier, the *entire* 7 years of the 7-year Tribulation is a time when God pours out His wrath, not just 3½ years as the Mid-Trib position would have you and I believe. (See sections on the problems of Post-Trib and Pre-Wrath). God's wrath begins clearly with the opening of the first seal in Revelation 6 and continues throughout up to the final climactic bowl judgments toward the end of the 7-year Tribulation. To say that the first half of the 7-year Tribulation is not God's wrath but man's is a serious error, as these researchers point out:

"This flies in the face of the fact that the entire Tribulation period is the wrath of God, not just the last half. The Mid-Tribulationist will often try to confuse when the wrath of God starts. The two sided scroll in Revelation is ALWAYS a sign of wrath in the Bible. The scroll encompasses the judgments of Revelation which are the seal, trumpet, and bowl judgments.

So there is no sound and theological way to conclude that the Church will go through some of the wrath of God, but not the worst of it. That is simply not correct.

The Mid-Tribulation Rapture view assumes that God's wrath will not begin until the second half of the Tribulation period. This assumption exists in the minds of some on the grounds that the Antichrist will rule the world in peace and prosperity for the first half of the Tribulation period, and the rest of the apocalyptic judgments will not come upon the world until the second half of the Tribulation period.

However, God's wrath will take place during the first half as well as the second half of the Tribulation period. During the first half of the Tribulation period, the Antichrist will be unveiled. Consequently, his coming will be just as much a judgment upon the world as will be the remaining judgments, many of which will take place during the second half of the Tribulation period.

The revelation of the Antichrist will be a spiritual judgment sent by God for the purpose of deceiving many of those who have rejected the gospel. Just as the opening of seals 2 through 7 will bring horrific judgments upon the world, the opening of the first seal, which will reveal the Antichrist, will also bring forth horrible divine judgment upon the world."[4]

So much for a peaceful "first half" or beginning to the 7-year Tribulation! It's all God's wrath through and through, that's why the Church is exempt from it. In fact, see for yourself in the Biblical order of events concerning the first half of the 7-year Tribulation:

"The events of Revelation 6-10, reveal a very terrible time for the Earth. Note the terrible events of the seven seal judgments and the six trumpet judgments.

Verse 2 White horse: This rider goes forth conquering and to conquer. It is probably the Antichrist who appears to be white in that he offers peace to the world. He deceives the nations and all the while he is talking peace he is conquering the nations of earth and setting up himself as the world dictator. It is imperative to acknowledge who it is that is opening the Seals and directing the Seal Judgments. It is plainly the Lamb who is the Lord Jesus Christ. It is ridiculous to conclude that these terrible judgments are the 'wrath of man' and not part of God's wrath. Without question Revelation 6:1 is telling us that the Seal Judgments are the beginning of God's pouring His wrath on the earth. They are initiated by Jesus Christ and under His direction and control and part of His plan. On this point alone the Mid-Trib view is shown to be in error.

Verse 4 Red horse: Rider is given power to take peace from the earth, the people kill one another in war. It is Jesus Christ, the Lamb who gives the power for the rider of the red horse to take peace from the earth and bring war.

Verse 5-6 The Lord Jesus Christ opens the third seal and the **Black horse** rider is allowed to cause famine on earth.

Verse 8 The Lamb opens the fourth seal and the **Pale horse** comes forward. The Pale horse rider is named 'death' and Hell follows him. One fourth of the earth is killed with the sword, hunger, death, and beasts of earth. It seems inconceivable that anyone would conclude that these seals are not directed and brought on earth by the Lord Jesus. It is He that is opening the seals and the riders are going forth in power to perform the Lord's plan. Once again the Mid-Trib view fails to take this important truth into consideration.

Verse 9-11 The Tribulation saints cry out to God, 'How long before you judge the earth and avenge our blood.' These are said to be saints slain for the Word of God because they would not recant their testimony of salvation in Jesus Christ. Verse 11 further identifies them with their 'brethren' still on the earth and states those too would be killed. Clearly these are people who are saved during the first half of the Tribulation and there is nothing to identify them as believers of the Church Age. They are crying out to God to avenge their deaths plainly recognizing that the Lord is in control and He is bringing about these devastating events.

Verse 12 Sixth Seal: Great earthquake, sun becomes as black as sackcloth, moon as blood. (Volcanic eruptions) Stars fall from heavens. (Meteors) Every mountain and island is moved by the earthquake. Everyone on earth flees to caves and rocks in mountains, begging them to fall on them and hide them from the face of Christ and His wrath. Without question only God can do these catastrophic things in nature. These terrible catastrophes in nature are being brought about by God, not man and it is self-evident they are part of God's purging of the earth and of His wrath.

Verse 17 'For the great day of his wrath is come; and who shall be able to stand?' This statement contextually comes after these cataclysmic events and is intended to sum up what has been revealed. The next statement is Revelation 7:1 and begins with the statement 'And after these things I saw four angels.' Grammatically, the thought is changed and a new event is to be revealed. This restricts the statement of Revelation 6:17 to referring to the five seals that have been just described. There can be no question that the Lord is saying the seal judgments are part of God's wrath and this negates the Mid-Trib view as being accurate.

First Angel: It rains hail, fire mingled with blood and a third part of the trees and grass are burned up. (Rev. 8:7) Who is it that directs angels?

Second Angel: A great mountain burning with fire cast into the sea and third part of the waters turned to blood.(Rev. 8:8-9) Who is it that directs nature?

Third Angel: Third of creatures in the sea killed and third of all ships. Great Star from heaven falls and third part of all fresh water is made bitter. (Rev. 8:10-11)Who is it that controls the universe and the stars of heaven?

Fourth Angel: Third of the sun, moon and stars smitten. Third part of the day is darkened. (Rev. 8:12) Who only has the power to smite the sun, moon and stars?

The angel flying through heaven saying with a loud voice, Woe, woe, woe. Clearly all that is happening is a continuation of the Seal Judgments and is part of God's wrath.

Fifth Angel: (First Woe) Bottomless pit opened and scorpions that have power to kill men by tormenting them five months till they die.

Sixth Angel: Four demons loosed from Euphrates River. They kill a third part of all men on earth. Revelation 9:20, 'And the rest of the men which were not killed by these plagues yet repented not of the works of their hands, that they should not worship devils, and idols of gold, and silver, and brass, and stone, and of wood: which neither can see, nor hear, nor walk' (Revelation 9:20).

Even a casual reading of Revelation 6-10 reveals these terrible events are a part of the wrath of God poured down on the earth. The time of God's wrath begins with the first Seal and continues through the sixth Trumpet judgments. *This surely is not a time of 'peace on earth' as the Mid-Tribulationalists would try to have us believe.*

It is completely erroneous to say that the first three and half years of the Tribulation are not part of the wrath of God and are only the 'wrath of man.'"[5]

That is, that's what you come away with if you stick with the Bible. Unfortunately that's not what the Mid-Trib position does. To make matters worse, rather than concede this Biblical truth, the Mid-Trib proponents then try to bolster their faulty position on the Rapture by having you and I believe that the 7-

year Tribulation isn't even really 7 years to begin with, it's only 3½. Say what? Are you serious?

As we saw before in great detail, the reason why we have a 7-year Tribulation in the first place is because it's Daniel's final week of his 70ᵗʰ week prophecy. The first 69 weeks have come and passed culminating in Christ's Triumphal entry, with one week or 7 years to go, hence the 7-year Tribulation. How can you say a "week" a "7" isn't really a 7? Also, this would destroy the dating and timing of the first 69 weeks and Jesus' Triumphal entry. If a "7" is not really a 7 then the timing of the 69 weeks is totally off! All because you want to "compromise" your position, you make mincemeat out of the rest of the Scripture, as this researcher states:

"The Mid-Trib position holds that the first three and one half years of Daniel's seventieth week belong to the end of the Church age. However, the literal fulfillment of Daniel's seventieth week calls for a future period of seven years, and Daniel 9:25-27 clearly identifies this "week" with the Tribulation period and the rule of Antichrist. The "prince that shall come" confirms the covenant for one week, not for half of that time.

It is impossible to get away from a literal seven year Tribulation period without making one of two concessions: First, if the entire last "week" is to be fulfilled in three and one half years, the important chronology of the rest of Daniel's prophecy of seventy weeks is destroyed.

Second, if only the last half of a seven year "week" falls in the Tribulation period, then the first half must overlap the Church age. Yet as it has been seen from Matthew 24 and Revelation 6-19, the Tribulation is highly Jewish in content, and during this period the Church is never seen. To cast even half of such a period back into the Church age would result in the greatest of confusion.

For instance, how could God seal 144,000 for service from the twelve tribes of Israel in an age when His witnessing body is the Church, when converted Jews enter into the Church, into the unity of the body of Christ, and lose their former identity as Israelites? In summary the Mid-Tribulation Rapture timing view is not sound and Biblical."[6]

Why? Because you went into the Bible with an "attitude of compromise" and you came out with a "tangled mess." Yet, the Scripture is clear. The 7-year Tribulation is a *full* 7 years, not just 3½. Let the Bible speak for itself and define the terms itself and everything will turn out just fine. And isn't that what we're supposed to do if we're not going to be deceived?

The **third problem** with the Mid-Trib teaching of the Rapture is that **It Places the Rapture in the 7-year Tribulation**. Now, in order to "make" their timing of the Rapture "fit into" the 7-year Tribulation, the Mid-Tribulationist must find some sort of verse to twist into a Rapture event, specifically at the mid-way point. And that's precisely what they've done with Revelation Chapter 11. The only problem is, as we will soon see, Revelation 11 has nothing to do with the Rapture of the Church. Once again, the Mid-Tribulationalist has "compromised" the Scripture to "make" their position work. But all they've effectively done is create an even bigger mess of problems.

For instance, they would have you and I believe that the account of the Two Witnesses mentioned in Revelation Chapter 11 is actually speaking of the Rapture of the Church in the middle of the 7-year Tribulation.

Revelation 11:11-12 "But after the three and a half days a breath of life from God entered them, and they stood on their feet, and terror struck those who saw them. Then they heard a loud voice from heaven saying to them, 'Come up here.' And they went up to heaven in a cloud, while their enemies looked on."

Well, there you have it. The Church just got Raptured in the middle of the 7-year Tribulation. I know....say what? I'm telling you, once you enter into the Scripture with an "attitude of compromise" you'll try anything to "make" your position work. Saying that the Two Witnesses in Revelation Chapter 11 are "symbolic" of the Church being Raptured during this time is not only ludicrous, it's flat out unbiblical, as these researchers point out:

"According to the Mid-Tribulational theory, the Rapture of the Church is seen symbolized in the resurrection and ascension of the two witnesses, but the two witnesses are not symbols. The normal, literal interpretation of the passage, including as it does the details of their dress, their prophecy, and their plagues, indicates that they are individual men.

They are spoken of as "two prophets," and when they are killed, their dead bodies lie a definite period of time in a literal city which is identified as Jerusalem. It would not make good sense to say that *symbolic* bodies were killed, only to lie on *literal* streets, any more than to deny them *literal* burial in *symbolic* graves. The narrative of the two witnesses is evidently meant to be taken *literally*.

Also, it is claimed that these two witnesses symbolize the two classes at the Rapture – the 'Dead' and the 'Alive.' However, this idea breaks down when it is remembered that *both witnesses die* and must be raised. How could one of the two witnesses symbolize the Church that is alive at the Rapture and the other symbolize the Church that is asleep (dead)? In Revelation 11, both witnesses are killed. How do you kill saints that are already dead?

Furthermore, the 'cloud' of Revelation 11:12 that the Mid-Tribulationalist identifies with that of 1 Thessalonians 4:17, 'a definite reference to the Lord's presence' is exceedingly precarious. Many times in Scripture the presence of God is indicated by a cloud, but that is no indication that two such references in two *distinct* books by *different* authors necessarily speak of the same appearing of the Lord.

Nor is the 'great voice' which bids the witnesses to 'Come up hither' of any necessity even remotely connected with the 'shout,' or even with the 'voice of the archangel' of the Pauline passage.

And a very important distinction that is left out is that at the Rapture 'the Lord himself shall descend from heaven,' while here in Revelation 11, the voice comes *from heaven* and calls them up *thither*."[7]

In other words, the whole thing falls apart because you're "compromising" the Scripture to make it "fit" your position. But it gets even worse. To further try to "sell us" on the idea that Revelation Chapter 11 is really speaking of the Rapture of the Church, they would then say that the trumpet "blown" in this Chapter is the same trumpet "related" to the Rapture.

Revelation 11:15 "The seventh angel sounded his trumpet, and there were loud voices in heaven, which said: 'The kingdom of the world has become the kingdom of our Lord and of his Christ, and He will reign for ever and ever.'"

Well, there you have it. The Rapture trumpet blew in the middle of the 7-year Tribulation and therefore the Church exited at the mid-way point. I know, I know…say what? First of all as we saw in the previous section dealing with the problems with the Pre-Wrath position of the Rapture, just because you see the word "trumpet" in the Scripture, doesn't' mean it's the same one as another trumpet in Scripture, let alone serving the same purpose. As was stated:

"There are several 'last trumpets' in Bible and Jewish tradition. When you have trumpets commonly used throughout the Bible, it's foolish to just assume any two of the 62 trumps or trumpets are prophetically related.

In the movies Ben-Hur and The Wizard of Oz, I recall hearing the sounding of trumpets. Are both these trumpets somehow prophetically related?

If your friend John said he went to his favorite restaurant last night, and another friend Larry said he also went to his favorite restaurant last night, is it logical for you to assume they both went to the same restaurant? Obviously not, because even though John and Larry went to their favorite restaurants, they may have had two different eating establishments in mind.

The same logic should apply with the word trumpet. With such a blind devotion to this one similarity, I have to wonder if these last tumpeters are able to distinguish the difference between Tylenol and Exlax. They're both over-the-counter drugs, they come in pill form, and they can also be found in a medicine cabinet. Of course, one will make your headache disappear and the other will make your toilet paper disappear."[8]

So just because you see the word "trumpet" doesn't mean it's the same "trumpet" as another, let alone serving the same purpose. In fact, once you carefully look at the Bible concerning the 7th trumpet mentioned in Revelation Chapter 11 and comparing it to the Rapture trumpet, you'll see clearly that there is no way you can say these are one and the same trumpet, let alone the same event, as these researchers also conclude:

"The identification of the *seventh trumpet* of Revelation 11:15 with the *last trump* of I Corinthians 15:52 and I Thessalonians 4:16 is probably the most important key to the Mid-Tribulation Rapture theory. The entire structure of this view stands or falls with the ability of its adherents to prove three related propositions: first, that the seventh trumpet falls in the middle of the week; second, nothing before this trumpet is Tribulation; and third, that the seventh trumpet is identical with the 'last trump.'

However, it is assumed without any particular proof that the seventh trumpet falls in the middle of the week. Yet, in 11:17-19, the sounding of the seventh trumpet is clearly associated with the reign of Christ, the judging of the dead, and the rewarding of 'thy servants the prophets,' all of which occur at the end of the

Tribulation with the revelation of Christ and the resurrection of Israel, at which time 'The kingdoms of this world are become the kingdoms of our Lord, and of his Christ; and he shall reign for ever and ever' (Rev. 11:15). It is most evident that the seventh trumpet brings the chronology of the book right up toward the time of the end, and makes it exceedingly difficult to identify it with a supposed Mid-Tribulational Rapture.

Also, Mid-Tribulationalists must labor to explain why they believe nothing *preceding* the seventh trumpet belongs to the Tribulation, which is clearly not true. Both difficulties grow out of a fallacious identifying of the seventh trumpet of John with the 'last trump' of Paul.

However, Pre-Tribulationalists, who make no such assumption, are free to give the seventh trumpet a normal and natural place in the chronology of the Tribulation, evidently well toward the end of the period, yet not on the last day, and certainly not in the middle of the week.

The fact is, any identification of these two trumpets is, at best, based on the surface similarity that one is designated 'last,' while the other completes a series of seven. In rather a naïve way, Mid-Tribulationalists assume that this is sufficient evidence to prove that they are identical.

There are many references to trumpets in the Word of God. Unless there is clear and concrete evidence, it is most precarious to identify trumpets found in different parts of the Bible. Paul's 'last trump' need not be the same as John's 'seventh trumpet,' and particularly so, since different subjects are in view.

Then too, trumpets serve for various purposes. In Leviticus 23:24, there is 'a memorial of blowing of trumpets, a holy convocation' (Num. 29:1-6). From Numbers 10:1-10 it is apparent that the same trumpets were used for vastly different purposes: 'the calling of the assembly,' 'the journeying of the camps,' the gathering together of the 'princes of Israel,' to 'blow an alarm,' and to 'blow with trumpets over your burnt-offerings, and over the sacrifices.'

The actual blowing of the trumpets was not the central issue. The important question is, 'what tune did the trumpets play?' Even though two trumpets may be clearly identified as the same, that in itself does not suffice to prove that each trumpet blast commands the same action.

Moreover, there are distinct points of dissimilarity between these trumpets. The contexts in question are vastly different. The trumpets of Revelation introduce judgments of God; they bring into being a time of unparalleled suffering, and comprehend the godless nations of the earth.

The trumpet of 1 Corinthians 15 and 1 Thessalonians 4, distinctly for the Church, implies nothing of judgment or anything else connected with the godless, and introduces for the believer in Christ a time of unprecedented glory and privilege, even the joy of His presence.

In the trumpet portion of the Revelation, there is no hint of translation, but a rushing *onward* toward the climax of God's fearful wrath and certain judgment.

There is no parallel here to a trumpet signal for the hosts of the redeemed to ascend, characterized as it must be: 'in a moment, in the twinkling of an eye, at the last trump.' All this speaks of brevity, of speed, of an instantaneous translation, and certainly not of a prolonged trumpet blast.

And finally, if you look at the text closely in Revelation 11, the ascending of the Two Witnesses to heaven occurs *prior* to the blowing of the 7th Trumpet. They're going to heaven occurs 3 verses prior to the blowing of the 7th trumpet judgment. That, then, means that their ascension into heaven occurs as part of the 6th Trumpet. So even the Mid-Tribulationalist gets their timing wrong!

The fact is, the 7th trumpet has nothing to do with the Rapture. A Revelation 11 Rapture makes havoc with any attempt of understanding the chronology of Biblical eschatology."[9]

Why? Because you went into the Bible with an "attitude of compromise" and you came out with a "tangled mess." Yet, the Scripture is clear. The Rapture of the Church does not take place during *any time* of the 7-year Tribulation and it has nothing to do with the Two Witnesses and the 7th Trumpet judgment. Let the Bible speak for itself and define the terms itself and everything will turn out just fine. And isn't that what we're supposed to do if we're not going to be deceived?

The **fourth problem** with the Mid-Trib teaching of the Rapture is that **It Removes Imminency before the 7-year Tribulation**. As with all the other positions on the Rapture, save the Pre-Trib position, the Mid-Tribulational positon totally destroys the doctrine of Imminency. That is, the Rapture could occur at any moment, it is imminent. Therefore I better get busy living for Jesus and sharing the Gospel as fast as I can. (See sections on the problems of Post-Trib and Pre-Wrath as well as the section defining and defending Pre-Trib)

Yet, based on what we just saw, the Mid-Trib position robs the Christian of this wonderful "motivating" truth. By their own definition of their "timing" on the Rapture I can now "calculate" the departure and hence get lazy and goof off until such event occurs (something that the other positions ironically accuse the Pre-Trib position of doing even though it is the *only one* that maintains the imminent 'unknown hour'). This rejection of the Imminent return of Christ is not only unscriptural, it's harmful to the believer, as these researchers admit:

"The Mid-Tribulational position rejects an imminent return of Christ, while fostering an unscriptural emphasis upon date-setting. If the Rapture occurs in the middle of the Tribulation, the date of the Rapture can be set, and if it can be set, believers today need not be in constant preparation for, or concerned about, Christ's imminent return.

According to Daniel the first three and a half years begin with the specific event of the signing of the covenant between Israel and the Gentile Antichrist. This surely will be an international event that all will know of and therefore anyone could then easily calculate when the Rapture would take place.

If the Rapture is at the middle of the Tribulation, then it is not imminent, but at least three and one half years away at any point in time prior to the beginning of the Tribulation. Christians would know that when the treaty with the Antichrist is signed it is three and a half years before Christ comes for them. Clearly this destroys the teaching of the imminent return of Christ.

Yet, we Christians are to look for the imminent return of Jesus Christ, not the Antichrist. The Churches are told to live in the light of the imminent coming of the Lord, the Rapture. Believers are to always be ready, living godly lives and be looking for Christ to come. The teaching is that Christ could return at any time, therefore we are to be ready. There is an urgent need in being ready now because Christ could come at any time.

Philippians 3:20 "But our citizenship is in heaven. And we eagerly await a Savior from there, the Lord Jesus Christ."

Colossians 3:4 "When Christ, who is your life, appears, then you also will appear with Him in glory."

1 Thessalonians 1:10 "And to wait for his Son from heaven, whom He raised from the dead – Jesus, Who rescues us from the coming wrath."

1 Timothy 6:14 "To keep this command without spot or blame until the appearing of our Lord Jesus Christ."

James 5:8 "You too, be patient and stand firm, because the Lord's coming is near."

1 Thessalonians 5:6 "So then, let us not be like others, who are asleep, but let us be alert and self-controlled."

Titus 2:13 "While we wait for the blessed hope – the glorious appearing of our great God and Savior, Jesus Christ."

Revelation 3:3 "Remember, therefore, what you have received and heard; obey it, and repent. But if you do not wake up, I will come like a thief, and you will not know at what time I will come to you."

Notice how no signs are given to look for, but rather we are to be watchful and ready for His coming. Churches today that are living in the period of time *before* the 7-year Tribulation are to be actively doing the work of the Lord through missions and being sound in doctrine. Christ tells His Church that it will not go through the 'hour of temptation, which shall come upon all the world, to try them that dwell upon the earth.'

Clearly the Lord is telling us to be expecting the Rapture at any moment."[10]

Why? Because it's a real event that's really going to happen when you least expect it. The Rapture's Imminency will "cleanse you" of any and all "procrastination" and will certainly spur on a much more "fruitful" attitude towards the commands of the Lord, like getting busy sharing the Gospel and living a holy life, being the best positive example for Jesus before the lost.

However, if you listen to the other positions on the Rapture, including the Mid-Trib position, all of these positive benefits are destroyed. Why? Because you went into the Bible with an "attitude of compromise" and you came out with a "tangled mess." You destroyed this Imminency!

Yet, the Scripture is clear. The Rapture is Imminent and you better get ready! It's high time to make the most of our time for Jesus, and get busy sharing the Gospel as fast as we can to as many as we can. There's no time to waste! The reason why is because this is *urgent*! People's lives are on the line and how much suffering and pain could they avoid if we'd get seriously motivated to share what's most important in life, the Gospel, like this man shares.

"There is a true story told of an Indian missionary. The young man was in India during a great festival in which all of the Hindus travel to the river Ganges to wash themselves for the forgiveness of sins. Thousands of Hindus traveled for miles to wash themselves in this river.

The story goes that this missionary was crossing a bridge over the river when he saw a woman weeping uncontrollably. He approached her to see what was wrong.

'My six month old baby boy. I just threw him into the river.' She told him that her husband was unable to work. They had no money to provide for the family.

She told him that her sins were so many that no one knew about. She was burdened with guilt and shame. She needed forgiveness and blessings. In order to receive the blessing and forgiveness of the goddess Ganges, she said, 'I have given her the most valuable offering I could give her. My six month old baby boy. I just threw him into the river.'

The missionary proceeded to explain the gospel to her. To tell her that she didn't have to kill her son. God had sent his son in order to save mankind.

When he was done the woman looked at him. 'Why didn't you come a half hour sooner?' She asked. 'I didn't have to kill my son.' And with that she began weeping again.

She's not the only one, you know. There are millions crying out, 'Why?' Longing and searching for an answer to the void in their heart. Looking for forgiveness and salvation."[11]

How many people do we know that would say the same thing to us? "Why didn't you come to me a half hour sooner, Christian co-worker, Christian neighbor, Christian family member? (We're all missionaries, you know?) Why did you let yourself get so distracted! I didn't have to lose my job. I didn't have to divorce my spouse. I didn't have to ruin my body with drugs or immorality...I didn't have to go into the 7-year Tribulation....I didn't have to go to hell...Why didn't you come a half hour sooner?

Folks, if we're too busy to share the Gospel...*we're too busy*! Have we become lazy and distracted from what's really important in life? And contrary to the critics of the Pre-Trib postion, that's precisely what these other positions on the Rapture do to us! They destroy this Imminency! They rob us of the cleansing effects of the Pre-Trib Biblical Rapture. That Christ could come back and get us at any time! I don't have time to goof off! I've got to get busy sharing the Gospel with as many as I can as fast as I can! It's actually the other positions *encouraging me* to *be lazy* and to *not care* as much and to *lose* any and all sense of urgency, when people like that woman there, in their last hours, are in desperate need of a Savior. Time is ticking! I don't have time to waste.

Therefore, let us not be deceived. Rather, let us allow the Bible to speak for itself on the timing of the Rapture so as to not miss out on this wonderful blessing. Let us allow the Scripture to cleanse us with this truth of the Imminent Return of Jesus Christ, as the Bible and Pre-Trib position states, and let us be that Church, those missionaries, that *make it there in time* for people like that lady and her child, amen?

Part V

The Point of the Rapture

Chapter Seventeen

The Proper Attitude Towards the Rapture

Which brings us to the **seventh thing** we're going to look at to avoid being deceived and that is **What is Our Attitude Towards the Rapture**? I say that because, as we just saw, the whole point of the Biblical teaching of the Rapture is to "encourage" the individual believer to *always* be ready for the Lord's return. How will He find you when He comes, as this story illustrates:

"The story is told about a certain man who visited a small one-room country school. He made the promise that he would give a prize to the student whose desk was found in the very best order when he came back. He gave no indication, not even a hint, when he would return.

He had no more than left the room when one of the students announced that she meant to win the prize. She was a girl whose desk was usually a mess. Her schoolmates laughed at her saying, 'Why Mary, your desk is always out of order. It's never clean.'

'But, starting right now,' Mary responded, 'I'm going to clean it every Monday morning.'

'But, supposing our visitor comes at the end of the week?' someone asked.

'Well then,' Mary said, 'I'll clean it up every morning.'

'But, what if he comes at the *end* of the day?' another questioned.

At that thought, Mary was silent for a moment. Then her face lit up and she said, 'I know what I'll do. I'll just keep it clean all the time!'

Christ may come at any time. Therefore we must keep our lives clean ALL THE TIME!

Our Heavenly Visitor is coming, but we do not know when. It could be soon. We need to be ready always. He is not coming to stay in our home. He is coming to take us to His home. We need to be ready and prepared for His coming. When He comes we do not want to be found in the wrong place, doing wrong things, saying wrong things. Wouldn't you want Him to find you serving Him, pleasing Him, thanking Him and obeying Him? WILL YOU BE READY? IT MAY BE TODAY!"[1]

Furthermore, as we saw, the teaching of the Rapture is likewise meant to "motivate" the Church to get busy doing what Jesus commanded us to do. That is, share the Gospel and be that godly example for Him in the midst of a world full of lost people. Unfortunately, this seems to no longer be the case. Not from a fault of the teaching of the Rapture, but rather a certain unfortunate "attitude" towards the Rapture.

Instead of working together as Christians in these Last Days sharing the Gospel to as many as we can, the logical response to the "Blessed Hope," it has now been turned into the "Big Beating." Instead of allowing the teaching of the Rapture to "motivate" us to share the Gospel even more, some people are now using it as a hammer to "divide us" and "distract us" from the main task at hand.

For instance, I have personally received emails saying that I am not only "working for satan" because I hold to the Pre-Trib position on the Rapture, but I am also being informed that I am a "horrible Pastor," "not even saved," and "headed to the Lake of Fire." Say what? All because I hold to the Pre-Trib Rapture position?

And yet, herein lies the problem. The doctrine of the Rapture is not a "salvific" issue in the Church. Rather, it's a "secondary" issue. Your position on the Rapture does not determine your salvation. You can be a Pre-Trib, Mid-Trib, Pre-Wrath, Post-Trib and if you are still solely trusting in the work of Jesus Christ alone on the Cross for the forgiveness of all your sins, you're going to heaven. (Although as we saw if a person thinks they will be "made pure" and "acceptable" to God through their suffering in the 7-year Tribulation then it might have "become" a salvific issue) But by and large, Eschatology (the study of last things) including a person's position on the Rapture does not determine their salvation.

So here's the point. How can you say then, "I'm not saved" and "I'm going to the Lake of Fire" because I hold to the Pre-Trib position, a secondary issue? Why would you take the "blessing" and turn it into a "beating?" You do realize that it's perfectly fine to disagree on a "secondary" issue and walk away still being brothers, right? Now, a "salvific" issue, I agree, we need to "go to town on" so to speak because we're dealing with a person's eternal destiny here. I get that. It's a serious "salvific" issue on the line here. However, a "secondary" issue, like a position on the Rapture, does not determine one's salvation.

This is precisely why we have the classic saying in the Church that states, "A mark of *maturity* in the Church is to agreeably disagree on "secondary" issues and yet not divide." Why? Because there's bigger fish to fry! There's a greater mission at hand. It's called the Great Commission. Souls are in need of saving all around us and time is ticking. We all agree that we're living in the Last Days, therefore should we not *demonstrate our maturity* by vigorously debating on "secondary" issues yet not dividing? We don't have time to beat each other up or get distracted when souls all around us are in need of saving. That's *true Christian maturity*.

Yet, again, this *mature* attitude towards the Rapture positions seems to be on the *decline*. The following researcher shares his encounter as well with this "offensive attitude" towards the teaching of the Rapture:

"In any investigation where there is a sharp cleavage of opinion, there are always those who resort to unwise and intemperate language. Such has been the case with the issue at hand. However, anyone who reads widely in the literature of the four viewpoints involved will be forced to conclude that much of the harsh language and offensive attitudes stem from the Post-Tribulational camp.

Some of those who argue so strenuously that they must go through the Tribulation reflect in their writings an attitude of bravado, mingled with contempt for those who, either from ignorance or cowardice, do not share that conviction. They put forth such statements as:

'Is there not a strain of weak-kneed, invertebrate, spineless sentiment in this idea of escaping tribulation?'

'Pre-Tribulationalists are 'Darbyites,' who follow 'the Rapture craze, fathered by theorists,' and whose views are held to be 'supreme rubbish.''

'We need to carry 'the war into the enemy's country' and 'bring guns to bear' on these 'deceptive doctrines' and 'rank absurdities' and 'fight against this latter-day delusion.''

Certainly, this is not the way to convince the brethren of their love. The reader will have to judge if these statements are "cruel or churlish," or if it manifests the fruit of the Spirit which is 'good temper, kindliness, generosity' (Gal. 5:22). Indeed, if in dealing with his fellow brethren, a man fails to manifest such fruit of the Spirit, including as it does *love, longsuffering, gentleness*, and *self-control*, is he to be trusted as one who is Spirit-taught in the understanding of things to come? (John 16:13).

It is one thing to rebuke false doctrine. It is entirely another to whip the brethren."[2]

And all of this is going on in front of the lost over a "secondary" issue. No wonder they don't want to "believe" in the Gospel. What kind of "unbelievable" examples are we setting them? Have we *lost* our way? The doctrine of the Rapture is meant to "encourage" and "motivate" us to live for Jesus and share the Gospel like never before, not to "divide" and "destroy" us at the *expense* of the Gospel, as this man shares:

"Out of curiosity a few weeks ago, I started doing a little experiment by typing just the word 'Rapture' into my internet search engine. Different results appeared with links to various websites that highlighted discussion and information about the Rapture of the Church.

Lately however, another troubling search result has started to appear that take you directly to the Alex Jones YouTube channel, automatically playing videos of Alex Jones himself condemning the Pre-Trib Rapture doctrine.

The latest link (as of the time of this writing) is to a video on The Alex Jones Channel called 'How the Pre-Trib Rapture Is a Deception.' The video description says it all: 'Elite Use the Rapture as a Cop-Out for Christians.'

Now I am not writing this as an attack on The Alex Jones Channel or the InfoWars website. My intention is to provide reassurance and comfort to those of my fellow sheep who may have watched these videos and who are also trying to maintain their hope in the Pre-Tribulation return of our Lord Jesus Christ for His true Church.

I had this thought while listening to the videos I referenced above: If the primary source of the fuel for those who attack the Pre-Trib Rapture is their belief that it is the will of God for them to carry out such attacks in order to 'rescue' the 'deceived,' then would they also be willing to put forth that same effort to rescue those who are lost and have never heard the true gospel message, let alone the doctrine of the Pre-Trib Rapture?

In other words, for those who find it to be God's will that they 'convert' those of us who are 'deceived' into believing that we will be 'rescued' from the horrors of the 7-year Tribulation, are you willing to also use equal effort to join in God's will to convert those who are truly lost and are being deceived into spending eternity in hell?

Do you share the same enthusiasm as the apostle Paul did when he quoted from the book of Isaiah in Romans 10:15? 'And how shall they preach, except they be sent? as it is written, How beautiful are the feet of them that preach the gospel of peace, and bring glad tidings of good things!'

I don't know about you, but I would much rather labor in bringing a warning that includes a message of hope, rather than labor in bringing a message of ridicule and condemnation aimed to destroy hope."[3]

That sounds like a *mature attitude* to me! That's what we *all* should be doing as Christians! Therefore, let's get a mature "attitude check" and remind ourselves as Christians *why we're ALL still here on earth* awaiting the Rapture. The Bible is clear. We are on a rescue mission to save people from hell. And contrary to our world's opinion, hell is real, and they *need to know that*. I didn't say that. Jesus did:

Luke 16:22-24 "The time came when the beggar died and the angels carried him to Abraham's side. The rich man also died and was buried. In hell, where he was in torment, he looked up and saw Abraham far away, with Lazarus by his side. So he called to him, Father Abraham, have pity on me and send Lazarus to dip the tip of his finger in water and cool my tongue, because I am in agony in this fire."

So here we see Jesus clearly informing us that a place of eternal torment, or in other words, hell really does exist, right? Please keep in mind Whom it was that said this. It was Jesus. But herein lies our problem. Instead of listening to Jesus and taking heed of His warning about hell and getting saved, most people put forth objections to hell as to why they say it cannot be true.

For instance, the **first objection** to hell is called **Universalism**. What universalism would have you and I believe is that everybody will universally get saved regardless of their actions or beliefs and thus nobody goes to hell because there's no need for one. But if this were true then why do we need to share the gospel? I mean, if everybody's going to heaven then why evangelize? But the truth is, Jesus did tell us to evangelize. Furthermore, if universalism is true then wouldn't this mean that the devil himself will eventually go to heaven? Yet, the Bible says that Jesus came to destroy the works of the devil, not to save him. Besides, universalism denies the clear teaching as we've already read about two eternal places, heaven and hell, not just one.

The **second objection** to hell is that **If there is a hell, it's only temporary**. You see, some people think that those who end up in hell will somehow someway eventually be able to get out. They say it's just too harsh to be tormented forever. But that's not what the Bible says.

Matthew 25:46 "Then they will go away to eternal punishment, but the righteous to eternal life."

Now, you can't get any more cut and dry than that. How long is eternal life? Forever, right? Therefore, in the exact same text there, how long is eternal punishment? Just as long isn't it? Hell is not temporary. It's just as forever as heaven is forever.

The **third objection** to hell is called **Annihilationism**. Here is what people do. Since they can't deny the texts that clearly reveal that hell exists, they once again try to soften the harshness of God's retribution by saying something like this. "Well, if hell does exist, then people who go there don't suffer endlessly. No! They simply cease to be or in other words they're annihilated." But that's not what the Bible says.

Revelation 20:7,10 "When the thousand years are over, Satan will be released from his prison. And the devil, who deceived them, was thrown into the lake of burning sulfur, where the beast and the false prophet had been thrown. They will be tormented day and night for ever and ever."

Now according to our text, it's pretty obvious that the beast and the false prophet haven't been annihilated there in hell, have they? No! They're still alive suffering torment in hell after being there for 1,000 years! Besides, annihilation would not be a punishment. It would be a release from punishment. And since the Bible declares that hell is a place of punishment, annihilation can't be true.

The **fourth objection** to hell is this, "**Why doesn't God just reform people?**" And yes, this may sound logical but it totally misses the point. You see, the Bible does teach that God tries to reform people. It's just that the time for this reformation is called *right now*. It's simple. If you don't want to experience God's forgiveness and if you don't want to experience His personal reformation right now in this life, then God will honor your decision. That's why, in reality, people send themselves to hell!

The **fifth objection** to hell is this, "**Isn't eternal damnation a bit overkill?**" I have to admit that this seems to make sense at least from man's point of view. But think about it from God's point of view:

"Here stands God on the day of creation. He looks at stars and He says, 'All you stars move yourself to this place and start in this order and move in a circle and move exactly as I tell you until I give you another word.' And they all obey Him.

'Planets pick yourself up and whirl, make this formation at My command until I give you another word.'

He looks at mountains and He says, 'Be lifted up" and they obey Him. He tells valleys, 'Be cast down' and they obey Him.

He looks at the sea and He says, 'You will come this far' and the sea obeys.

And then He looks at you and says, 'Come' and you go, 'No!'"[4]

This is why hell is not overkill. Do you have any idea how wicked our rebellion against God is? Everything in the world obeys Him except us. Who do we think we are? Hell isn't overkill! It has to exist just as long as a Righteous God exists. Why? Because only eternal punishment can suffice for sins against an Eternal God. Besides, without eternal separation there could be no heaven. Why? Because evil cannot exist in heaven otherwise it would cease to be heaven!

The **sixth objection** to hell is that **Hell has no redeeming value**. But again, stop and think about it. *An awful punishment fits the nature of an awe-inspiring God.* Those who by choice refuse to give God glory in this life will be forced to give Him glory in the afterlife via torment. Besides, the Bible is clear. God is Holy and all of us have committed unholy sins against Him! Therefore, hell satisfies the justice of God for sins committed against the Holiness of God. That's how great and fearful a standard His Holiness is. Furthermore, the Bible says that hell's primary purpose or "value" if you will was not for people. It was for the devil and his demons.

Matthew 25:41 "Then the King will turn to those on the left and say, 'Away with you, you cursed ones, into the eternal fire prepared for the devil and his demons."

The Bible is clear. Hell was originally created for the devil and his demons, not people. But since people have rebelled against God just like the devil then to hell you will go, like this man shares:

"Think a moment of what the devil has done. And if you could design a place to make him pay for what he's done in your life and the lives around you, what kind of place would you design?

Well God, has designed just a place. It's called hell. And hell was originally designed by God to make the devil pay for bringing evil and rebellion into His creation. It was a place where God's anger, His rage, His wrath would go uncut, unbridled, and uncensored.

It was designed with the devil in mind, not people. But hell does not discriminate between a person and a demon. It's like a wood chipper that you throw big logs and branches into to grind them up into mulch.

And this is what hell is. It's God's divine wood chipper. Nobody cringes when they see a log ground up. But imagine if someone grabbed a log and as they throw it in there, a piece of the limb grabs their pants and starts to pull them in. What would you do?

Would you not grab them? Would you not pull them? Would you not scream, 'Turn it off! Turn the machine off!' Why? Because that chipper was not designed for grinding humans, but that chipper doesn't care if it's a human or if it's a log or if it's a rock or a stone. It is designed to crush!

And so it is with hell. It doesn't care if it's a demon or a human. It was designed to crush and destroy and heap pain, suffering, and agony on rebellious angels that dared to rebel against God.

There is no escape. There is no turning back. They are doomed! And so it is with anyone who has the audacity to rebel against God, human or devil. The divine wood chipper is there to suck them in!"[5]

Even though hell was originally created for the devil and his demons, there is no discrimination! If you don't want to receive God's gracious offer of forgiveness through Jesus Christ, then to hell you will go! You'll get sucked in just like the demons!

The **seventh objection** to hell is that **Hell is life on earth**. You can hear others say, "Besides, if there is a hell, I'll get to party with all my buddies." But anybody who makes this statement has obviously never read the Bible, let alone studied what the Bible says hell is like. Personally, I like this man's study on hell:

"Picture a time that just continues to tumble on and on forever, never ending, never slowing down, the same years and decades of torment, regret, sorrow, pain, blanketed darkness, nights never ending, constant consciousness, lostness, aloneness, loneliness, rumblings from the pit, groans, torturing fire, choking smells, unending and unending, no letting-up, no relief, no comfort, never resting, never ceasing, never relenting, no end in sight, one hundred years rolling into another one hundred years, slowly turning over into a thousand years, painstakingly evolving into another thousand years, and finally into a million years, the same grinding pain, the continual bone-racking agony, screams upon screams, weeping upon weeping, echoing sighs upon sighs!"[6]

Now, I don't know about you, but if that's your idea of a party, I'm not going. I don't care how many times you invite me. But seriously, the point is this. Those who end up in hell will wish it was only as bad as life on earth. I guarantee you, there won't be any partying.

The **eighth objection** to hell is that **Only "rotten" people go to hell**. But this is actually one of the biggest lies from the pit of hell! You see, the Bible teaches that all people are currently headed for hell and that there is no neutral position.

John 8:42,44 "Jesus told them, If God were your Father, you would love me, because I have come to you from God. For you are the children of your father the devil, and you love to do the evil things he does."

The Bible is clear. We either belong to God or we belong to who? The devil, right? There is no "middle road." We are all considered rotten because of our rotten sin! We only cease to become a child of the devil and become a child of God when we get saved. Not one second sooner, not one second later. And how ironic it is that those who think there's a "neutral" position out there, not only still belong to the devil, but they're still on the way to hell. Gee, I'd say that's a pretty good trick of the devil, how about you?

The **ninth objection** to hell is that **Hell is unfair.** In other words, you hear people say, "A good and loving God would never allow for such a place." Now even though that sounds so wonderful, it's absolutely unbiblical. You see, it's precisely because God is good that He must judge all. God must punish wickedness, otherwise He couldn't be loving or good. For instance, would it be loving if God allowed people to get away with the murder, rape, torture, etc. that we all know never makes it to court or even gets found out? Would it be loving or good for God to allow Hitler or the perpetrators of 9-11 to enjoy eternal bliss in heaven without having to deal with their wicked deeds? How loving is that? Rather, it's precisely because God is good and loving that He not only will judge all, but He's also provided a way of out of it, even though He didn't have to.

Therefore the point is this. Throw up any objection you want, but if you're going to be true to the Scripture you cannot deny the necessity of a hell. If you deny hell, it only shows you don't understand the Holiness of God. You see, what makes hell so horrible is not merely its necessity, but it's nature as well. It's the worst place you could ever dream of, yet it's not a dream. It's your worst nightmare! No wonder Jesus spoke more about hell than He ever did about heaven. I mean, it only makes sense that if God really loved us He would warn us about such a place, right? That's precisely what He did!

Matthew 5:22 "But I tell you that anyone who is angry with his brother will be subject to judgment. Again, anyone who says to his brother, 'Raca,' is answerable to the Sanhedrin. But anyone who says, 'You fool!' will be in danger of the fire of HELL."

Matthew 5:29 "If your right eye causes you to sin, gouge it out and throw it away. It is better for you to lose one part of your body than for your whole body to be thrown into HELL."

Mark 9:43 "If your hand causes you to sin, cut it off. It is better for you to enter life maimed than with two hands to go into HELL, where the fire never goes out."

Mark 9:45 "And if your foot causes you to sin, cut it off. It is better for you to enter life crippled than to have two feet and be thrown into HELL."

Matthew 10:28 "Do not be afraid of those who kill the body but cannot kill the soul. Rather, be afraid of the One who can destroy both soul and body in HELL."

Matthew 23:15 "Woe to you, teachers of the law and Pharisees, you hypocrites! You travel over land and sea to win a single convert, and when he becomes one, you make him twice as much a son of HELL as you are."

Matthew 23:33 "You snakes! You brood of vipers! How will you escape being condemned to HELL?"

Luke 12:5 "But I will show you whom you should fear: Fear him who, after the killing of the body, has power to throw you into HELL. Yes, I tell you, fear him."

Now here's my point. If you're going to believe Jesus when He talks about a heaven, then how much more should you listen to Him when He talks about a hell? How sad it is that even though Jesus out of love for you and I clearly warned about the horrible nature of a hell, that some people still ignore Him!

But what's even more shocking than that is that it's not only non-Christians who are refusing to believe in hell, but even so-called Christians are refusing to believe in hell, or as in the case of the Rapture positions, spend all their time beating up other Christians over a "secondary" issue and never witnessing to the lost in the first place. This is such an obvious horrible witness to the lost, that even an atheist knows better!

"An atheist said to a Christian one time, 'If I believe what you Christians say you believe about a coming judgment, and that rejecters of Christ will be lost eternally in hell, then I would crawl on my bare knees on crushed glass all over the city, warning men, night and day, to flee from the coming day of God's wrath!'"7

But that's not what we're doing today, is it? This is how we're being deceived about the Rapture. How sad it is that we Christians who have been entrusted with the Gospel, God's message of love and grace and forgiveness through Jesus Christ so that people could escape hell, could actually give a rip about sharing that same message with the lost because you're too busy beating each other up over a "secondary" issue. That's not only deceitful, it's deadly!

Again, that's why we stated at the very beginning of this book, *Don't be deceived*! The Rapture is real, but so is Hell! This is not a game! There may be a multitude of opinions out there concerning the *timing* of the Rapture, but it should *never* detour us from the *purpose* of the Rapture. We've got to get busy working together saving as many as we can from the dangers of HELL. It's real! It's time to be *wise sheep* not *ravenous wolves* as this man shares:

"Just in case those who claim to be doing 'the Lord's work' by condemning the so-called 'heresy' of the Pre-Trib Rapture think that those of us who have hope to escape the horrors of the Tribulation are wimps, then I have a thought for you to ponder.

You think that it takes a certain degree of intestinal fortitude to stand up and be strong enough to proclaim a message of bad news to those who don't want to hear a message of bad news and warning. Well there is another message that takes *an even higher degree of courage* to proclaim:

The Gospel message is no message to be told by wimps, to wimps. It is a very strong message of bad news, forewarning the coming danger of eternity in hell. Yet *at the same time* it is also a message of *good* news because it offers the hope of escaping hell and spending eternity in heaven through faith in Jesus Christ.

Anyone who endeavors to proclaim, and then actually follows through with the *action* of proclaiming the Gospel, is no wimp. They are subjecting themselves to ridicule, further condemnation, rejection, and possibly even worse.

We who hold to the hope of the Pre-Tribulation Rapture also share in proclaiming the same warnings about the upcoming judgment of the Tribulation to those who would rather we just held our tongues. But we season our message with the salt of the hope of the Rapture through faith in the blood of Jesus Christ and the promise of the seal of His Holy Spirit.

That's the difference between *wolves* and *sheep*. Wolves are always on the attack, offering no hope of salvation. But true sheep follow the command of their Shepherd and *always* endeavor to bring the good news of the Gospel unto all nations.

'My sheep hear my voice, and I know them, and they follow me' (John 10:27)."[8]

Are you "hearing" what we're trying to say in this book? It's time to get busy "following" Jesus by being faithful sheep declaring salvation, not ravenous wolves attacking with no hope. We need to get busy endeavoring to work together, sharing the Gospel unto all nations. That's why we're *all* still here *all* awaiting the Rapture. Don't be deceived. It's time to get busy sharing the Gospel as fast as we can. Hell is real, and you wouldn't ever want your worst enemy to go there. It's horrible! Therefore, this is not a time to call each other satanic over a "secondary" issue like your position on the Rapture. Rather it's a time to join hands to work together and "rescue" as many as we can from that horrible place.

Remember what the atheist said, "If I believed what you Christians say you believe about a coming judgment, and that rejecters of Christ will be lost eternally in hell, then I would crawl on my bare knees on crushed glass all over the city, warning men, night and day, to flee from the coming day of God's wrath!" As we saw, the world already scoffs at hell. Let's not give them something else to scoff at by being a bad witness on top of it, by beating each other up over a "secondary" issue like the Rapture. Don't be deceived. We need to make sure the non-Christians are ready for eternity too!

Speaking of which, if you are reading this book and you're not saved, that is, you're not a Christian, then what more can we do to get your attention? Don't be deceived either. Yes, the Rapture is real but so is Hell. Please don't go there. Call upon the name of Jesus Christ today and ask Him to forgive you of all your sins before it's too late. *Don't be deceived for all eternity.* Today may be your last day. Don't risk your soul into the Lake of Fire! Take the only way out through Jesus, and be rescued today! Amen?

How to Receive Jesus Christ:

1. Admit your need (I am a sinner).

2. Be willing to turn from your sins (repent).

3. Believe that Jesus Christ died for you on the Cross and rose from the grave.

4. Through prayer, invite Jesus Christ to come in and control your life through the Holy Spirit. (Receive Him as Lord and Savior.)

What to pray:

Dear Lord Jesus,

I know that I am a sinner and need Your forgiveness. I believe that You died for my sins. I want to turn from my sins. I now invite You to come into my heart and life. I want to trust and follow You as Lord and Savior.

In Jesus' name. Amen.

Notes

Chapter 1 *The Importance of the Rapture*

1. *Last Days News Report on the Rapture*
   (https://www.youtube.com/watch?v=TTC_TGShmNk)
2. *Last Days Weather Report*
   (https://www.youtube.com/watch?v=peXo1tRzvqc)
3. *Time Line of 7-year Tribulation Events*
   (Bible Study by Billy Crone)

Chapter 2 *The Basis of the Rapture*

1. *Definition of the Word Rapture*
   (http://www.biblestudytools.com/lexicons/greek/nas/harpazo.html)
   (http://www.raptureready.com/rr-pre-trib-rapture.html)
2. *The Rapture Taught by Jesus & Paul Chart*
   (http://www.middletownbiblechurch.org/proph/raptjn14.htm)
   (http://www.middletownbiblechurch.org/proph/rapture.htm)

Chapter 3 *The Purpose of the Rapture*

1. *To Comfort the Living About the Dead*
   (https://www.raptureready.com/terry/james3.html)
   (http://www.middletownbiblechurch.org/proph/rapture.htm)
   (http://www.pre-trib.org/articles/view/an-overview-of-pretribulational-arguments)
2. *To Comfort the Living About the Day of the Lord*
   (https://www.raptureready.com/terry/james3.html)
   (https://www.raptureready.com/resource/stanton/k4.htm)
3. *Quote The Rapture is a Soothing Balm to a Troubled Heart*

  (http://www.pre-trib.org/articles/view/an-overview-of-pretribulational-arguments)
4. *The Meaning of the Word Maranatha*
  (http://www.raptureready.com/rr-imminency.html)
  (http://www.gotquestions.org/maranatha.html)
5. *Joke Benefits of a New Body*
  (Email story) – Source unknown
6. *Characteristics of Heaven*
  (Bible Study by Billy Crone)
7. *Quote Dr. Kent Hovind on Heaven*
  (http://www.wiseoldgoat.com/papers-creation/hovind-seminar_part2b_2007.html)
8. *Characteristics on the Millennial Kingdom*
  (http://www.biblestudytools.com/commentaries/revelation/related-topics/summary-of-the-millennial-kingdom.html)
  (http://www.biblestudytools.com/commentaries/revelation/related-topics/millennial-reign-of-messiah.html)
  (http://webcache.googleusercontent.com/search?q=cache:pOQz0-5Af2MJ:https://bible.org/seriespage/4-millennial-kingdom-and-eternal-state&num=1&hl=en&gl=us&strip=1&vwsrc=0)
  (http://www.matthewmcgee.org/millen.html)
  (http://www.wordexplain.com/millenniumcharacteristics.html)
9. *Quote The Millennium is Our Greatest Adventure*
  (https://books.google.com/books?id=xCW8fjiEDYC&pg=PA179&lpg=PA179&dq=The+greatest+adventure+we+could+ever+imagine+awaits+us+in+the+reality+of+the+Kingdom+of+Christ&source=bl&ots=V29plgl3us&sig=sqseOlNR0VYLJ8uICRhwBw8rrDo&hl=en&sa=X&ved=0ahUKEwjf0Ivej63MAhXMLSYKHb43DhUQ6AEIHDAA#v=onepage&q=The%20greatest%20adventure%20we%20could%20ever%20imagine%20awaits%20us%20in%20the%20reality%20of%20the%20Kingdom%20of%20Christ&f=false)
10. *Quote That's My King*
  (https://thatsmyking.wordpress.com/words/)
11. *Quote The Destiny of Christians*
  (https://www.raptureready.com/terry/james3.html)

Chapter Four *The Jewish Wedding Ceremony*

1. *Quote The Importance of the Timing of the Rapture*
   (http://www.pre-trib.org/articles/view/an-overview-of-
   pretribulational-arguments)
2. *The Custom of the Groom Wearing Gold, Incense, & Myrrh*
   Fred H. Wight, *Manners & Customs of Bible Lands*,
   (Chicago: Moody Press, 1953, Pg.130)
3. *The Different Phases of a Jewish Marriage Ceremony*
   (Excerpts taken from a study by William P. Risk, *The Ultimate
   Wedding*, http://www.ldolphin.org/risk/ult.shtml)
   (http://www.biblestudytools.com/commentaries/revelation/related-
   topics/the-jewish-wedding-analogy.html)
   (https://www.raptureready.com/soap2/wriston1.html)

Chapter Five   *The Unknown Hour*

1. *Events Preceding the Second Coming*
   (http://christinprophecy.org/articles/why-i-believe-in-a-pre-tribulation-
   rapture/)
2. *Example of Events that Can Be Calculated in 7-year Tribulation*
   (http://www.raptureready.com/rr-pretribulation-rapture.html)
3. *Quote Will We Know the Hour of the Second Coming?*
   (http://www.gty.org/resources/sermons/2373/ready-or-nothere-i-come-part-
   1)
   (http://www.gty.org/resources/sermons/2374/ready-or-nothere-i-come-part-
   2)
4. *Differences Between the Rapture & Second Coming*
   (http://christinprophecy.org/articles/why-i-believe-in-a-pre-tribulation-
   rapture/)
   (http://www.pre-trib.org/articles/view/an-overview-of-pretribulational-
   arguments)
   (http://chafer-cstn.org/BaseT/ESCHA/Rapture/PreTrib50Args.Walvoord.
   103A2A.htm)
   (http://www.thepropheticyears.com/reasons/rapture.htm)
   (http://www.omegaletter.com/articles/articles.asp?ArticleID=6882)
   (https://www.tms.edu/m/tmsj13i.pdf)
   (http://www.middletownbiblechurch.org/proph/rapt2com.htm)

Chapter Six   *The Absence of the Church*

1. *The Book of Revelation Outline*
   (http://www.middletownbiblechurch.org/proph/rapture.htm)
2. *The Use of the Word Church in the Book of Revelation*
   (http://www.pre-trib.org/articles/view/an-overview-of-pretribulational-arguments)
3. *The Importance of the Absence of the Word Church in Revelation*
   (http://www.pre-trib.org/articles/view/an-overview-of-pretribulational-arguments)
4. *Proof the Church is Absent in Matthew 24*
   (http://www.nowtheendbegins.com/our-top-5-reasons-why-matthew-24-cannot-be-talking-about-the-rapture-of-the-church/)
5. *Olivet Discourse & Revelation 6 Chart*
   (http://www.credocourses.com/blog/2015/the-first-6-seal-judgments-of-revelation/)
6. *Differences Between 1 Thessalonians & Matthew 24*
   (http://www.pre-trib.org/articles/view/matthew-2431-rapture-or-second-coming)
7. *The Finality of the Angel Harvest*
   (http://www.gty.org/resources/sermons/66-53/the-final-reaping-of-the-earth)
8. *Why the Angel Harvest is Not Referring to the Rapture of the Church*
   (http://www.pre-trib.org/articles/view/matthew-2431-rapture-or-second-coming)

Chapter Seven *The Location of the Church*

1. *What the Church Does in Heaven During 7-Year Tribulation*
   (http://christinprophecy.org/articles/why-i-believe-in-a-pre-tribulation-rapture/)
2. *Background Study of the Twenty-Four Elders*
   (http://www.pre-trib.org/articles/view/an-overview-of-pretribulational-arguments)
   (http://www.thepropheticyears.com/reasons/rapture.htm)
   (http://tribulationrisingcom.fatcow.com/scriptural-evidence-of-a-pre-tribulation-rapture/)
   (http://www.gotquestions.org/24-elders.html)

(http://christinprophecy.org/articles/why-i-believe-in-a-pre-tribulation-rapture/)

3. *Quote the Location of the Twenty-Four Elders* (http://www.pre-trib.org/articles/view/an-overview-of-pretribulational-arguments)

4. *Quote Why are There Twenty-Four Elders* (http://www.pre-trib.org/articles/view/an-overview-of-pretribulational-arguments)

5. *Quote the Difference in Clothing of the Twenty-Four Elders* (http://tribulationrisingcom.fatcow.com/scriptural-evidence-of-a-pre-tribulation-rapture/)

Chapter Eight *The Promises to the Church*

1. *Background Study of Revelation 3:10* (http://www.blogos.org/organicfruit/pre-tribulation-rapture.php) (http://gracebiblestudies.org/Resources/Web/www.duluthbible.org/g_f_j/Rapture_Zeller2.htm) (http://www.pre-trib.org/articles/view/an-overview-of-pretribulational-arguments) (http://www.thepropheticyears.com/reasons/rapture.htm) (https://www.tms.edu/m/tmsj13i.pdf) (http://www.middletownbiblechurch.org/proph/rapture.htm)

2. *Quote Kept from the Hour of Trial is the Rapture* (http://www.blogos.org/organicfruit/pre-tribulation-rapture.php)

3. *Quote the War Analogy & Being Removed* (http://www.middletownbiblechurch.org/proph/rapture.htm)

4. *Quote the Test Analogy & Being Removed* (http://www.pre-trib.org/articles/view/an-overview-of-pretribulational-arguments)

5. *Quote Miscellaneous Analogies & Being Removed* (http://www.middletownbiblechurch.org/proph/rapture.htm)

6. *Quote Final Comments on Revelation 3:10* (http://gracebiblestudies.org/Resources/Web/www.duluthbible.org/g_f_j/Rapture_Zeller2.htm)

7. *Background Study on the Wrath of God* (https://www.facebook.com/notes/sharon-moles/the-rapture-a-stunning-event-is-quickly-approaching-for-our-world-part-2-

by-davi/10151412947049824/)
(http://www.blogos.org/organicfruit/pre-tribulation-rapture.php)
(http://www.pre-trib.org/articles/view/an-overview-of-
pretribulational-arguments)
(https://www.raptureready.com/resource/stanton/k2.htm)
(http://www.raptureready.com/rr-pretribulation-rapture.html)
(https://www.tms.edu/m/tmsj13i.pdf)
(http://christinprophecy.org/articles/why-i-believe-in-a-pre-
tribulation-rapture/)

8. *Quote Objections to Church Rescued from 7-year Tribulation*
   (http://www.pre-trib.org/articles/view/an-overview-of-
   pretribulational-arguments)
9. *Quote Difference Between General Tribulation & The Tribulation*
   (http://www.pre-trib.org/articles/view/an-overview-of-
   pretribulational-arguments)
10. *Quote Two Groups of People Mentioned in 1 Thessalonians 5*
    (http://www.pre-trib.org/articles/view/an-overview-of-
    pretribulational-arguments)
11. *Quote God Saves His Church from His Wrath*
    (http://www.pre-trib.org/articles/view/an-overview-of-pretribulational-
    arguments)
12. *Quote God Saves His Bride from His Wrath*
    (http://www.pre-trib.org/articles/view/an-overview-of-pretribulational-
    arguments)
13. *Quote the Nature of the 7-Year Tribulation Excludes the Church*
    (http://www.pre-trib.org/articles/view/an-overview-of-pretribulational-
    arguments)

Chapter Nine *The Removal of the Church*

1. *Different Theories of Who the Restrainer Is*
   (http://www.pre-trib.org/articles/view/an-overview-of-pretribulational-
   arguments)
2. *Quote What the World Will Be Like When Restrainer is Removed*
   (http://www.pre-trib.org/articles/view/an-overview-of-pretribulational-
   arguments)
3. *Quotes Ministry of Holy Spirit on Earth After Church is Removed*

(http://www.pre-trib.org/articles/view/an-overview-of-pretribulational-arguments)
(https://www.raptureready.com/rr-pre-trib-rapture.html)
4. *Quotes Why Church Must Be Removed Before Antichrist Appears*
    (http://www.middletownbiblechurch.org/proph/rapture.htm)
    (http://christinprophecy.org/articles/why-i-believe-in-a-pre-tribulation-rapture/)
    (https://www.raptureready.com/abc/antichrist.html)
5. *Quote Similarities Between the Rapture & Noah & Lot's Day*
    (http://www.jesus-is-savior.com/End%20of%20the%20World/pretrib_proof.htm)
6. *Examples of God Transferring People*
    (http://www.middletownbiblechurch.org/proph/questrap.htm)
7. *Quotes Similarities Between the Rapture & Enoch*
    (http://www.middletownbiblechurch.org/prophecy/prophe3.htm)
    (https://www.raptureready.com/featured/ice/Rapture-in-history.html)

Chapter Ten   *The Purpose of the Tribulation*

1. *Quote The Gap of the Church Age*
    (https://www.raptureready.com/terry/james3.html)
2. *Quote The Activity of the Gap of the Church Age*
    (http://www.middletownbiblechurch.org/proph/rapture.htm)
3. *Quote The Purpose of the 70th Week*
    (https://www.raptureready.com/terry/james3.html)
    (http://christinprophecy.org/articles/why-i-believe-in-a-pre-tribulation-rapture/)
4. *Quote The Concern of the 70th Week*
    (https://www.raptureready.com/resource/stanton/k2.htm)
5. *Quote The Meaning of the Greek Word Katoikeo*
    (https://www.raptureready.com/resource/stanton/k2.htm)
6. *Quote The Bad News of Being in the 7-year Tribulation*
    (https://www.raptureready.com/resource/stanton/k2.htm)
7. *Quote The 7-year Tribulation Concerns the Gentile Nations*
    (https://www.raptureready.com/featured/ice/tt9.html)
8. *Quote The Conversions of the Multitudes in the 7-year Tribulation*

(http://www.jesus-is-savior.com/End%20of%20the%20World/pretrib
_proof.htm)
(https://www.raptureready.com/terry/james3.html)

Chapter Eleven *The Red Herring Objections*

1. *Quote The Rapture Passage in the Original Greek*
   (http://rapture22.tripod.com/rr-pre-trib-rapture.html)
2. *Quote The Word Rapture is Found in the Bible*
   (http://www.pre-trib.org/articles/view/rapture-myths)
3. *Quote The Amazement of People Rejecting the Rapture*
   (https://www.raptureready.com/rr-pre-trib-rapture.html)
   (http://www.raptureforums.com/Rapture/defendingthepretrib
   rapture.cfm)
4. *Quote Accusations that the Rapture is a Secret Event*
   (http://www.pre-trib.org/articles/view/rapture-myths)
5. *Quote Shocked at So Much Error in One Sentence*
   (http://www.pre-trib.org/articles/view/rapture-myths)
6. *Quote The Usage of the Word Rapture Prior to 1830*
   (http://www.pre-trib.org/articles/view/rapture-myths)
7. *Quote People Fighting with a Strawman*
   (http://www.pre-trib.org/articles/view/rapture-myths)
8. *Quote Pretribulationalists Never Called the Rapture a Secret*
   (http://www.pre-trib.org/articles/view/rapture-myths)
9. *Quote Evidence the Rapture Will Not Be a Secret Event*
   (https://www.raptureready.com/rr-thief.html)
10. *Quote More Evidence the Rapture Will Not Be a Secret Event*
    (https://www.raptureready.com/rr-secret-rapture.html)
11. *Quote Evidence Pretribbers are Not Hiding the Rapture Event*
    (https://www.raptureready.com/rr-secret-rapture.html)
12. *Quote Evidence the Critics of Pre-Trib are Keeping Rapture Secret*
    (https://www.raptureready.com/rr-pre-trib-rapture.html)
13. *Quote The Rapture Will Be a Widely Known Global Event*
    (https://www.raptureready.com/rap72.html)
14. *Quote The Lunacy of Saying There is No Verse on the Rapture*
    (http://www.sumnerchristianfellowship.org/the-pretribulation-
    rapture-of-the-church/)
    (https://www.raptureready.com/resource/stanton/k2.htm)

15. *Quote The Hypocrisy of the Critics of the Pre-Trib Rapture*
    (http://www.raptureforums.com/Rapture/defendingthepretrib
    rapture.cfm)

Chapter Twelve   *The Unfair Objections*

1. *Quote Craziness of People Wanting to Be in the 7-year Tribulation*
    (https://www.raptureready.com/rr-pre-trib-rapture.html)
2. *Quote The Church & Israel are Two Separate Entities*
    (https://www.gty.org/resources/pdf/sermons/1325)
3. *Quote The Shock of Being Left Behind*
    (https://www.raptureready.com/soap/heron2.html)
4. *Quote The Activity Caused by the Pre-Trib Rapture*
    (https://www.raptureready.com/terry/james3.html)
    (http://www.jesus-is-savior.com/End%20of%20the%20World/
    pretrib_proof.htm)
5. *Quote The False Challenges Against Imminency*
    (http://www.pre-trib.org/articles/view/an-overview-of-
    pretribulational-arguments)
6. *Quote The Gladness Produced by the Pre-Trib Rapture*
    (http://www.pre-trib.org/articles/view/an-overview-of-pretribulational-
    arguments)

Chapter Thirteen   *The Spurious Objections*

1. *Quote Robert Van Kampen's Promotion of Pre-Wrath Teaching*
    (https://www.raptureready.com/who/Robert_Van_Kampen.html)
2. *Quote Dave MacPherson's Hatred Toward Pre-Trib Teaching*
    (https://www.raptureready.com/faq/faq789.html)
3. *Quote Margaret McDonald's Vision of the Tribulation Period*
    (http://www.pre-trib.org/data/pdf/Wilkinson-LeftBehindorLed Astra1 .pdf)
4. *Quote Margaret McDonald's Vision Does Not Support Pre-Trib*
    (http://www.raptureready.com/rr-margaret-mcdonald.html)
5. *Quote Edward Irving's Beliefs on the Tribulation Period*
    (http://www.raptureforums.com/Rapture/mythsoriginspretrib
    rapture2.cfm)

6. *Quote The Nazis Big Lie & Dave MacPherson's Big Lie* (http://www.pre-trib.org/articles/view/part-2-myths-of-origin-rapture)
7. *Quote John Darby Distanced Himself from Margaret McDonald* (https://en.wikipedia.org/wiki/Margaret_MacDonald_(visionary))
8. *Quote Margaret McDonald Theory of Pre-Trib Origin Falls Apart* (https://www.raptureready.com/faq/faq789.html)
9. *Quote Example of People Losing Money Betting Against Pre-Trib* (http://www.raptureready.com/rr-margaret-mcdonald.html)
10. *Quote Historical Evidence of Pre-Trib Teaching* (https://www.raptureready.com/featured/ice/MythsoftheOriginof Pretribulationism_1.html) (https://www.raptureready.com/terry/james3.html) (http://www.raptureready.com/rr-margaret-mcdonald.html) (http://christinprophecy.org/articles/why-i-believe-in-a-pre-tribulation-rapture/) (http://www.thepropheticyears.com/reasons/rapture.htm) (http://www.grantjeffrey.com/article/why_some_reject.htm) (http://www.raptureme.com/terry/james27.html) (http://www.essentialchristianity.com/pages.asp?pageid=21918) (http://royalheir.blogspot.com/2012/03/early-church-fathers-were-pre.html) (http://www.pre-trib.org/articles/view/part-2-myths-of-origin-rapture) (https://www.raptureready.com/faq/faq789.html)
11. *Quote History Vindicates Pre-Trib Teaching* (https://www.facebook.com/notes/terri-wonder/the-pre-tribulation-rapture-was-taught-by-the-early-church/4786473940917/) (http://www.raptureme.com/terry/james27.html)
12. *Quote False Accusations Made Against Pre-Trib* (http://www.essentialchristianity.com/pages.asp?pageid=21918)
13. *Quote The Rapture of the Church is Not a New Teaching* (http://www.omegaletter.com/briefs/briefings.asp?BID=3902)

Chapter Fourteen   *Problems with Post-Trib*

1. *Quote Definition of the Post-Trib Rapture Position* (https://en.wikipedia.org/wiki/Post-tribulation_rapture)

(http://www.posttribpeople.com/Post-Tribulation-Belief.html)

2. *Quote God's Plan for Israel vs. the Church*
(http://www.grantjeffrey.com/article/why_some_reject.htm)
(https://www.raptureready.com/rr-pre-trib-rapture.html)

3. *Quote The Rapture Comes Before the Day of the Lord*
(http://www.pre-trib.org/articles/view/an-overview-of-pretribulational-arguments)

4. *Differences Between the Rapture & Second Coming*
(http://christinprophecy.org/articles/why-i-believe-in-a-pre-tribulation-rapture/)
(http://www.pre-trib.org/articles/view/an-overview-of-pretribulational-arguments)
(http://chafer-cstn.org/BaseT/ESCHA/Rapture/PreTrib50Args.Walvoord.103A2A.htm)
(http://www.thepropheticyears.com/reasons/rapture.htm)
(http://www.omegaletter.com/articles/articles.asp?ArticleID=6882)
(https://www.tms.edu/m/tmsj13i.pdf)
(http://www.middletownbiblechurch.org/proph/rapt2com.htm)

5. *Quote The Argument from Silence*
(http://kentcrockett.com/biblestudies/posttribbers.htm)

6. *Quote the Post-Trib Problem with the Millennium Population*
(http://www.pre-trib.org/articles/view/an-overview-of-pretribulational-arguments)
(https://www.raptureready.com/featured/ice/tt1.html)
(https://www.raptureready.com/featured/ice/RaptureBefore Tribulation.html)

7. *Quote The Post-Trib Problem with the Sheep & the Goats*
(http://www.pre-trib.org/articles/view/an-overview-of-pretribulational-arguments)
(http://www.khouse.org/articles/1995/35/)
(https://www.raptureready.com/featured/ice/tt1.html)
(https://www.tms.edu/m/tmsj13i.pdf)

8. *Quote The Timing of the Bema Seat Judgment*
(https://www.raptureready.com/resource/stanton/k11.htm)

9. *Quote The Post-Trib Belief on the First Resurrection*
(http://www.freestockphotos.com/COMING1/FirstResurrection Rapture.htm)
(https://en.wikipedia.org/wiki/Post-tribulation_rapture)

10. *Quote Multiple Resurrections Mentioned in the Bible*

(http://www.pre-trib.org/articles/view/the-resurrection-single-or-multiple)

11. *Quote The Resurrection & the Rapture Are Not One & the Same*
    (http://www.pre-trib.org/articles/view/the-resurrection-single-or-multiple)

12. *Quote There Are No Contradiction in the Bible*
    (http://www.pre-trib.org/articles/view/the-resurrection-single-or-multiple)

13. *Quote The Church is Removed Before the Antichrist Appears*
    (http://www.raptureready.com/rr-pretribulation-rapture.html)
    (https://www.raptureready.com/resource/stanton/k11.htm)

14. *Quote Jesus Returns from a Wedding*
    (http://www.raptureready.com/rr-pretribulation-rapture.html)
    (https://www.raptureready.com/resource/stanton/k11.htm)
    (https://www.tms.edu/m/tmsj13i.pdf)

15. *Quote The Post-Trib Position Makes the Rapture Meaningless*
    (http://www.pre-trib.org/articles/view/an-overview-of-pretribulational-arguments)

16. *Quote The Post-Trib Position Destroys Imminency*
    (http://www.pre-trib.org/articles/view/doctrine-of-imminency-is-it-biblical)
    (http://theologicalmatters.com/2012/08/17/tackling-tough-theological-matters-problems-with-post-tribulationalism/)
    (https://www.raptureready.com/resource/stanton/k11.htm)
    (http://informedchristians.com/index.php/Articles/50-reason-why-the-rapture-must-happen-before-the-7-year-tribulation)
    (http://home.earthlink.net/~ronrhodes/PostTribProblems.html)

17. *Quote The Post-Trib Position Destroys the Comfort of the Rapture*
    (http://www.raptureforums.com/FeaturedCommentary/wheresthecomfort.cfm)

Chapter Fifteen *Problems with Pre-Wrath*

1. *Quote The Origins of the Pre-Wrath Theory*
   (http://www.lamblion.com/articles/articles_rapture10.php)

2. *Quote The Explanation of the Pre-Wrath Theory*
   (http://thechristianbbs.com/cgi-bin/ultimatebb.cgi?ubb=get_topic;
   f=53;t=000497)

3. *Quote The Errors of the Pre-Wrath Theory*
   (http://www.middletownbiblechurch.org/proph/prewrath.htm)
4. *Quote The Motive of the Pre-Wrath Theory*
   (http://www.ldolphin.org/prewrath.html)
5. *The Confusing Name of the Pre-Wrath Theory*
   (http://www.lamblion.com/articles/articles_rapture10.php)
6. *Quote God's Wrath Involves the Whole 7-year Tribulation*
   (http://christinprophecy.org/articles/why-i-believe-in-a-pre-tribulation-rapture/)
7. *Quote The Day of the Lord Involves the Whole 7-year Tribulation*
   (http://bible-truth.org/Pre-Wrath.html)
   (https://www.raptureready.com/who/Robert_Van_Kampen.html)
   (http://thechristianbbs.com/cgi-bin/ultimatebb.cgi?ubb=get_topic;
   f=53;t=000497)
   (http://www.pre-trib.org/articles/view/three-quarters-rapture-theory)
   (http://compass.org/store/products/Article%3A-Dealing-with-Deceit-%252d-
   The-Pre%252dWrath-Deception.html)
8. *Pre-Trib Rapture Chart*
   (http://bible-truth.org/Pre-Wrath.html)
9. *Quote Summary of the Pre-Trib View*
   (http://bible-truth.org/Pre-Wrath.html)
10. *Pre-Wrath Rapture Chart*
    (https://www.raptureready.com/who/Robert_Van_Kampen.html)
11. *The Chronological Errors of the Pre-Wrath Theory*
    (http://www.lamblion.com/articles/articles_rapture10.php)
    (http://www.middletownbiblechurch.org/proph/prewrath.htm)
    (http://bible-truth.org/Pre-Wrath.html)
    (http://www.gotquestions.org/pre-wrath-rapture.html)
    (http://www.pre-trib.org/articles/view/an-overview-of-pretribulational-
    arguments)
12. *Quote The Identical View of the Pre-Wrath Theory*
    (http://www.middletownbiblechurch.org/proph/prewrath.htm)
13. *Quote The Birth Pang Confusion of the Pre-Wrath Theory*
    (http://www.middletownbiblechurch.org/proph/prewrath.htm)
14. *Quote Even More Chronological Errors of the Pre-Wrath Theory*
    (http://www.middletownbiblechurch.org/proph/prewrath.htm)
    (http://bible-truth.org/Pre-Wrath.html)
    (http://www.raptureforums.com/FeaturedCommentary/theprewrathrapturepar
    t3.cfm)

(https://www.raptureready.com/rr-pre-trib-rapture.html)
15. *Quote What God is Doing in the 2,000 year Church Gap*
    (http://www.middletownbiblechurch.org/proph/rapture.htm)
16. *Quote The Confusion of the Church & Israel in the Pre-Wrath Theory*
    (http://www.middletownbiblechurch.org/proph/prewrath.htm)
17. *Quote The Confusion of Identities in 7-Year Tribulation by Pre-Wrath Theory*
    (http://www.middletownbiblechurch.org/proph/prewrath.htm)
    (http://bible-truth.org/Pre-Wrath.html)
18. *Quote The Confusion of the Angel Harvest by Pre-Wrath*
    (http://www.middletownbiblechurch.org/proph/prewrath.htm)
    (http://www.ldolphin.org/prewrath.html)
19. *Quote The Confusion of the Millennium Population by Pre-Wrath*
    (http://www.ldolphin.org/prewrath.html)
20. *Quote The Confusion of Matthew 24 by Pre-Wrath*
    (http://www.ldolphin.org/prewrath.html)
    (http://www.middletownbiblechurch.org/proph/prewrath.htm)
21. *Quote The Confusion of the Church by Pre-Wrath*
    (http://bible-truth.org/Pre-Wrath.html)
22. *Quote The Replacement of the Church by Pre-Wrath*
    (http://www.middletownbiblechurch.org/proph/prewrath.htm)
23. *Quote The Confusion of the Church Promises by Pre-Wrath*
    (http://www.middletownbiblechurch.org/proph/prewrath.htm)
24. *Quote The Rotten Promises of the Pre-Wrath Theory*
    (http://www.middletownbiblechurch.org/proph/prewrath.htm)
25. *Quote The Destruction of Imminency by the Pre-Wrath Theory*
    (http://www.middletownbiblechurch.org/proph/prewrath.htm)
26. *Quote The Lack of Hope by the Pre-Wrath Theory*
    (http://compass.org/store/products/Article%3A-Dealing-with-Deceit-%252d-The-Pre%252dWrath-Deception.html)
27. *Quote The Heresy of Self-Cleansing by the Pre-Wrath Theory*
    (http://bible-truth.org/Pre-Wrath.html)
28. *Quote The Heresy of Self-Purification by the Pre-Wrath Theory*
    (http://bible-truth.org/Pre-Wrath.html)
    (http://www.lamblion.com/articles/articles_rapture10.php)

Chapter Sixteen   *Problems with Mid-Trib*

1. *Quote The Explanation of the Mid-Trib Theory*
    (http://www.nobts.edu/faculty/itor/lemkesw/personal/midtribulationism.html)
    (https://www.raptureready.com/resource/stanton/k9.htm)
2. *Quote The Minority View of the Mid-Trib Theory*
    (https://www.raptureready.com/resource/stanton/k9.htm)
3. *Quote The Compromise of God's Wrath by the Mid-Trib Theory*
    (http://www.raptureforums.com/Rapture/whatisthemidtribulationrapture.cfm)
4. *Quote The Compromise of Timing by the Mid-Trib Theory*
    (http://www.raptureforums.com/Rapture/whatisthemidtribulationrapture.cfm)
    (http://www.spiritandtruth.org/teaching/documents/articles/167/167.htm?
    x=x)
5. *Quote The Biblical Order of Events in the 7-year Tribulation*
    (http://bible-truth.org/mid-trib.html)
6. *Quote The Compromise of Daniel's 70th Week by the Mid-Trib Theory*
    (https://www.raptureready.com/resource/stanton/k9.htm)
7. *Quote The Compromise of Revelation 11 by the Mid-Trib Theory*
    (https://www.raptureready.com/resource/stanton/k9.htm)
8. *Quote The Real Purpose of the Biblical Trumpets*
    (https://www.raptureready.com/rr-pre-trib-rapture.html)
9. *Quote The Compromise of the Trumpets by the Mid-Trib Theory*
    (https://www.raptureready.com/resource/stanton/k9.htm)
10. *Quote The Compromise of Imminency by the Mid-Trib Theory*
    (http://bible-truth.org/mid-trib.html)
11. *Quote Missionary Story of Imminency*
    (http://www.thehaystack.tv/dont-be-fooled-by-a-counterfeit/)

Chapter Seventeen *The Proper Attitude*

1. *Quote Story of the Cleansing Benefits of Imminency*
    (http://www.middletownbiblechurch.org/prophecy/prophe3.htm)
2. *Quote Immature Comments Made by Anti-Pre-Trib Opponents*
    (https://www.raptureready.com/resource/stanton/k10.htm)
3. *Quote Divisive Comments Made by Anti-Pre-Trib Opponents*
    (https://www.raptureready.com/soap2/payne62.html)
4. *Quote Man's Rebellion Against God's Commands*
    (https://battle4truth.wordpress.com/2008/05/05/paul-washer-
    quotes/)
5. *Quote Hell is the Divine Wood Chipper*

(http://www.sermonaudio.com:80/sermoninfo.asp?SID=72706103314)

6. *Quote Biblical Description of Hell*
   (Mal Couch, *Revelation II Notebook,*
   (Fort Worth: Tyndale Seminary, Pgs. 150-151)

7. *Quote An Atheist's Comments on Hell*
   (http://www.churchchrist.net/Sermons/Witness.htm)

8. *Quote The Wolfish Behavior of the Anti-Pre-Trib Opponents*
   (https://www.raptureready.com/soap2/payne62.html)

Printed in Great Britain
by Amazon